STEPHEN COLBERT'S TEK JANSEN™

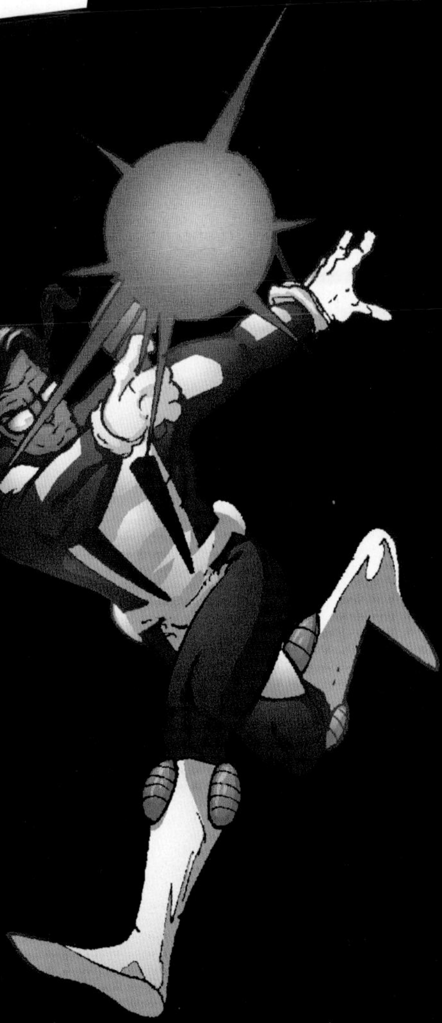

AN ONI PRESS PUBLICATION

Publisher **JOE NOZEMACK**

Editor in Chief **JAMES LUCAS JONES**

Managing Editor **RANDAL C. JARRELL**

Marketing Director **CORY CASONI**

Art Director **KEITH WOOD**

Assistant Editor **JILL BEATON**

Production Assistant **DOUGLAS E. SHERWOOD**

This volume collects Stephen Colbert's Tek Jansen issues 1-3.

Stephen Colbert's Tek Jansen, June 2008. Stephen Colbert's Tek Jansen is © 2008
Comedy Partners. All rights Reserved. Tek Jansen original character design by J.J.
Abrahams, plus unless otherwise specified, all other material © 2008 Oni Press,
Inc. Oni Press logo and icon are ™ & © 2008 Oni Press, Inc. All rights reserved.
Oni Press logo and icon artwork created by Dave Gibbons. Comedy Central logo is
™ & © Comedy Central.

www.onipress.com

First Edition, June 2008
ISBN 978-1-934964-16-3

13 9 7 8 6 5 4 3 2 1

Printed in China.

STEPHEN COLBERT'S TEK JANSEN

INVASION OF THE OPTIKLONS

WRITTEN BY **JOHN LAYMAN** & **TOM PEYER**

CHAPTER 1 ILLUSTRATED BY **SCOTT CHANTLER**

CHAPTERS 2-5 ILLUSTRATED BY **ROBBI RODRIGUEZ**

COLORED BY **PETE PANTAZIS** & **AURELIO ALFONSO**

LETTERED BY **DOUGLAS E. SHERWOOD**

EDITED BY **JAMES LUCAS JONES** & **RANDAL C. JARRELL**

DESIGNED BY **KEITH WOOD**

TEST COMPILED BY **RICHARD DAHM**

BASED ON CHARACTER BY **STEPHEN COLBERT**

APPROVED BY THE COLBERT NATION AUTHORITY

SQUAD

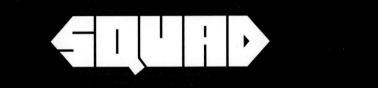

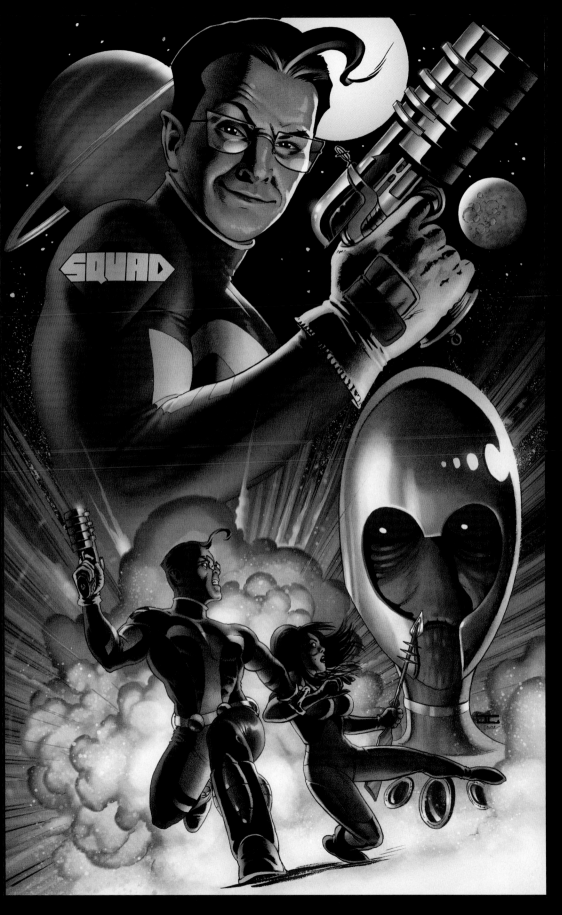

JOHN CASSADAY   LAURA MARTIN

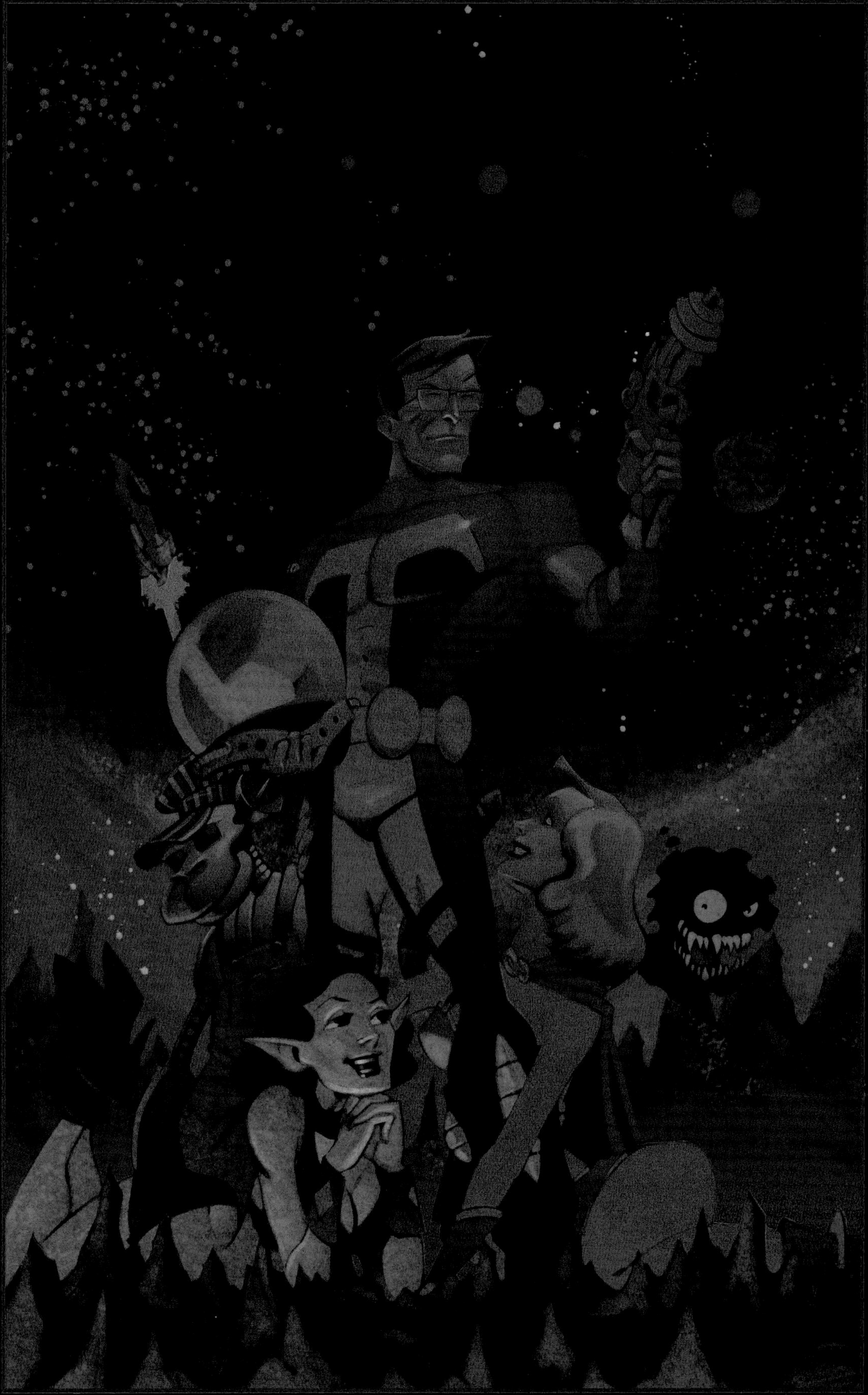

art by SCOTT CHANTLER with DAVE MCCAIG

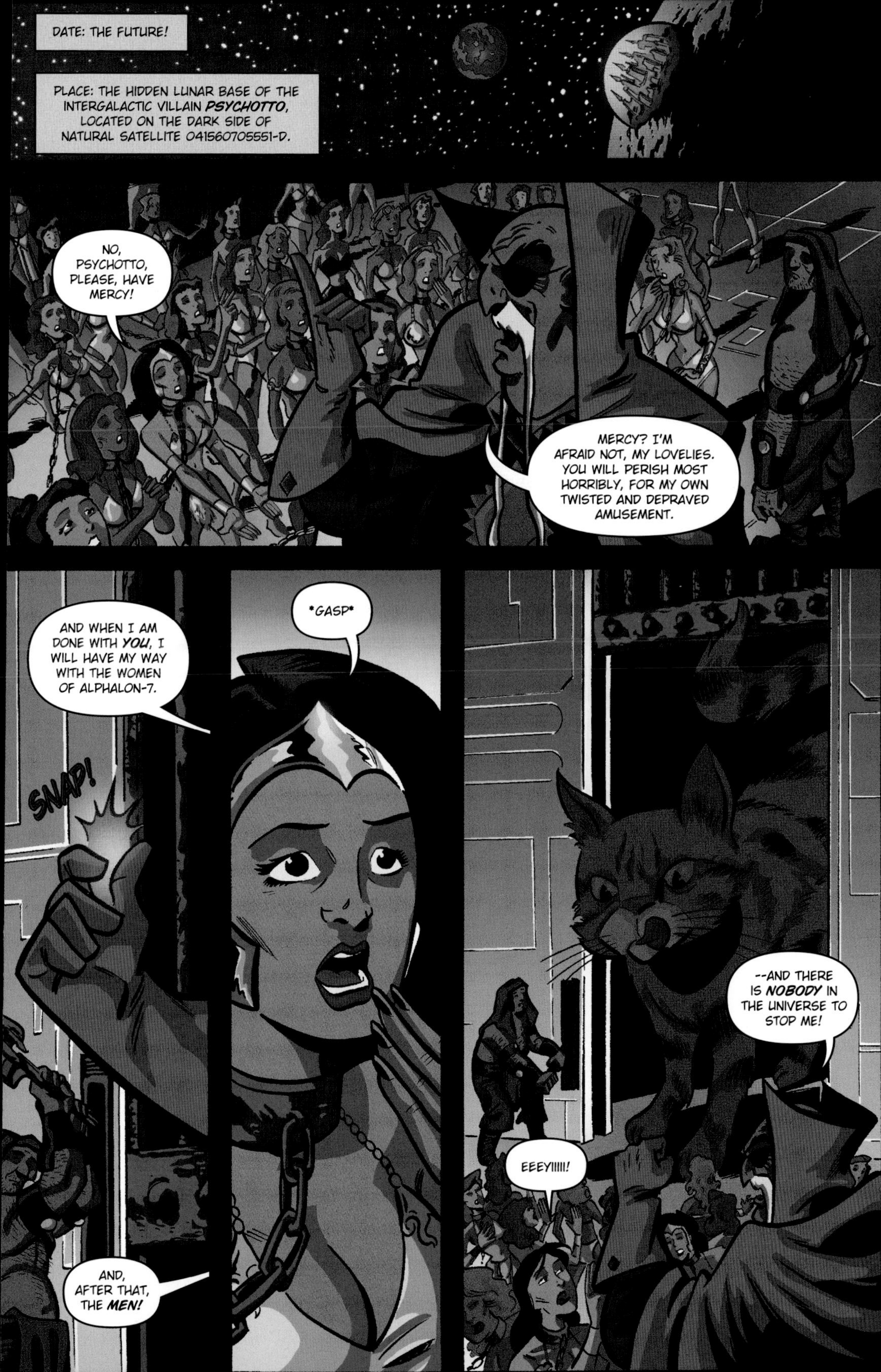

DATE: THE FUTURE!
PLACE: THE HIDDEN LUNAR BASE OF THE INTERGALACTIC VILLAIN ***PSYCHOTTO***, LOCATED ON THE DARK SIDE OF NATURAL SATELLITE 041560705551-D.
NO, PSYCHOTTO, PLEASE, HAVE MERCY!
MERCY? I'M AFRAID NOT, MY LOVELIES. YOU WILL PERISH MOST HORRIBLY, FOR MY OWN TWISTED AND DEPRAVED AMUSEMENT.
AND WHEN I AM DONE WITH ***YOU***, I WILL HAVE MY WAY WITH THE WOMEN OF ALPHALON-7.
SNAP!
AND, AFTER THAT, THE ***MEN!***
GASP
--AND THERE IS ***NOBODY*** IN THE UNIVERSE TO STOP ME!
EEEYIIIII!

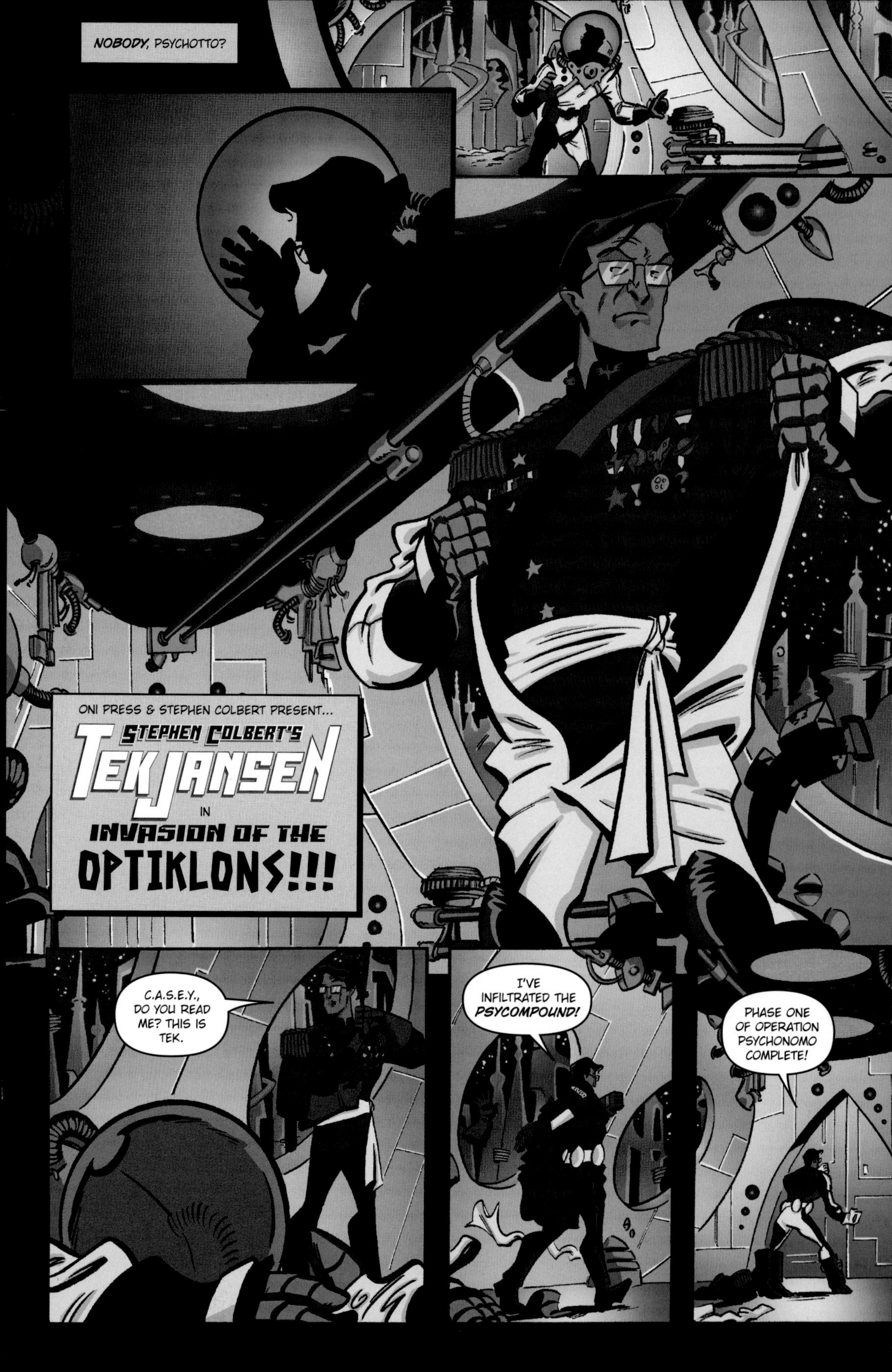

NOBODY, PSYCHOTTO?
ONI PRESS & STEPHEN COLBERT PRESENT...
STEPHEN COLBERT'S
TEK JANSEN
IN
INVASION OF THE
OPTIKLONS!!!
C.A.S.E.Y., DO YOU READ ME? THIS IS TEK.
I'VE INFILTRATED THE PSYCOMPOUND!
PHASE ONE OF OPERATION PSYCHONOMO COMPLETE!

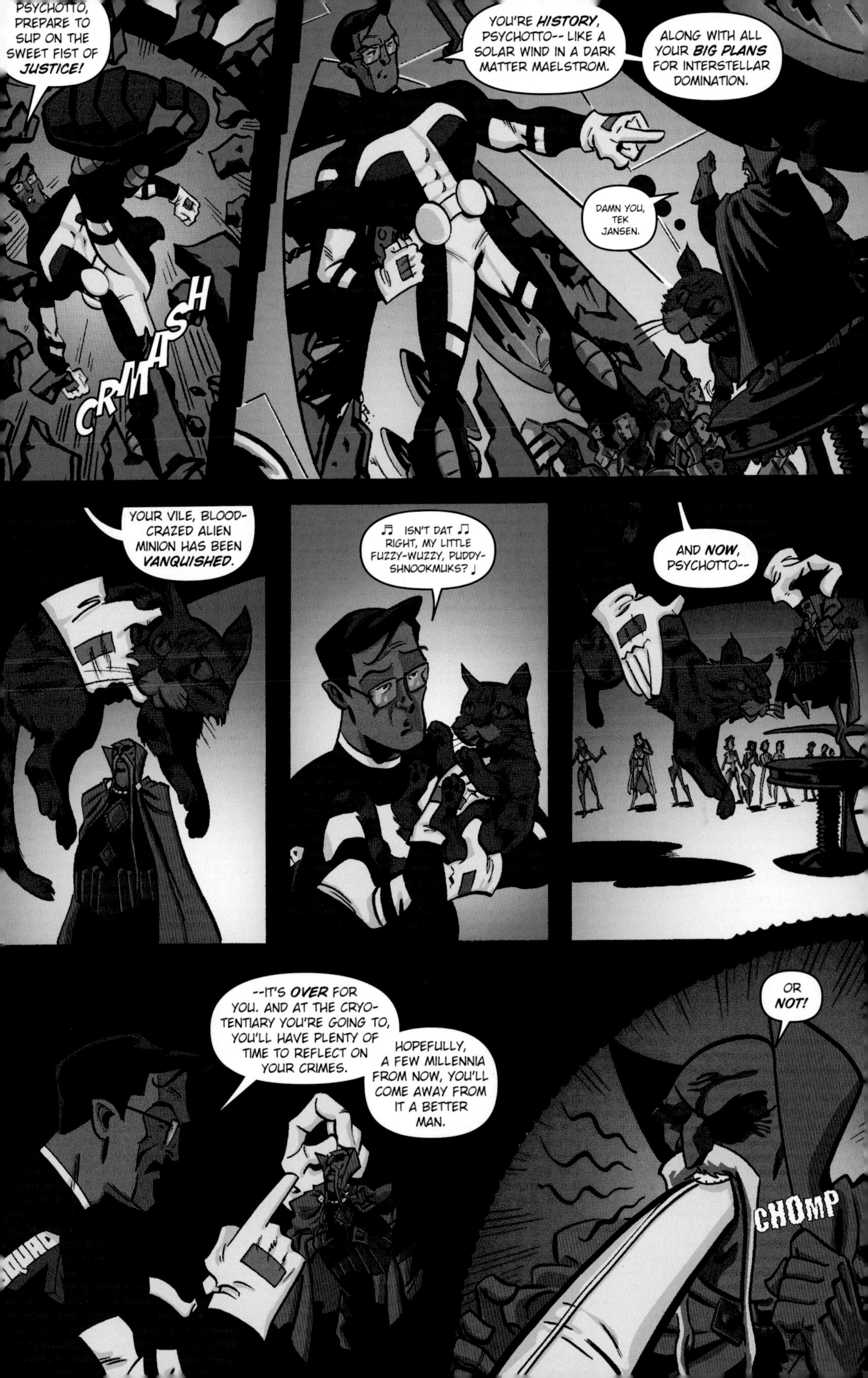
PSYCHOTTO, PREPARE TO SUP ON THE SWEET FIST OF JUSTICE!
CRMASH
YOU'RE HISTORY, PSYCHOTTO-- LIKE A SOLAR WIND IN A DARK MATTER MAELSTROM.
ALONG WITH ALL YOUR BIG PLANS FOR INTERSTELLAR DOMINATION.
DAMN YOU, TEK JANSEN.
YOUR VILE, BLOOD-CRAZED ALIEN MINION HAS BEEN VANQUISHED.
♫ ISN'T DAT ♫ RIGHT, MY LITTLE FUZZY-WUZZY, PUDDY-SHNOOKMUKS? ♩
AND NOW, PSYCHOTTO--
--IT'S OVER FOR YOU. AND AT THE CRYO-TENTIARY YOU'RE GOING TO, YOU'LL HAVE PLENTY OF TIME TO REFLECT ON YOUR CRIMES.
HOPEFULLY, A FEW MILLENNIA FROM NOW, YOU'LL COME AWAY FROM IT A BETTER MAN.
OR NOT!
CHOMP

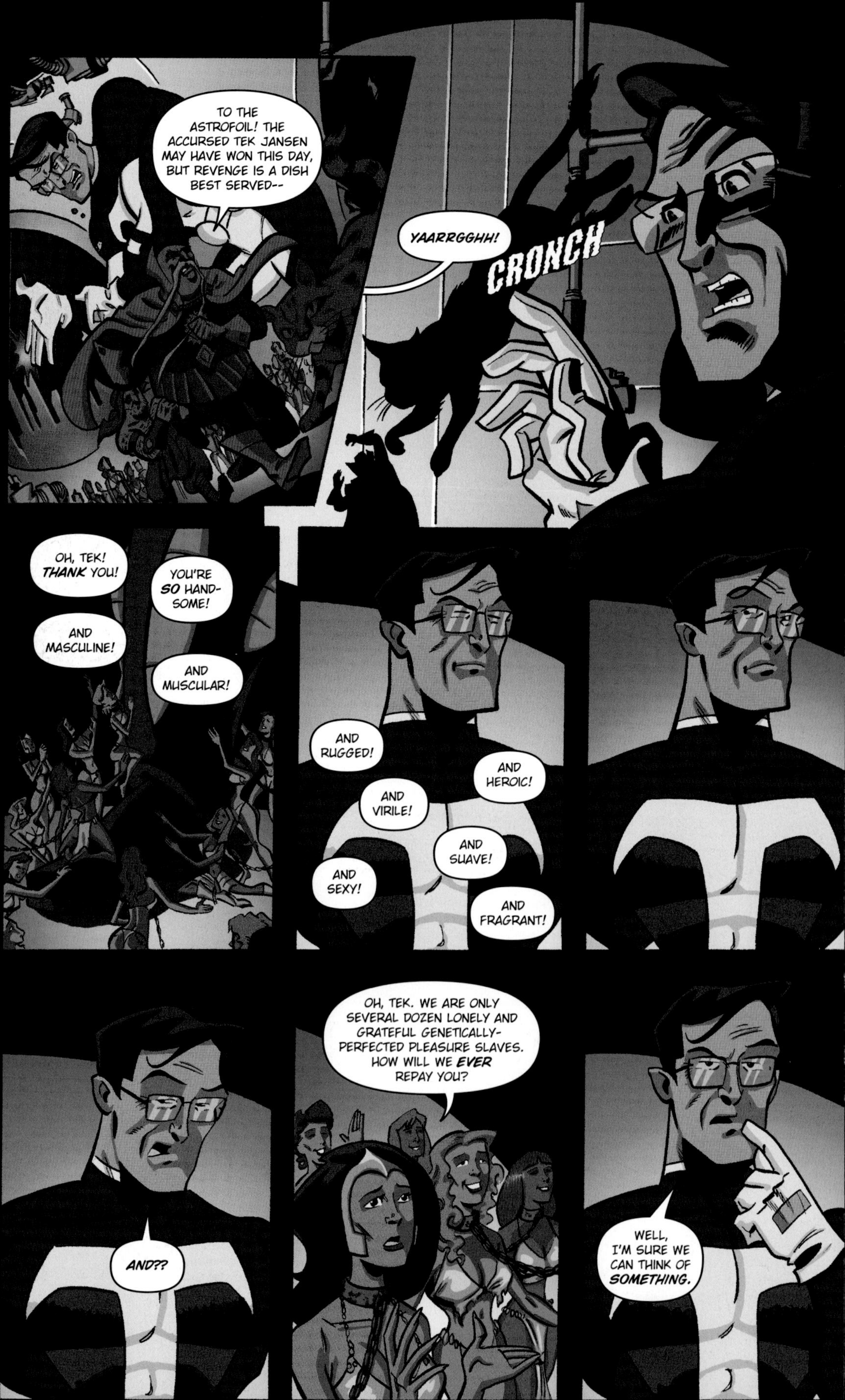
TO THE ASTROFOIL! THE ACCURSED TEK JANSEN MAY HAVE WON THIS DAY, BUT REVENGE IS A DISH BEST SERVED--
YAARRGGHH!
CRONCH
OH, TEK! *THANK* YOU!
YOU'RE *SO* HANDSOME!
AND MASCULINE!
AND MUSCULAR!
AND RUGGED!
AND HEROIC!
AND VIRILE!
AND SUAVE!
AND SEXY!
AND FRAGRANT!
AND??
OH, TEK. WE ARE ONLY SEVERAL DOZEN LONELY AND GRATEFUL GENETICALLY-PERFECTED PLEASURE SLAVES. HOW WILL WE *EVER* REPAY YOU?
WELL, I'M SURE WE CAN THINK OF *SOMETHING.*

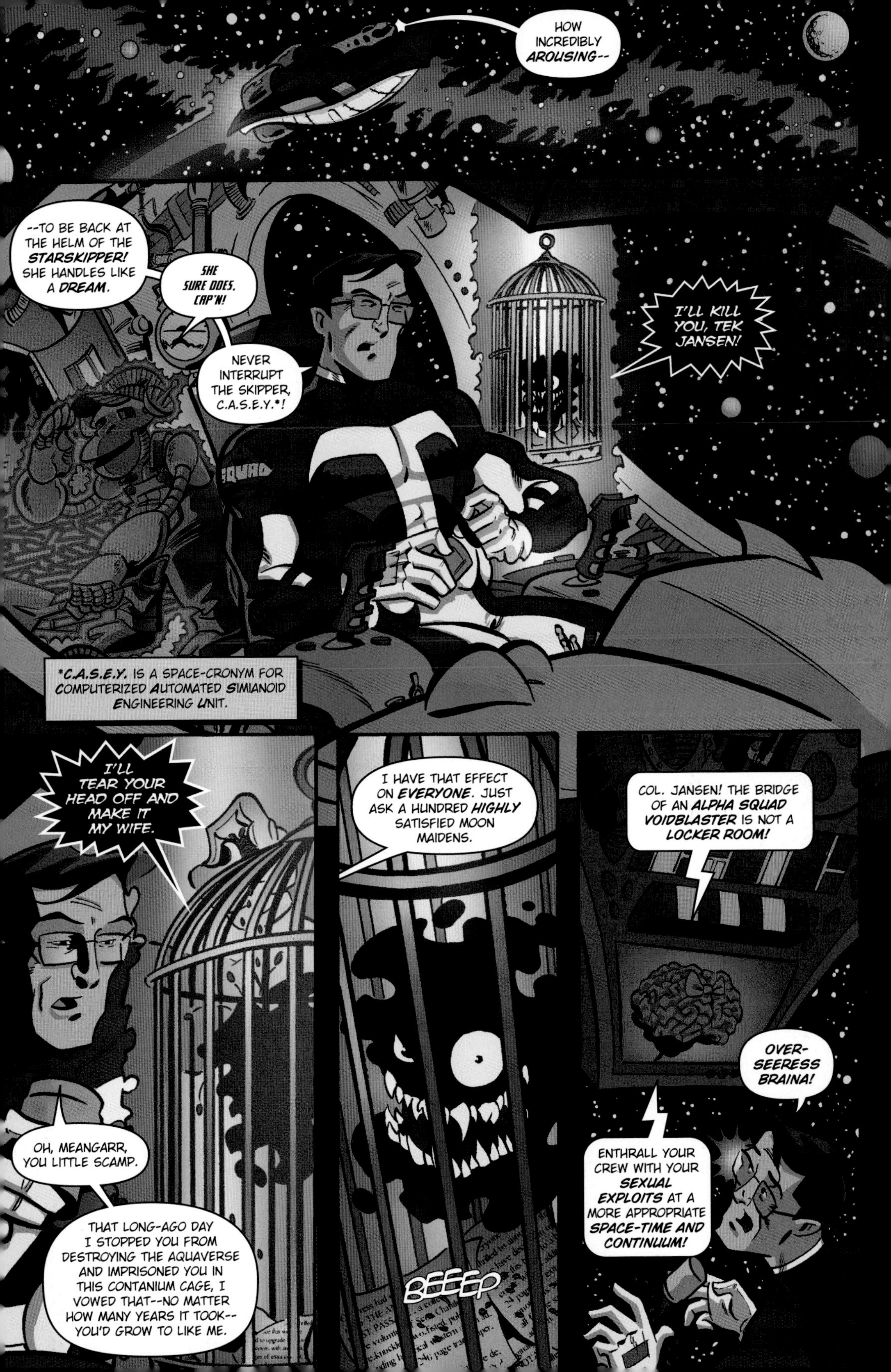
HOW INCREDIBLY AROUSING--
--TO BE BACK AT THE HELM OF THE STARSKIPPER! SHE HANDLES LIKE A DREAM.
SHE SURE DOES, CAP'N!
NEVER INTERRUPT THE SKIPPER, C.A.S.E.Y.*!
I'LL KILL YOU, TEK JANSEN!
SQUAD
*C.A.S.E.Y. IS A SPACE-CRONYM FOR COMPUTERIZED AUTOMATED SIMIANOID ENGINEERING UNIT.
I'LL TEAR YOUR HEAD OFF AND MAKE IT MY WIFE.
OH, MEANGARR, YOU LITTLE SCAMP.
THAT LONG-AGO DAY I STOPPED YOU FROM DESTROYING THE AQUAVERSE AND IMPRISONED YOU IN THIS CONTANIUM CAGE, I VOWED THAT--NO MATTER HOW MANY YEARS IT TOOK--YOU'D GROW TO LIKE ME.
I HAVE THAT EFFECT ON EVERYONE. JUST ASK A HUNDRED HIGHLY SATISFIED MOON MAIDENS.
BEEEP
COL. JANSEN! THE BRIDGE OF AN ALPHA SQUAD VOIDBLASTER IS NOT A LOCKER ROOM!
OVER-SEERESS BRAINA!
ENTHRALL YOUR CREW WITH YOUR SEXUAL EXPLOITS AT A MORE APPROPRIATE SPACE-TIME AND CONTINUUM!

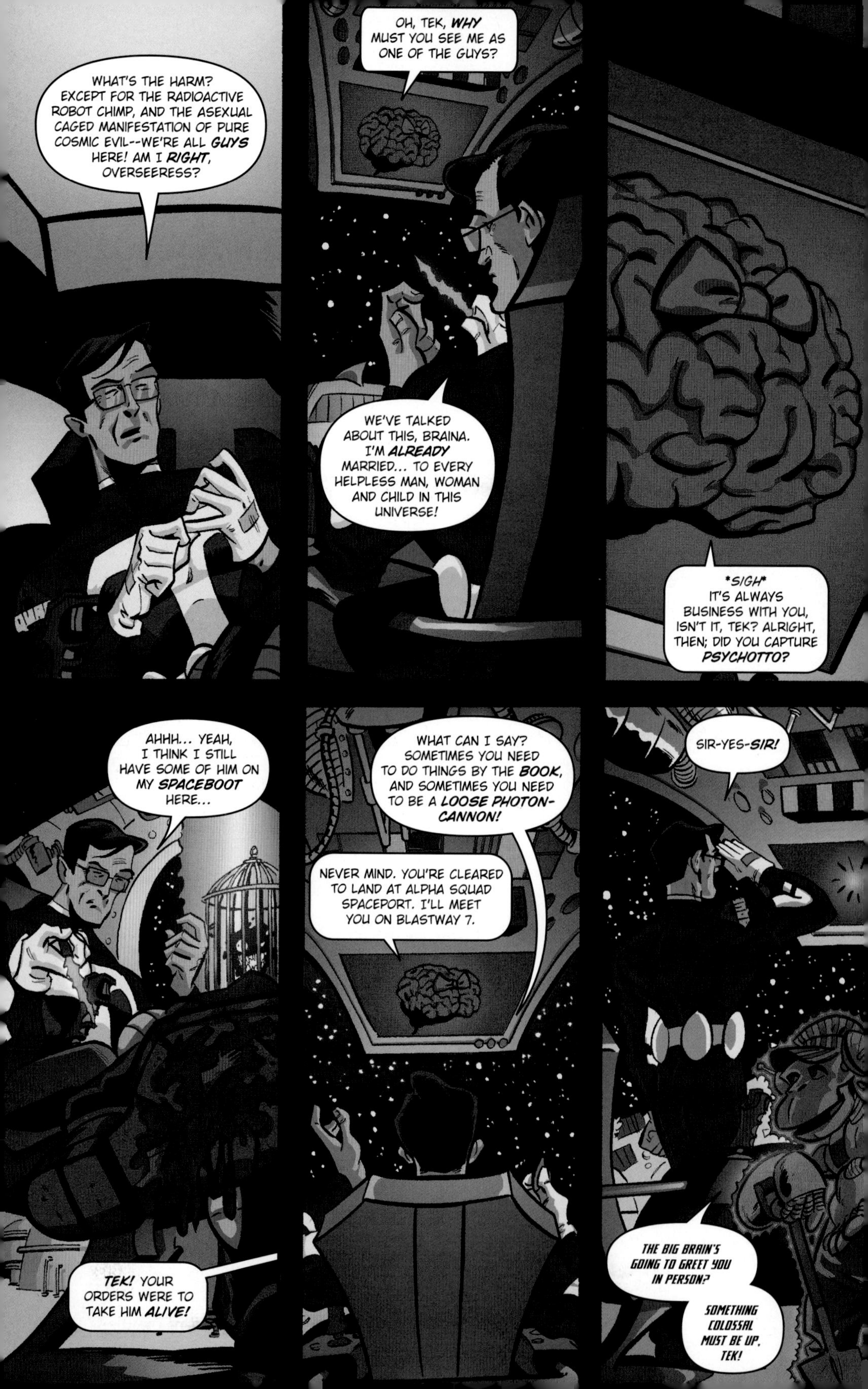
WHAT'S THE HARM? EXCEPT FOR THE RADIOACTIVE ROBOT CHIMP, AND THE ASEXUAL CAGED MANIFESTATION OF PURE COSMIC EVIL--WE'RE ALL GUYS HERE! AM I RIGHT, OVERSEERESS?
OH, TEK, WHY MUST YOU SEE ME AS ONE OF THE GUYS?
WE'VE TALKED ABOUT THIS, BRAINA. I'M ALREADY MARRIED... TO EVERY HELPLESS MAN, WOMAN AND CHILD IN THIS UNIVERSE!
SIGH IT'S ALWAYS BUSINESS WITH YOU, ISN'T IT, TEK? ALRIGHT, THEN; DID YOU CAPTURE PSYCHOTTO?
AHHH... YEAH, I THINK I STILL HAVE SOME OF HIM ON MY SPACEBOOT HERE...
TEK! YOUR ORDERS WERE TO TAKE HIM ALIVE!
WHAT CAN I SAY? SOMETIMES YOU NEED TO DO THINGS BY THE BOOK, AND SOMETIMES YOU NEED TO BE A LOOSE PHOTON-CANNON!
NEVER MIND. YOU'RE CLEARED TO LAND AT ALPHA SQUAD SPACEPORT. I'LL MEET YOU ON BLASTWAY 7.
SIR-YES-SIR!
THE BIG BRAIN'S GOING TO GREET YOU IN PERSON?
SOMETHING COLOSSAL MUST BE UP, TEK!

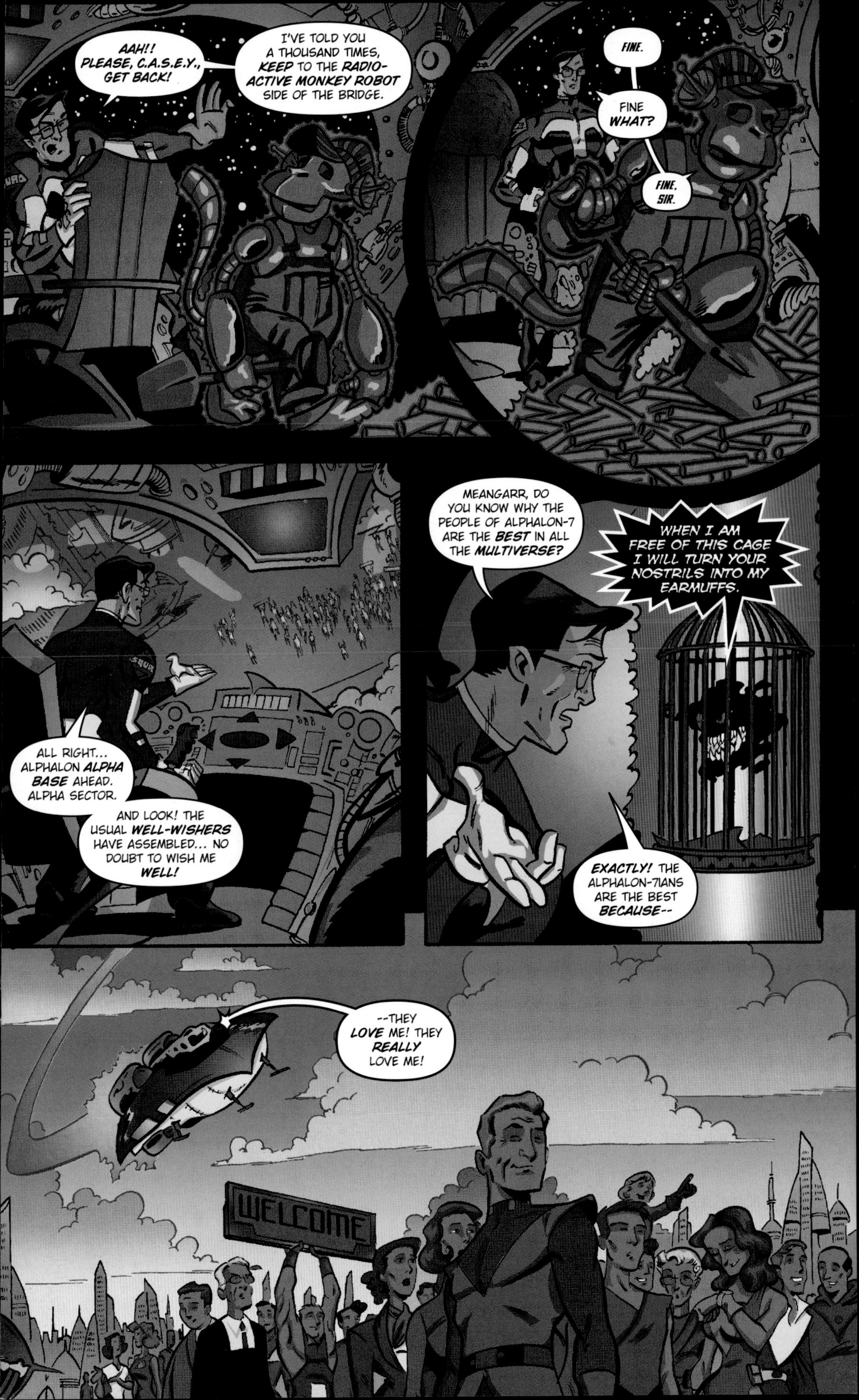
AAH!! PLEASE, C.A.S.E.Y., GET BACK!
I'VE TOLD YOU A THOUSAND TIMES, KEEP TO THE RADIO-ACTIVE MONKEY ROBOT SIDE OF THE BRIDGE.
FINE.
FINE WHAT?
FINE, SIR.
ALL RIGHT... ALPHALON ALPHA BASE AHEAD. ALPHA SECTOR.
AND LOOK! THE USUAL WELL-WISHERS HAVE ASSEMBLED... NO DOUBT TO WISH ME WELL!
MEANGARR, DO YOU KNOW WHY THE PEOPLE OF ALPHALON-7 ARE THE BEST IN ALL THE MULTIVERSE?
WHEN I AM FREE OF THIS CAGE I WILL TURN YOUR NOSTRILS INTO MY EARMUFFS.
EXACTLY! THE ALPHALON-7IANS ARE THE BEST BECAUSE--
--THEY LOVE ME! THEY REALLY LOVE ME!
WELCOME

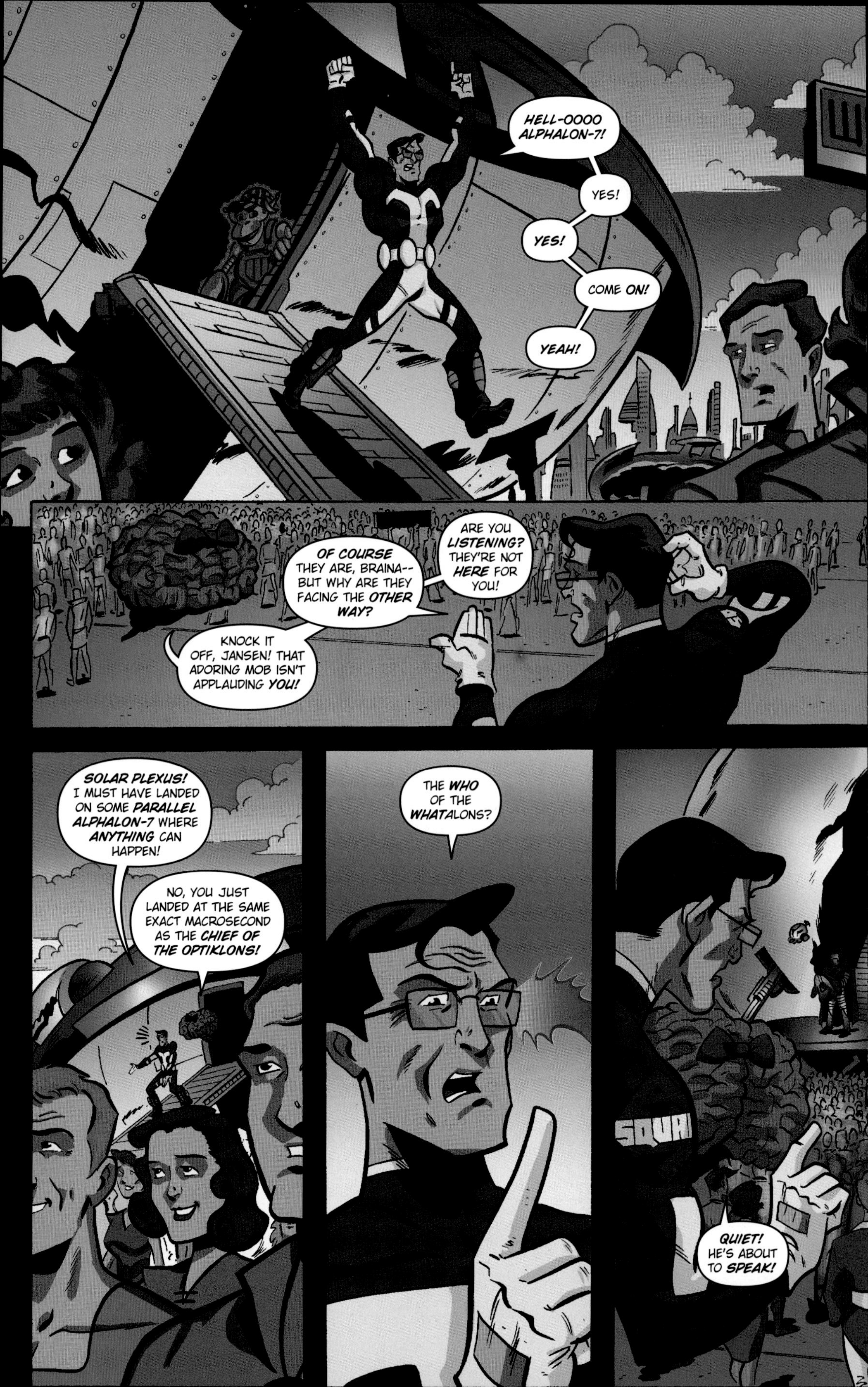
HELL-OOOO ALPHALON-7!
YES!
YES!
COME ON!
YEAH!
ARE YOU LISTENING? THEY'RE NOT HERE FOR YOU!
OF COURSE THEY ARE, BRAINA-- BUT WHY ARE THEY FACING THE OTHER WAY?
KNOCK IT OFF, JANSEN! THAT ADORING MOB ISN'T APPLAUDING YOU!
SOLAR PLEXUS! I MUST HAVE LANDED ON SOME PARALLEL ALPHALON-7 WHERE ANYTHING CAN HAPPEN!
NO, YOU JUST LANDED AT THE SAME EXACT MACROSECOND AS THE CHIEF OF THE OPTIKLONS!
THE WHO OF THE WHATALONS?
SQUA
QUIET! HE'S ABOUT TO SPEAK!

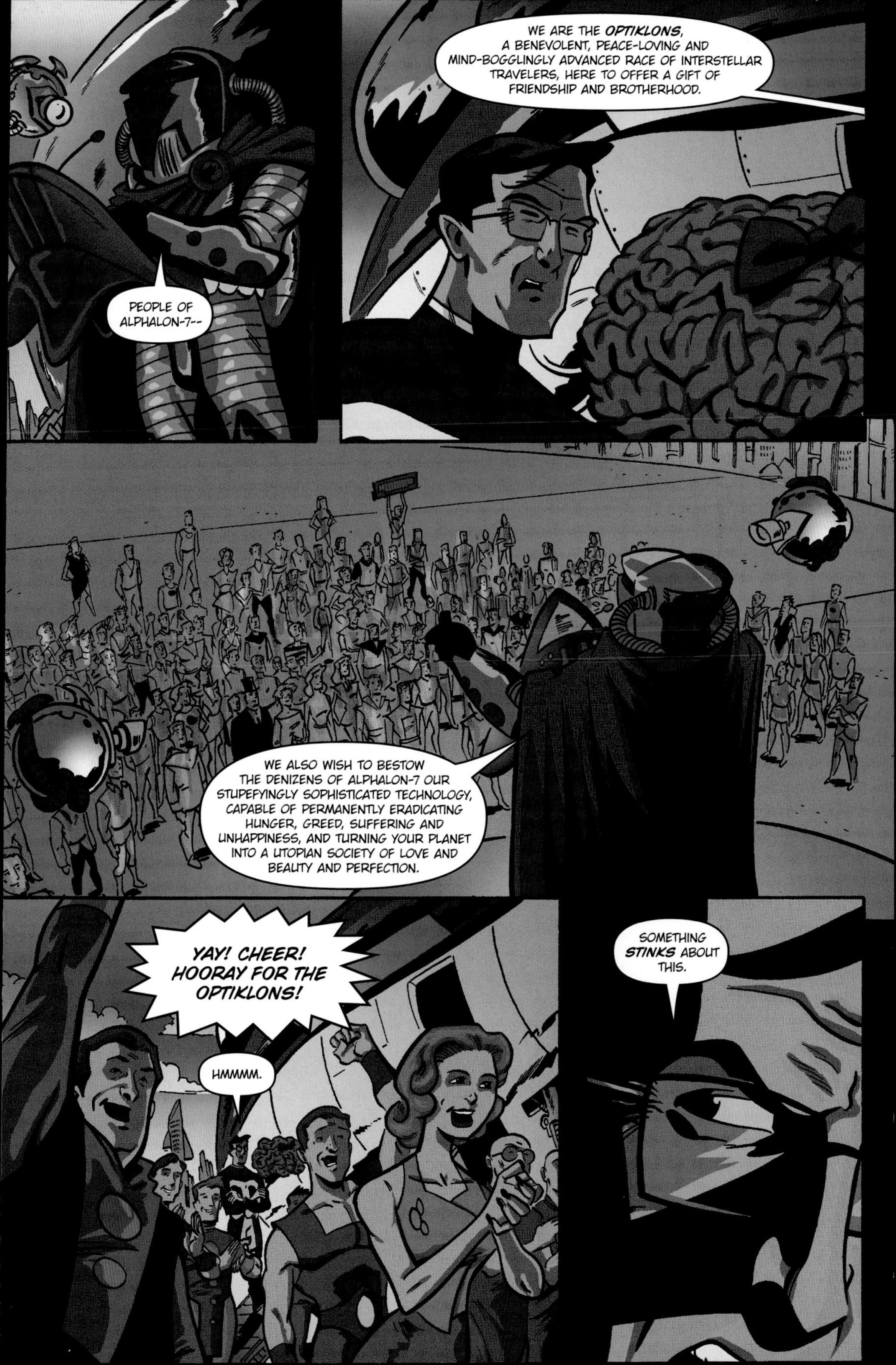
PEOPLE OF ALPHALON-7--
WE ARE THE OPTIKLONS, A BENEVOLENT, PEACE-LOVING AND MIND-BOGGLINGLY ADVANCED RACE OF INTERSTELLAR TRAVELERS, HERE TO OFFER A GIFT OF FRIENDSHIP AND BROTHERHOOD.
WE ALSO WISH TO BESTOW THE DENIZENS OF ALPHALON-7 OUR STUPEFYINGLY SOPHISTICATED TECHNOLOGY, CAPABLE OF PERMANENTLY ERADICATING HUNGER, GREED, SUFFERING AND UNHAPPINESS, AND TURNING YOUR PLANET INTO A UTOPIAN SOCIETY OF LOVE AND BEAUTY AND PERFECTION.
YAY! CHEER! HOORAY FOR THE OPTIKLONS!
HMMMM.
SOMETHING STINKS ABOUT THIS.

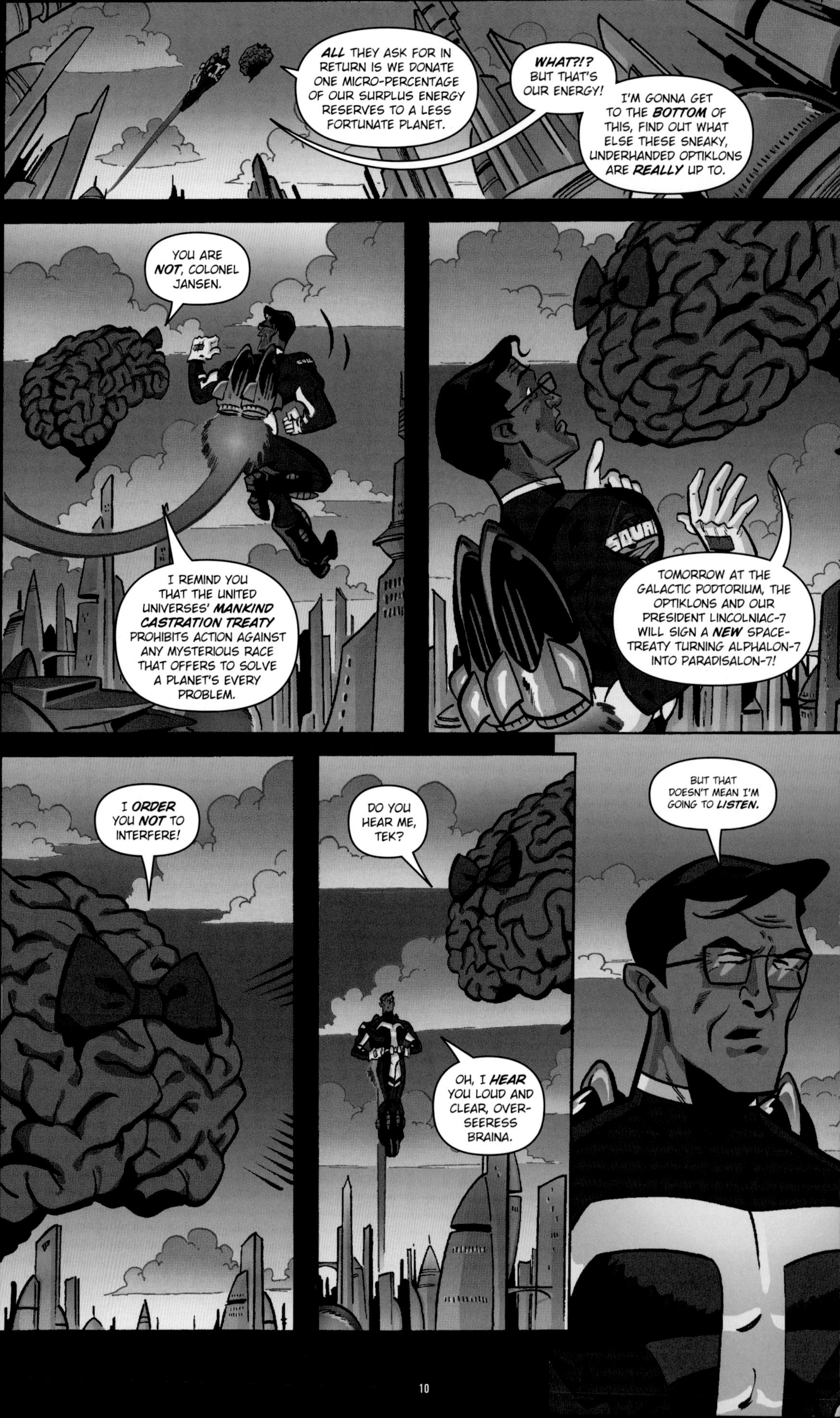

ALL THEY ASK FOR IN RETURN IS WE DONATE ONE MICRO-PERCENTAGE OF OUR SURPLUS ENERGY RESERVES TO A LESS FORTUNATE PLANET.
WHAT?!? BUT THAT'S OUR ENERGY!
I'M GONNA GET TO THE BOTTOM OF THIS, FIND OUT WHAT ELSE THESE SNEAKY, UNDERHANDED OPTIKLONS ARE REALLY UP TO.
YOU ARE NOT, COLONEL JANSEN.
I REMIND YOU THAT THE UNITED UNIVERSES' MANKIND CASTRATION TREATY PROHIBITS ACTION AGAINST ANY MYSTERIOUS RACE THAT OFFERS TO SOLVE A PLANET'S EVERY PROBLEM.
TOMORROW AT THE GALACTIC PODTORIUM, THE OPTIKLONS AND OUR PRESIDENT LINCOLNIAC-7 WILL SIGN A NEW SPACE-TREATY TURNING ALPHALON-7 INTO PARADISALON-7!
I ORDER YOU NOT TO INTERFERE!
DO YOU HEAR ME, TEK?
OH, I HEAR YOU LOUD AND CLEAR, OVER-SEERESS BRAINA.
BUT THAT DOESN'T MEAN I'M GOING TO LISTEN.

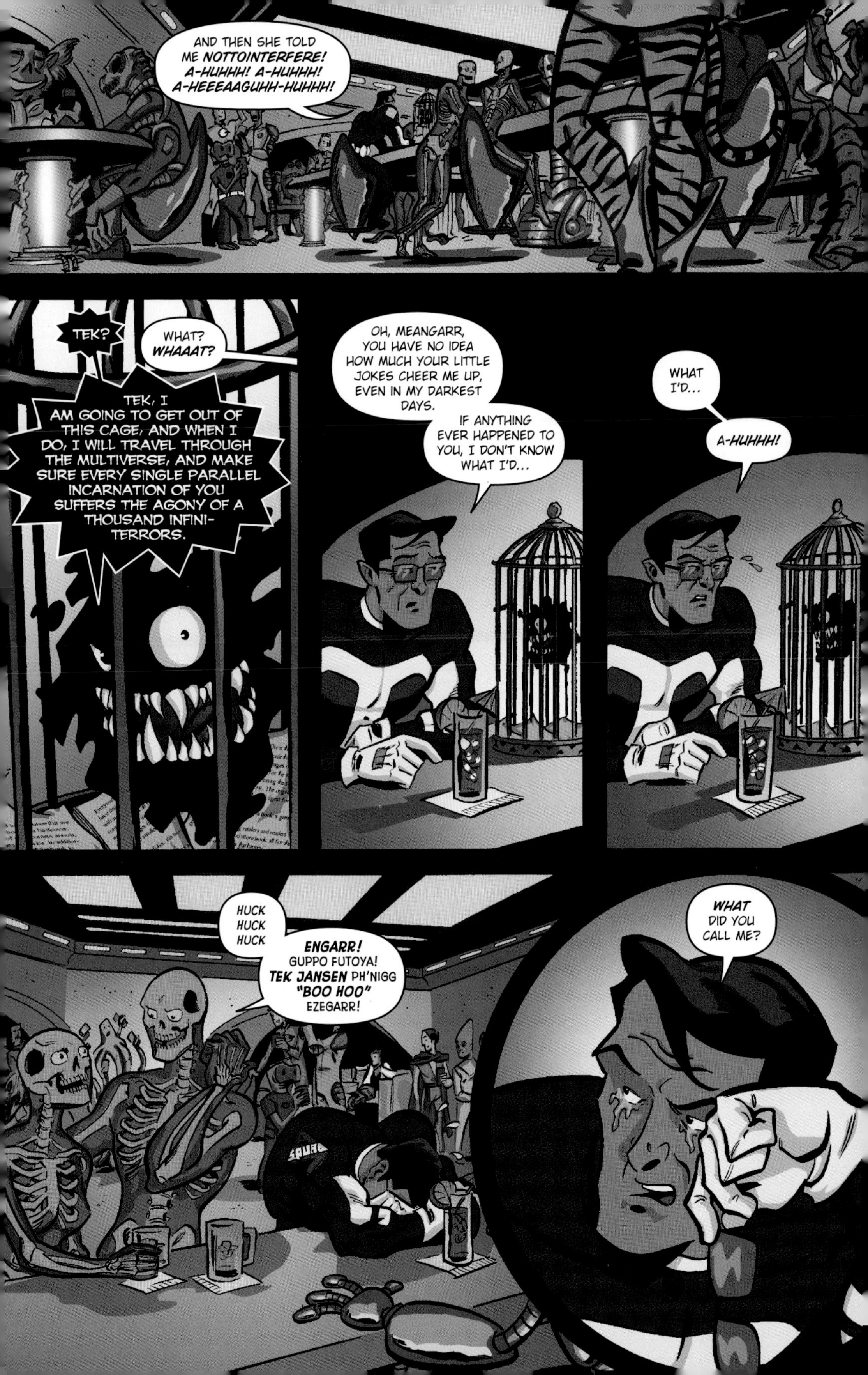
AND THEN SHE TOLD ME **NOTTOINTERFERE! A-HUHHH! A-HUHHH! A-HEEEAAGUHH-HUHHH!**
TEK?
WHAT? **WHAAAT?**
TEK, I AM GOING TO GET OUT OF THIS CAGE, AND WHEN I DO, I WILL TRAVEL THROUGH THE MULTIVERSE, AND MAKE SURE EVERY SINGLE PARALLEL INCARNATION OF YOU SUFFERS THE AGONY OF A THOUSAND INFINI-TERRORS.
OH, MEANGARR, YOU HAVE NO IDEA HOW MUCH YOUR LITTLE JOKES CHEER ME UP, EVEN IN MY DARKEST DAYS.
IF ANYTHING EVER HAPPENED TO YOU, I DON'T KNOW WHAT I'D...
WHAT I'D...
A-**HUHHH!**
HUCK HUCK HUCK
ENGARR! GUPPO FUTOYA! **TEK JANSEN** PH'NIGG **"BOO HOO"** EZEGARR!
WHAT DID YOU CALL ME?

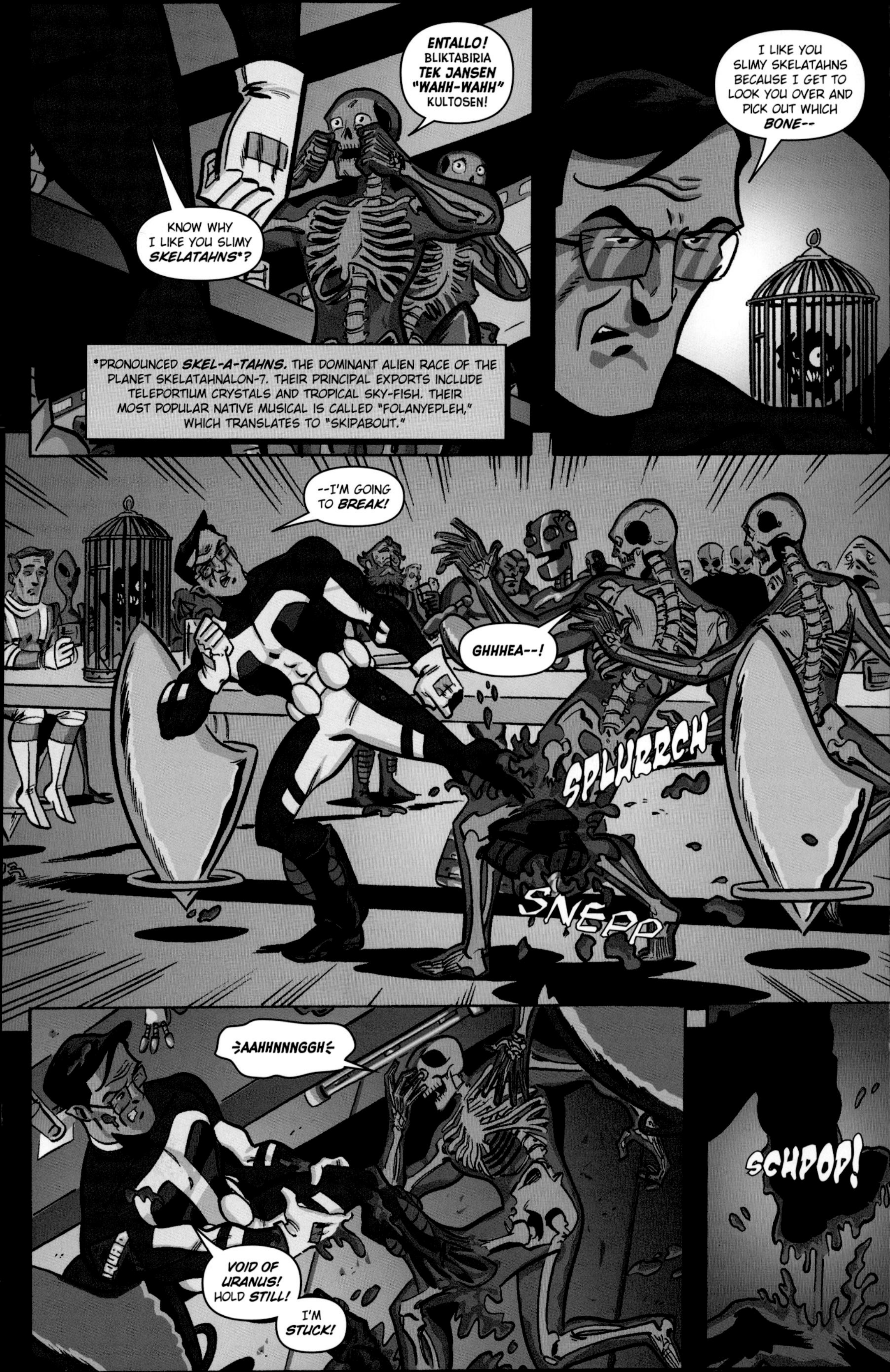
KNOW WHY I LIKE YOU SLIMY SKELATAHNS*?
ENTALLO! BLIKTABIRIA TEK JANSEN "WAHH-WAHH" KULTOSEN!
*PRONOUNCED SKEL-A-TAHNS. THE DOMINANT ALIEN RACE OF THE PLANET SKELATAHNALON-7. THEIR PRINCIPAL EXPORTS INCLUDE TELEPORTIUM CRYSTALS AND TROPICAL SKY-FISH. THEIR MOST POPULAR NATIVE MUSICAL IS CALLED "FOLANYEPLEH," WHICH TRANSLATES TO "SKIPABOUT."
I LIKE YOU SLIMY SKELATAHNS BECAUSE I GET TO LOOK YOU OVER AND PICK OUT WHICH BONE--
--I'M GOING TO BREAK!
GHHHEA--!
SPLURRCH
SNEPP
AAHHNNNGGH
VOID OF URANUS! HOLD STILL!
I'M STUCK!
SCHPOP!

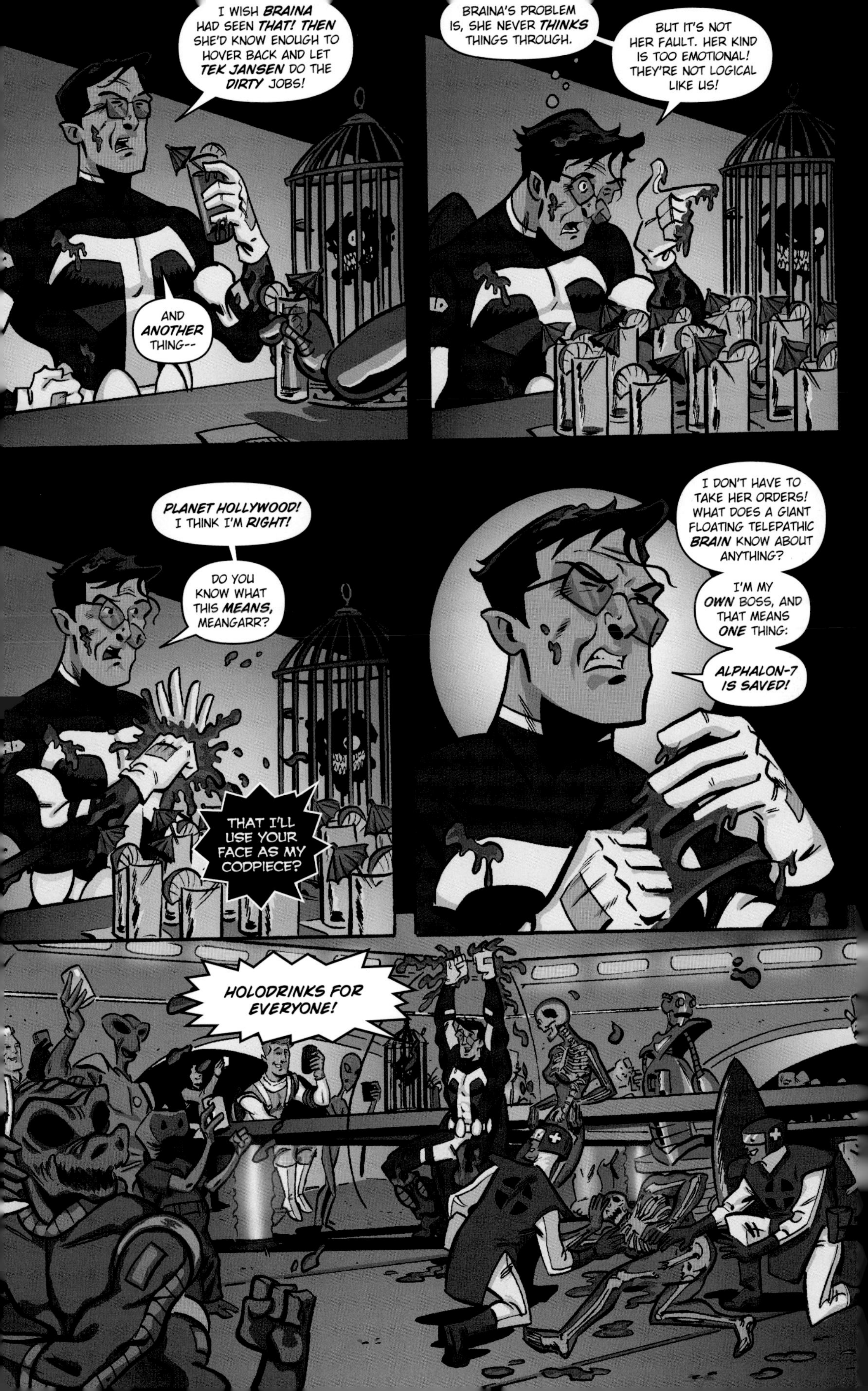
I WISH BRAINA HAD SEEN THAT! THEN SHE'D KNOW ENOUGH TO HOVER BACK AND LET TEK JANSEN DO THE DIRTY JOBS!
AND ANOTHER THING--
BRAINA'S PROBLEM IS, SHE NEVER THINKS THINGS THROUGH.
BUT IT'S NOT HER FAULT. HER KIND IS TOO EMOTIONAL! THEY'RE NOT LOGICAL LIKE US!
PLANET HOLLYWOOD! I THINK I'M RIGHT!
DO YOU KNOW WHAT THIS MEANS, MEANGARR?
THAT I'LL USE YOUR FACE AS MY CODPIECE?
I DON'T HAVE TO TAKE HER ORDERS! WHAT DOES A GIANT FLOATING TELEPATHIC BRAIN KNOW ABOUT ANYTHING?
I'M MY OWN BOSS, AND THAT MEANS ONE THING:
ALPHALON-7 IS SAVED!
HOLODRINKS FOR EVERYONE!

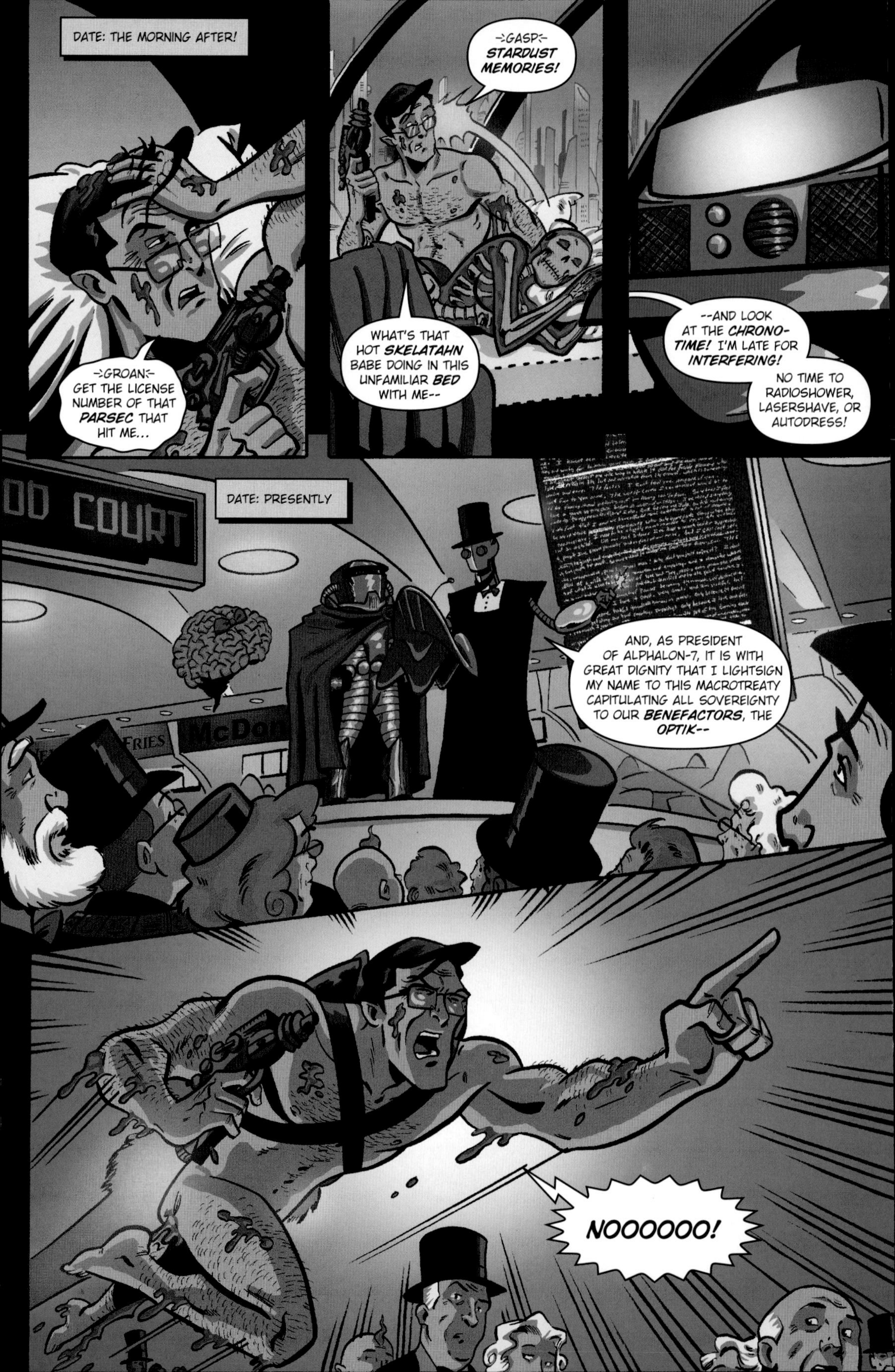
DATE: THE MORNING AFTER!
-GROAN- GET THE LICENSE NUMBER OF THAT PARSEC THAT HIT ME...
-GASP- STARDUST MEMORIES!
WHAT'S THAT HOT SKELATAHN BABE DOING IN THIS UNFAMILIAR BED WITH ME--
--AND LOOK AT THE CHRONO-TIME! I'M LATE FOR INTERFERING!
NO TIME TO RADIOSHOWER, LASERSHAVE, OR AUTODRESS!
OD COURT
DATE: PRESENTLY
FRIES
McDon
AND, AS PRESIDENT OF ALPHALON-7, IT IS WITH GREAT DIGNITY THAT I LIGHTSIGN MY NAME TO THIS MACROTREATY CAPITULATING ALL SOVEREIGNTY TO OUR BENEFACTORS, THE OPTIK--
NOOOOOO!

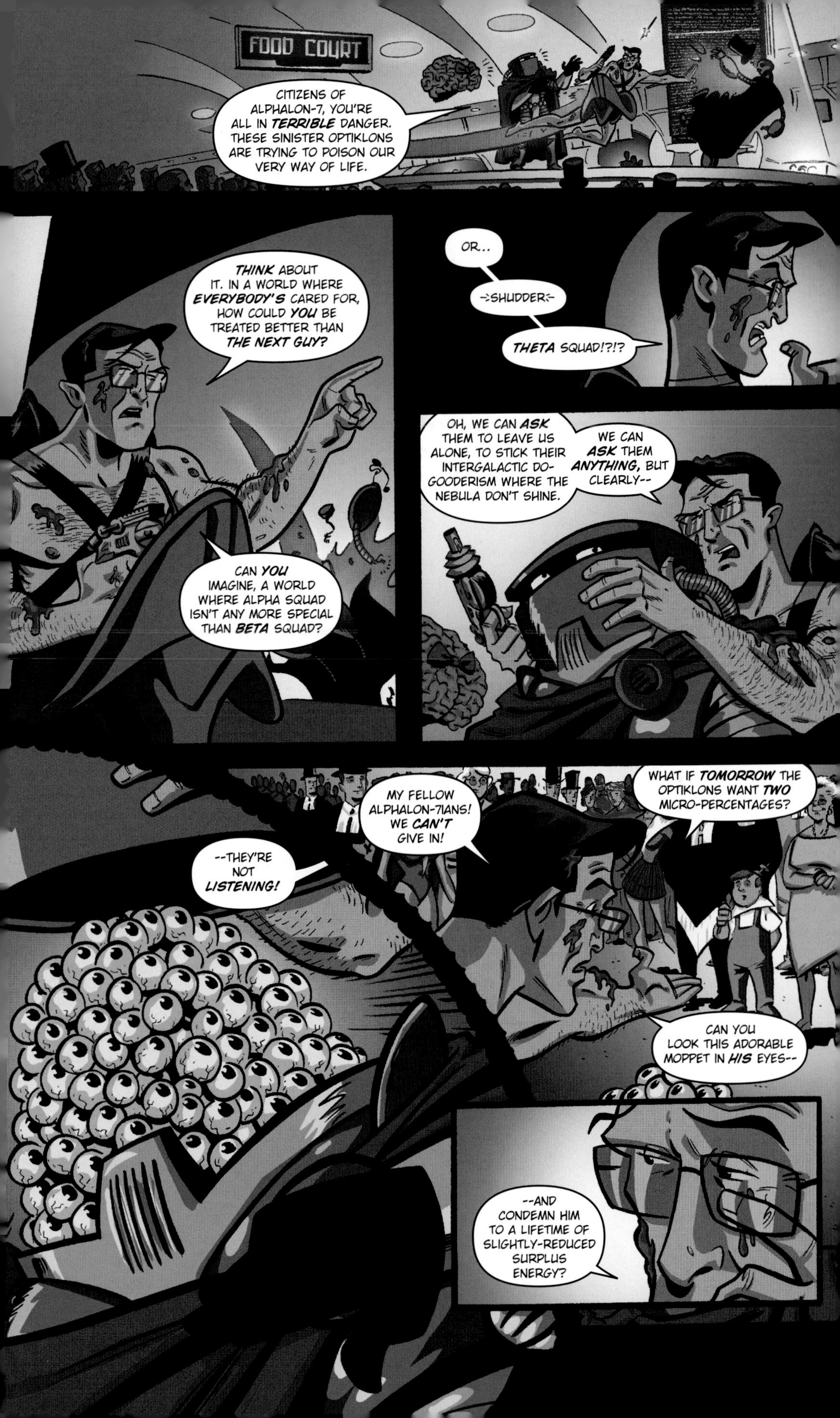
FOOD COURT
CITIZENS OF ALPHALON-7, YOU'RE ALL IN *TERRIBLE* DANGER. THESE SINISTER OPTIKLONS ARE TRYING TO POISON OUR VERY WAY OF LIFE.
THINK ABOUT IT. IN A WORLD WHERE *EVERYBODY'S* CARED FOR, HOW COULD *YOU* BE TREATED BETTER THAN *THE NEXT GUY?*
CAN *YOU* IMAGINE, A WORLD WHERE ALPHA SQUAD ISN'T ANY MORE SPECIAL THAN *BETA* SQUAD?
OR...
-SHUDDER-
THETA SQUAD!?!?
OH, WE CAN *ASK* THEM TO LEAVE US ALONE, TO STICK THEIR INTERGALACTIC DO-GOODERISM WHERE THE NEBULA DON'T SHINE.
WE CAN *ASK* THEM *ANYTHING,* BUT CLEARLY--
--THEY'RE NOT *LISTENING!*
MY FELLOW ALPHALON-7IANS! WE *CAN'T* GIVE IN!
WHAT IF *TOMORROW* THE OPTIKLONS WANT *TWO* MICRO-PERCENTAGES?
CAN YOU LOOK THIS ADORABLE MOPPET IN *HIS* EYES--
--AND CONDEMN HIM TO A LIFETIME OF SLIGHTLY-REDUCED SURPLUS ENERGY?

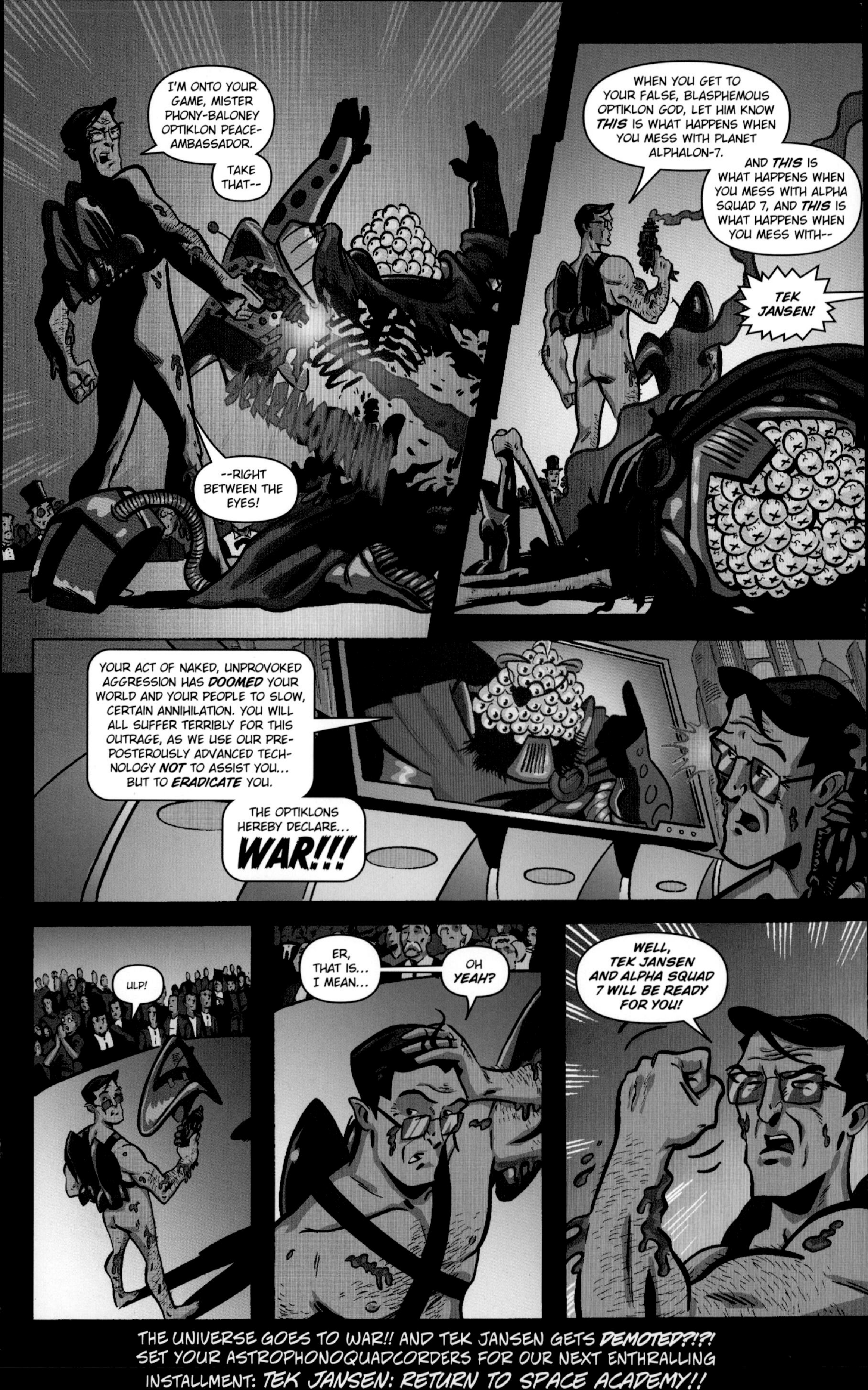
I'M ONTO YOUR GAME, MISTER PHONY-BALONEY OPTIKLON PEACE-AMBASSADOR.
TAKE THAT--
--RIGHT BETWEEN THE EYES!
WHEN YOU GET TO YOUR FALSE, BLASPHEMOUS OPTIKLON GOD, LET HIM KNOW ***THIS*** IS WHAT HAPPENS WHEN YOU MESS WITH PLANET ALPHALON-7.
AND ***THIS*** IS WHAT HAPPENS WHEN YOU MESS WITH ALPHA SQUAD 7, AND ***THIS*** IS WHAT HAPPENS WHEN YOU MESS WITH--
TEK JANSEN!
YOUR ACT OF NAKED, UNPROVOKED AGGRESSION HAS ***DOOMED*** YOUR WORLD AND YOUR PEOPLE TO SLOW, CERTAIN ANNIHILATION. YOU WILL ALL SUFFER TERRIBLY FOR THIS OUTRAGE, AS WE USE OUR PREPOSTEROUSLY ADVANCED TECHNOLOGY ***NOT*** TO ASSIST YOU... BUT TO ***ERADICATE*** YOU.
THE OPTIKLONS HEREBY DECLARE... **WAR!!!**
ULP!
ER, THAT IS... I MEAN...
OH ***YEAH?***
WELL, TEK JANSEN AND ALPHA SQUAD 7 WILL BE READY FOR YOU!

THE UNIVERSE GOES TO WAR!! AND TEK JANSEN GETS ***DEMOTED?!?!***
SET YOUR ASTROPHONOQUADCORDERS FOR OUR NEXT ENTHRALLING INSTALLMENT: ***TEK JANSEN: RETURN TO SPACE ACADEMY!!***

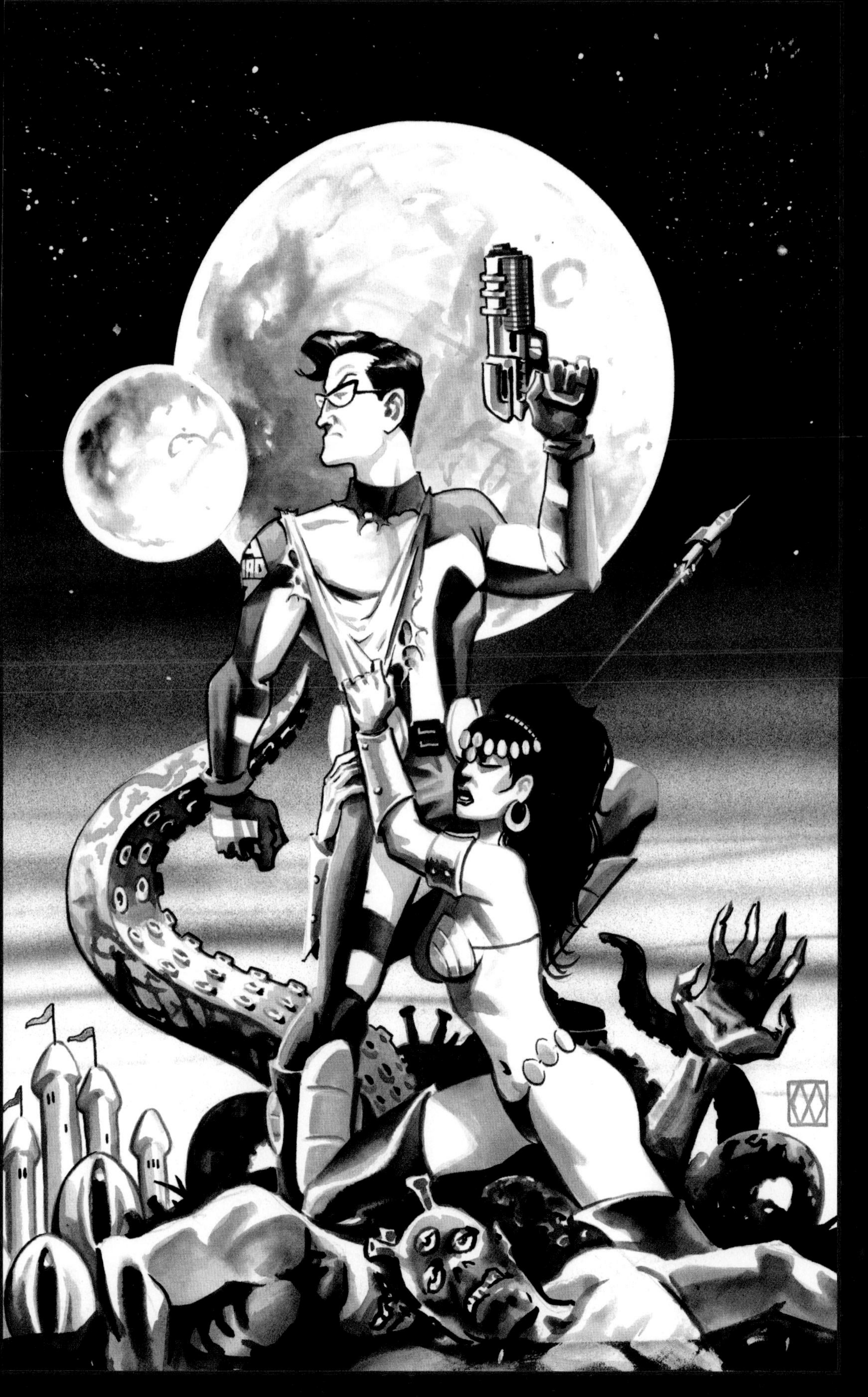

art by MATT WAGNER

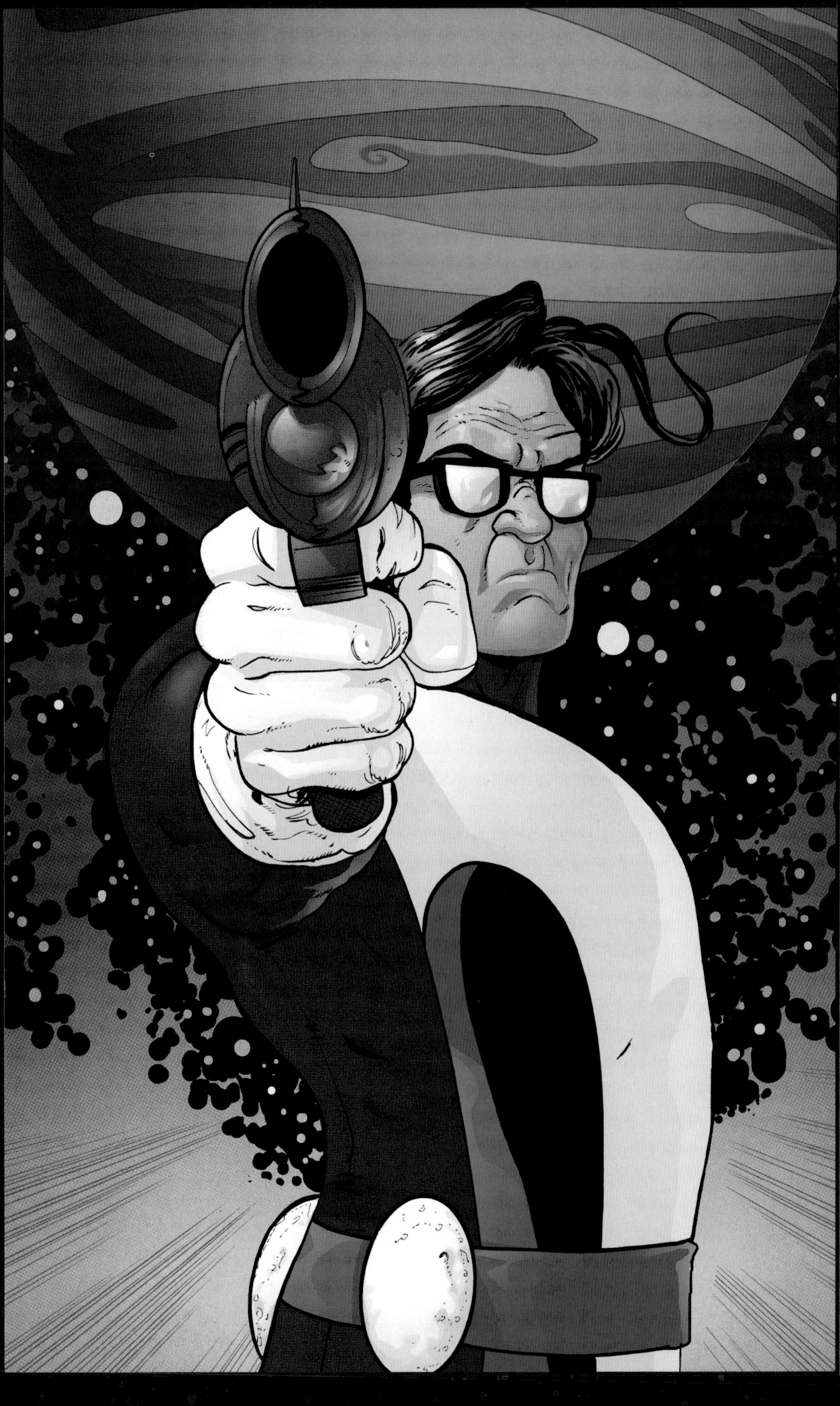

art by **ROBBI RODRIGUEZ** with **DAN JACKSON**

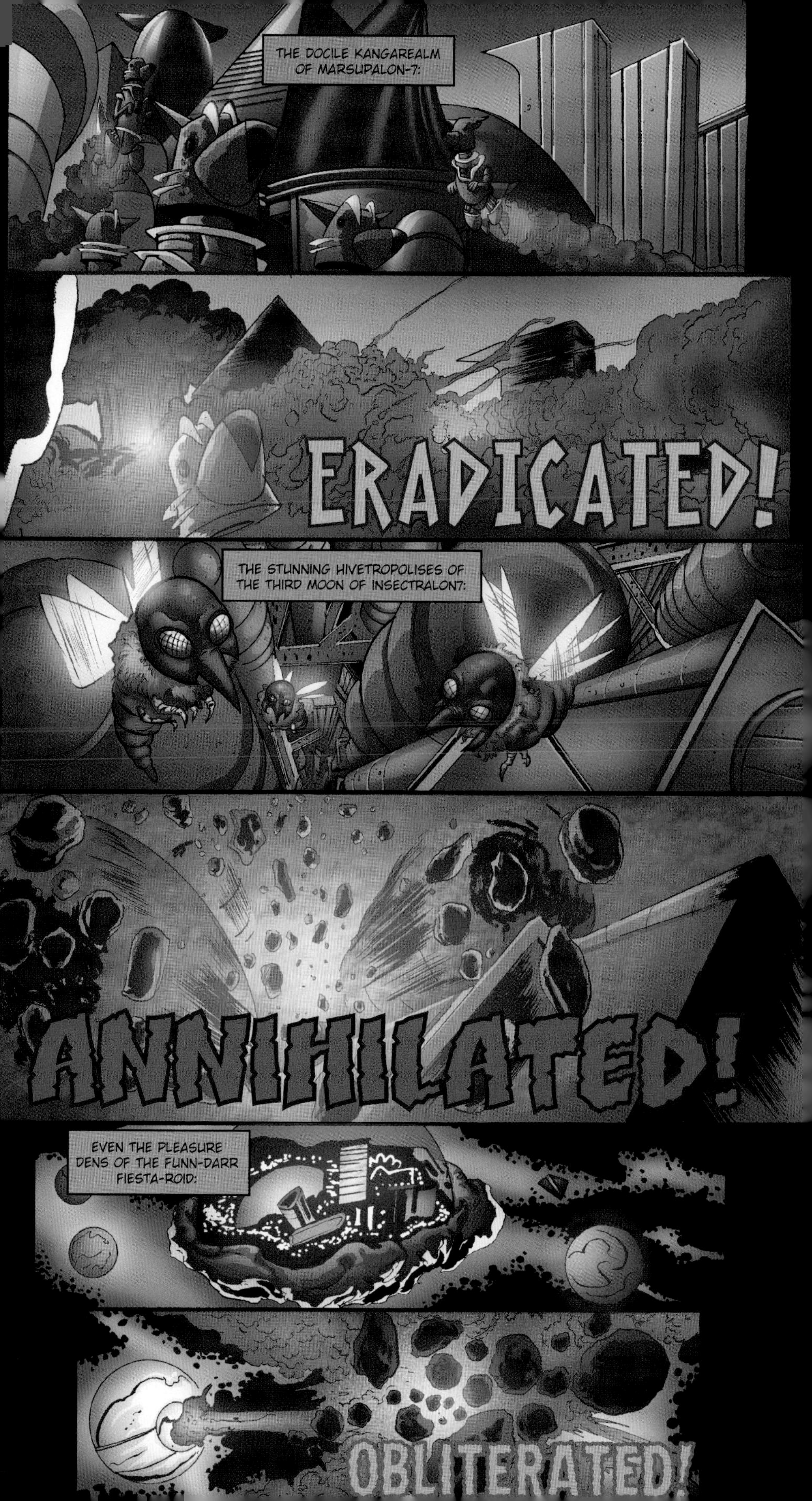
THE DOCILE KANGAREALM OF MARSUPALON-7:
ERADICATED!
THE STUNNING HIVETROPOLISES OF THE THIRD MOON OF INSECTRALON7:
ANNIHILATED!
EVEN THE PLEASURE DENS OF THE FUNN-DARR FIESTA-ROID:
OBLITERATED!

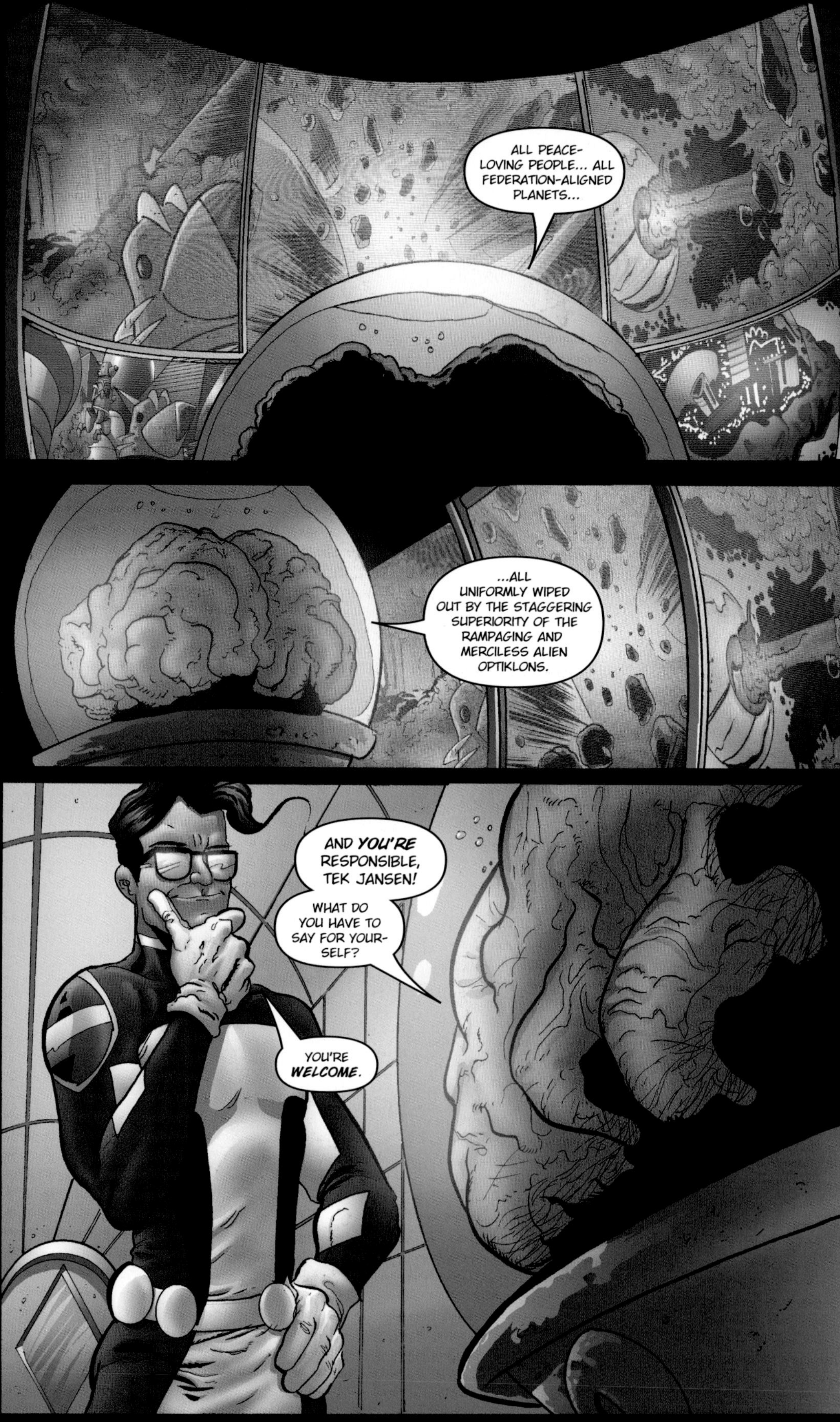
ALL PEACE-LOVING PEOPLE... ALL FEDERATION-ALIGNED PLANETS...
...ALL UNIFORMLY WIPED OUT BY THE STAGGERING SUPERIORITY OF THE RAMPAGING AND MERCILESS ALIEN OPTIKLONS.
AND YOU'RE RESPONSIBLE, TEK JANSEN!
WHAT DO YOU HAVE TO SAY FOR YOURSELF?
YOU'RE WELCOME.

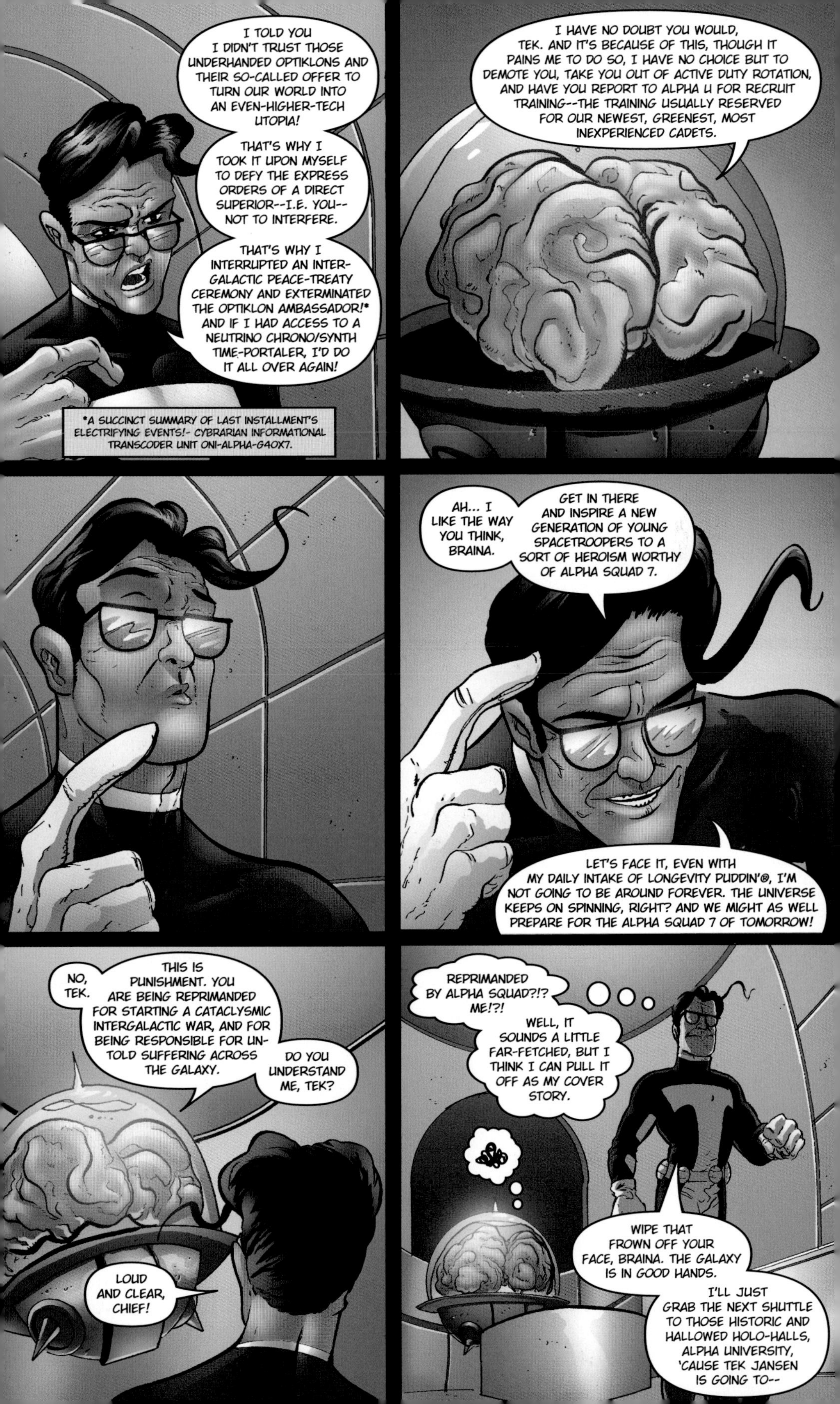
I TOLD YOU I DIDN'T TRUST THOSE UNDERHANDED OPTIKLONS AND THEIR SO-CALLED OFFER TO TURN OUR WORLD INTO AN EVEN-HIGHER-TECH UTOPIA!
THAT'S WHY I TOOK IT UPON MYSELF TO DEFY THE EXPRESS ORDERS OF A DIRECT SUPERIOR--I.E. YOU--NOT TO INTERFERE.
THAT'S WHY I INTERRUPTED AN INTER-GALACTIC PEACE-TREATY CEREMONY AND EXTERMINATED THE OPTIKLON AMBASSADOR!* AND IF I HAD ACCESS TO A NEUTRINO CHRONO/SYNTH TIME-PORTALER, I'D DO IT ALL OVER AGAIN!
*A SUCCINCT SUMMARY OF LAST INSTALLMENT'S ELECTRIFYING EVENTS!- CYBRARIAN INFORMATIONAL TRANSCODER UNIT ONI-ALPHA-G40X7.
I HAVE NO DOUBT YOU WOULD, TEK. AND IT'S BECAUSE OF THIS, THOUGH IT PAINS ME TO DO SO, I HAVE NO CHOICE BUT TO DEMOTE YOU, TAKE YOU OUT OF ACTIVE DUTY ROTATION, AND HAVE YOU REPORT TO ALPHA U FOR RECRUIT TRAINING--THE TRAINING USUALLY RESERVED FOR OUR NEWEST, GREENEST, MOST INEXPERIENCED CADETS.
AH... I LIKE THE WAY YOU THINK, BRAINA.
GET IN THERE AND INSPIRE A NEW GENERATION OF YOUNG SPACETROOPERS TO A SORT OF HEROISM WORTHY OF ALPHA SQUAD 7.
LET'S FACE IT, EVEN WITH MY DAILY INTAKE OF LONGEVITY PUDDIN'®, I'M NOT GOING TO BE AROUND FOREVER. THE UNIVERSE KEEPS ON SPINNING, RIGHT? AND WE MIGHT AS WELL PREPARE FOR THE ALPHA SQUAD 7 OF TOMORROW!
NO, TEK.
THIS IS PUNISHMENT. YOU ARE BEING REPRIMANDED FOR STARTING A CATACLYSMIC INTERGALACTIC WAR, AND FOR BEING RESPONSIBLE FOR UNTOLD SUFFERING ACROSS THE GALAXY.
DO YOU UNDERSTAND ME, TEK?
LOUD AND CLEAR, CHIEF!
REPRIMANDED BY ALPHA SQUAD?!? ME!?!
WELL, IT SOUNDS A LITTLE FAR-FETCHED, BUT I THINK I CAN PULL IT OFF AS MY COVER STORY.
WIPE THAT FROWN OFF YOUR FACE, BRAINA. THE GALAXY IS IN GOOD HANDS.
I'LL JUST GRAB THE NEXT SHUTTLE TO THOSE HISTORIC AND HALLOWED HOLO-HALLS, ALPHA UNIVERSITY, 'CAUSE TEK JANSEN IS GOING TO--

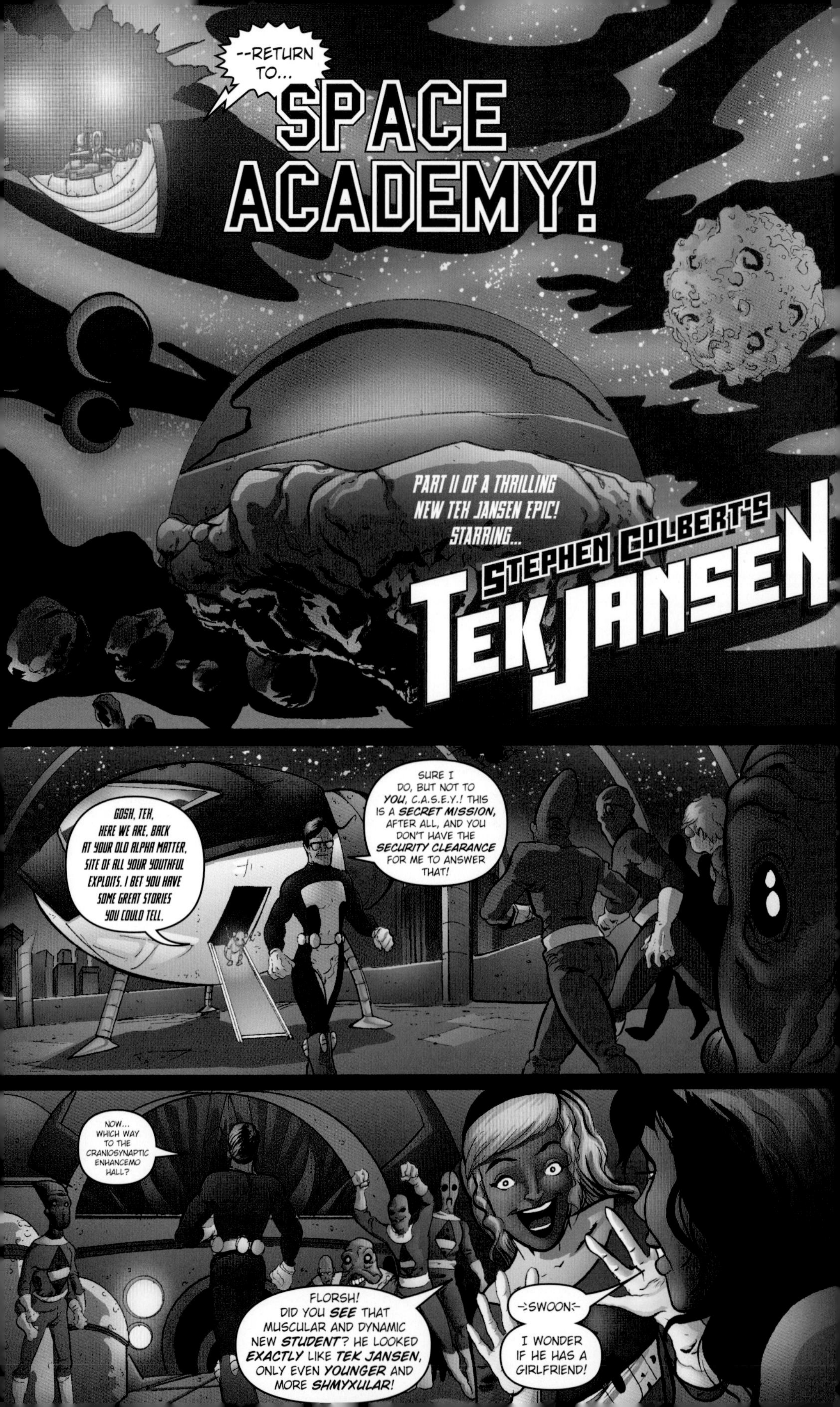
--RETURN TO...
SPACE ACADEMY!
PART II OF A THRILLING NEW TEK JANSEN EPIC! STARRING...
STEPHEN COLBERT'S
TEK JANSEN
GOSH, TEK, HERE WE ARE, BACK AT YOUR OLD ALPHA MATTER, SITE OF ALL YOUR YOUTHFUL EXPLOITS. I BET YOU HAVE SOME GREAT STORIES YOU COULD TELL.
SURE I DO, BUT NOT TO YOU, C.A.S.E.Y.! THIS IS A SECRET MISSION, AFTER ALL, AND YOU DON'T HAVE THE SECURITY CLEARANCE FOR ME TO ANSWER THAT!
NOW... WHICH WAY TO THE CRANIOSYNAPTIC ENHANCEMO HALL?
FLORSH! DID YOU SEE THAT MUSCULAR AND DYNAMIC NEW STUDENT? HE LOOKED EXACTLY LIKE TEK JANSEN, ONLY EVEN YOUNGER AND MORE SHMYXULAR!
SWOON
I WONDER IF HE HAS A GIRLFRIEND!

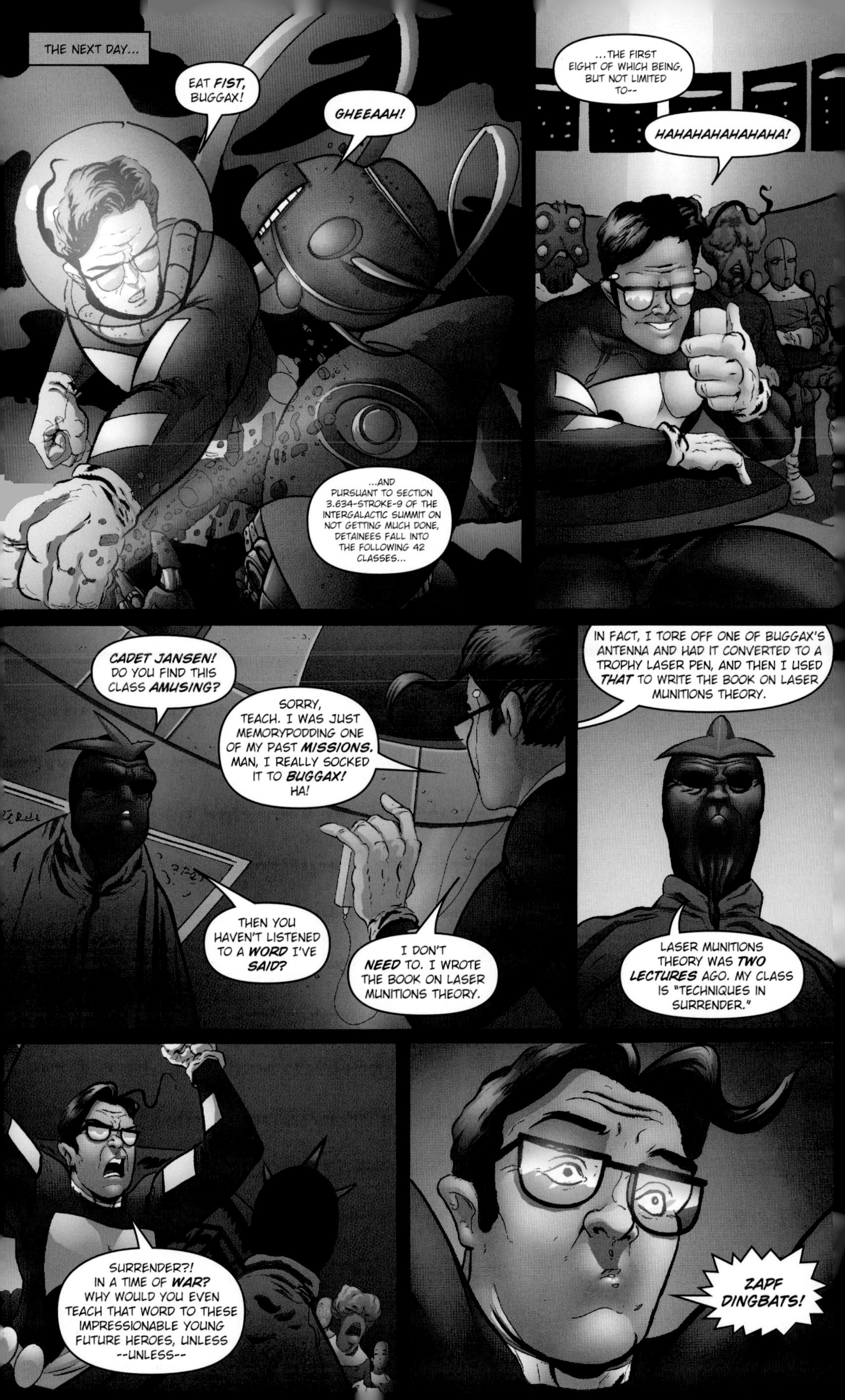
THE NEXT DAY...
EAT FIST, BUGGAX!
GHEEAAH!
...AND PURSUANT TO SECTION 3.634-STROKE-9 OF THE INTERGALACTIC SUMMIT ON NOT GETTING MUCH DONE, DETAINEES FALL INTO THE FOLLOWING 42 CLASSES...
...THE FIRST EIGHT OF WHICH BEING, BUT NOT LIMITED TO--
HAHAHAHAHAHAHA!
CADET JANSEN! DO YOU FIND THIS CLASS AMUSING?
SORRY, TEACH. I WAS JUST MEMORYPODDING ONE OF MY PAST MISSIONS. MAN, I REALLY SOCKED IT TO BUGGAX! HA!
THEN YOU HAVEN'T LISTENED TO A WORD I'VE SAID?
I DON'T NEED TO. I WROTE THE BOOK ON LASER MUNITIONS THEORY.
IN FACT, I TORE OFF ONE OF BUGGAX'S ANTENNA AND HAD IT CONVERTED TO A TROPHY LASER PEN, AND THEN I USED THAT TO WRITE THE BOOK ON LASER MUNITIONS THEORY.
LASER MUNITIONS THEORY WAS TWO LECTURES AGO. MY CLASS IS "TECHNIQUES IN SURRENDER."
SURRENDER?! IN A TIME OF WAR? WHY WOULD YOU EVEN TEACH THAT WORD TO THESE IMPRESSIONABLE YOUNG FUTURE HEROES, UNLESS --UNLESS--
ZAPF DINGBATS!

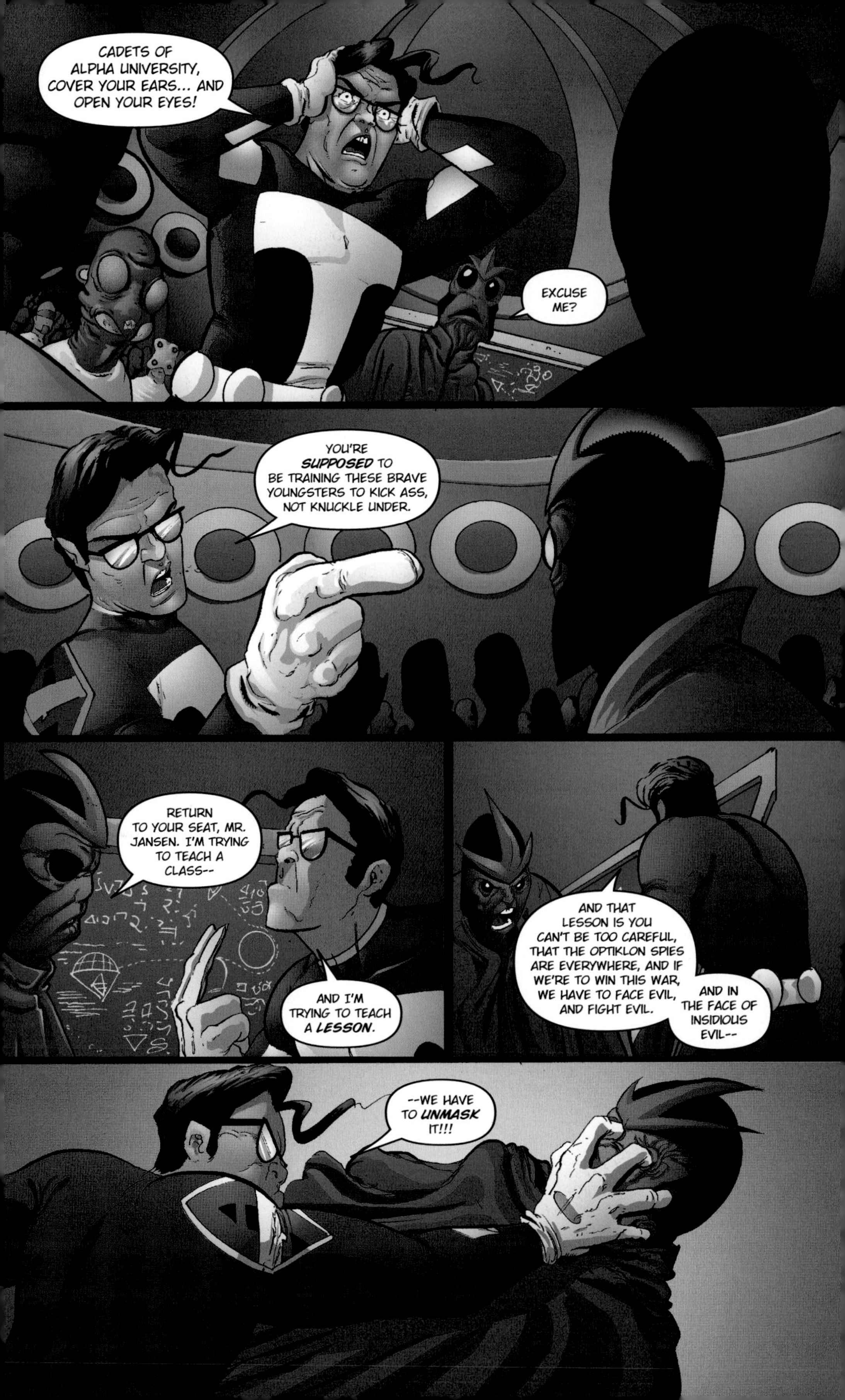
CADETS OF ALPHA UNIVERSITY, COVER YOUR EARS... AND OPEN YOUR EYES!
EXCUSE ME?
YOU'RE **SUPPOSED** TO BE TRAINING THESE BRAVE YOUNGSTERS TO KICK ASS, NOT KNUCKLE UNDER.
RETURN TO YOUR SEAT, MR. JANSEN. I'M TRYING TO TEACH A CLASS--
AND I'M TRYING TO TEACH A ***LESSON***.
AND THAT LESSON IS YOU CAN'T BE TOO CAREFUL, THAT THE OPTIKLON SPIES ARE EVERYWHERE, AND IF WE'RE TO WIN THIS WAR, WE HAVE TO FACE EVIL, AND FIGHT EVIL.
AND IN THE FACE OF INSIDIOUS EVIL--
--WE HAVE TO ***UNMASK*** IT!!!

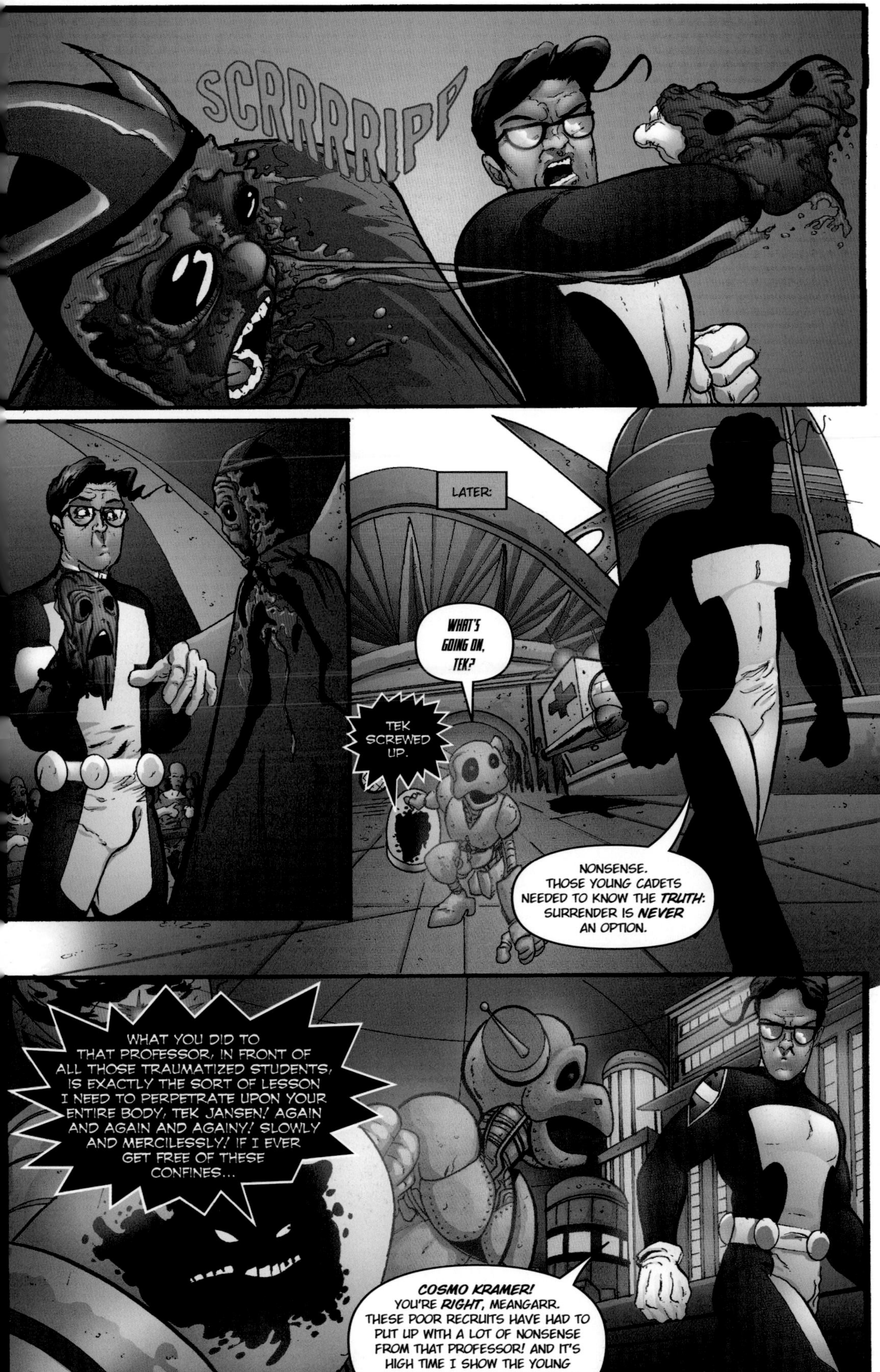

SCRRRRIPP
LATER:
WHAT'S GOING ON, TEK?
TEK SCREWED UP.
NONSENSE. THOSE YOUNG CADETS NEEDED TO KNOW THE *TRUTH*: SURRENDER IS *NEVER* AN OPTION.
WHAT YOU DID TO THAT PROFESSOR, IN FRONT OF ALL THOSE TRAUMATIZED STUDENTS, IS EXACTLY THE SORT OF LESSON I NEED TO PERPETRATE UPON YOUR ENTIRE BODY, TEK JANSEN! AGAIN AND AGAIN AND AGAIN! SLOWLY AND MERCILESSLY! IF I EVER GET FREE OF THESE CONFINES...
COSMO KRAMER! YOU'RE *RIGHT*, MEANGARR. THESE POOR RECRUITS HAVE HAD TO PUT UP WITH A LOT OF NONSENSE FROM THAT PROFESSOR! AND IT'S HIGH TIME I SHOW THE YOUNG SCAMPS WHAT IT REALLY MEANS TO BE AN ALPHA CADET!

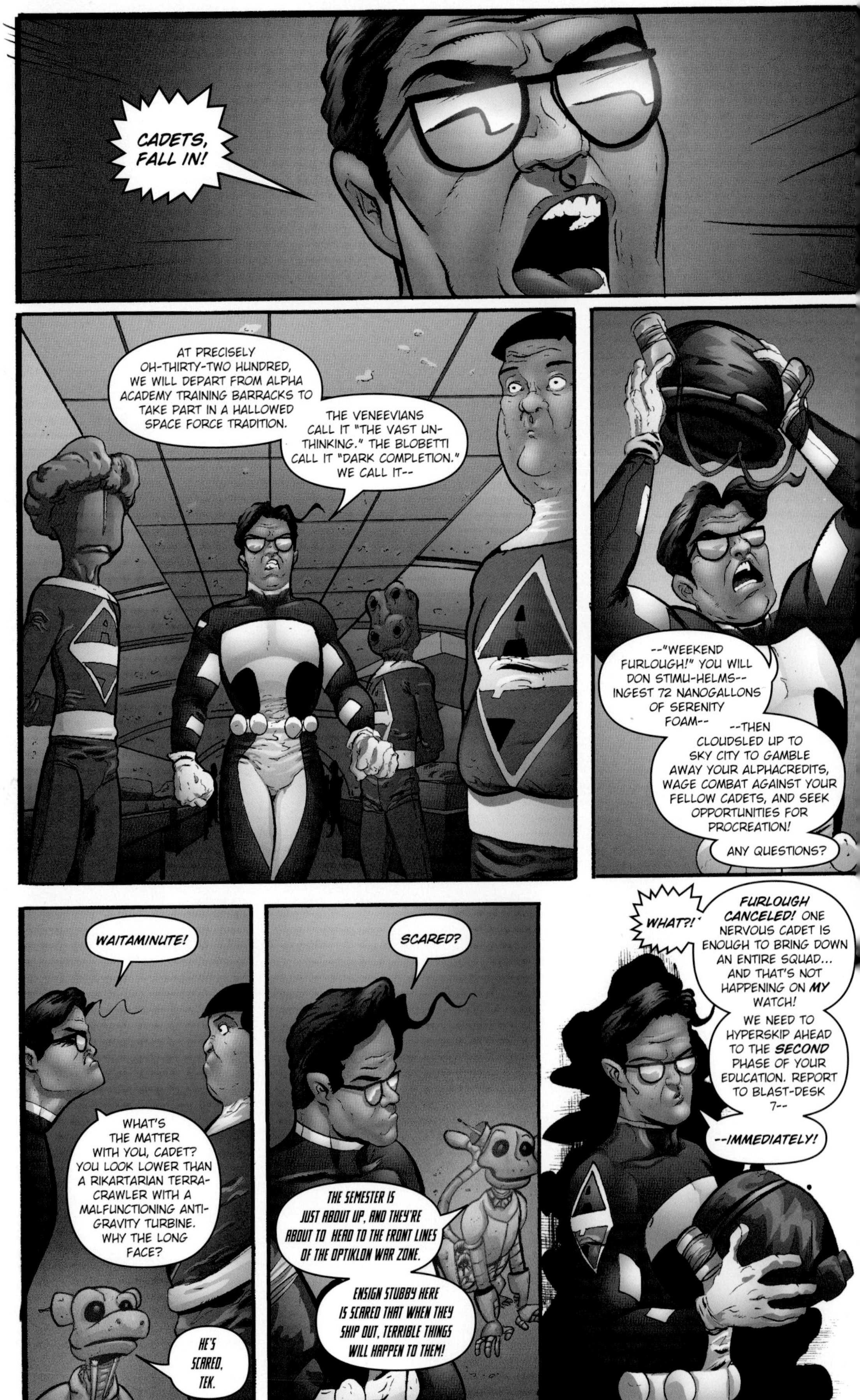
CADETS, FALL IN!
AT PRECISELY OH-THIRTY-TWO HUNDRED, WE WILL DEPART FROM ALPHA ACADEMY TRAINING BARRACKS TO TAKE PART IN A HALLOWED SPACE FORCE TRADITION.
THE VENEEVIANS CALL IT "THE VAST UN-THINKING." THE BLOBETTI CALL IT "DARK COMPLETION." WE CALL IT--
--"WEEKEND FURLOUGH!" YOU WILL DON STIMU-HELMS--INGEST 72 NANOGALLONS OF SERENITY FOAM--
--THEN CLOUDSLED UP TO SKY CITY TO GAMBLE AWAY YOUR ALPHACREDITS, WAGE COMBAT AGAINST YOUR FELLOW CADETS, AND SEEK OPPORTUNITIES FOR PROCREATION!
ANY QUESTIONS?
WAITAMINUTE!
WHAT'S THE MATTER WITH YOU, CADET? YOU LOOK LOWER THAN A RIKARTARIAN TERRA-CRAWLER WITH A MALFUNCTIONING ANTI-GRAVITY TURBINE. WHY THE LONG FACE?
HE'S SCARED, TEK.
SCARED?
THE SEMESTER IS JUST ABOUT UP, AND THEY'RE ABOUT TO HEAD TO THE FRONT LINES OF THE OPTIKLON WAR ZONE.
ENSIGN STUBBY HERE IS SCARED THAT WHEN THEY SHIP OUT, TERRIBLE THINGS WILL HAPPEN TO THEM!
WHAT?!
FURLOUGH CANCELED! ONE NERVOUS CADET IS ENOUGH TO BRING DOWN AN ENTIRE SQUAD... AND THAT'S NOT HAPPENING ON MY WATCH!
WE NEED TO HYPERSKIP AHEAD TO THE SECOND PHASE OF YOUR EDUCATION. REPORT TO BLAST-DESK 7--
--IMMEDIATELY!

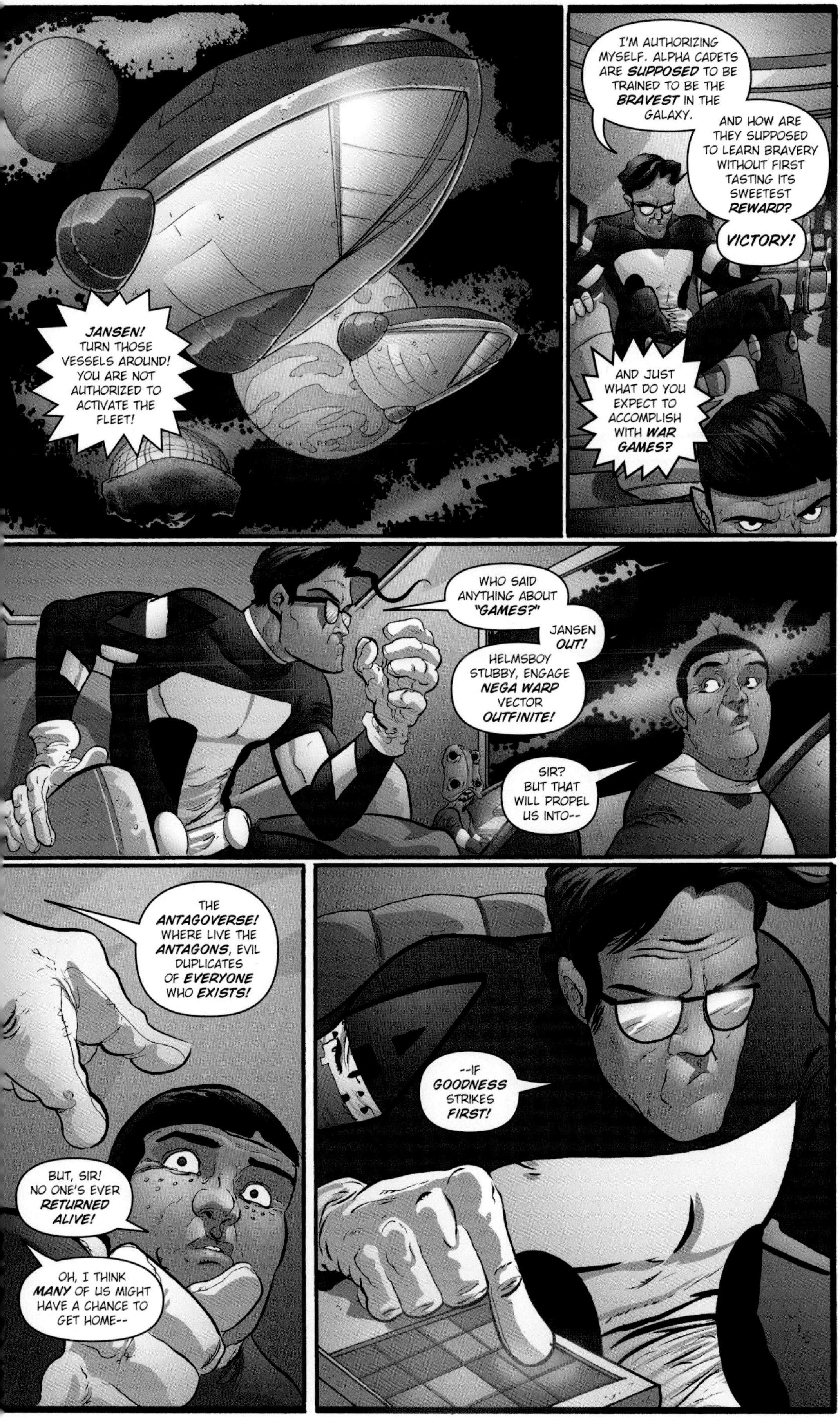
JANSEN! TURN THOSE VESSELS AROUND! YOU ARE NOT AUTHORIZED TO ACTIVATE THE FLEET!
I'M AUTHORIZING MYSELF. ALPHA CADETS ARE SUPPOSED TO BE TRAINED TO BE THE BRAVEST IN THE GALAXY.
AND HOW ARE THEY SUPPOSED TO LEARN BRAVERY WITHOUT FIRST TASTING ITS SWEETEST REWARD?
VICTORY!
AND JUST WHAT DO YOU EXPECT TO ACCOMPLISH WITH WAR GAMES?
WHO SAID ANYTHING ABOUT "GAMES?"
JANSEN OUT!
HELMSBOY STUBBY, ENGAGE NEGA WARP VECTOR OUTFINITE!
SIR? BUT THAT WILL PROPEL US INTO--
THE ANTAGOVERSE! WHERE LIVE THE ANTAGONS, EVIL DUPLICATES OF EVERYONE WHO EXISTS!
BUT, SIR! NO ONE'S EVER RETURNED ALIVE!
OH, I THINK MANY OF US MIGHT HAVE A CHANCE TO GET HOME--
--IF GOODNESS STRIKES FIRST!

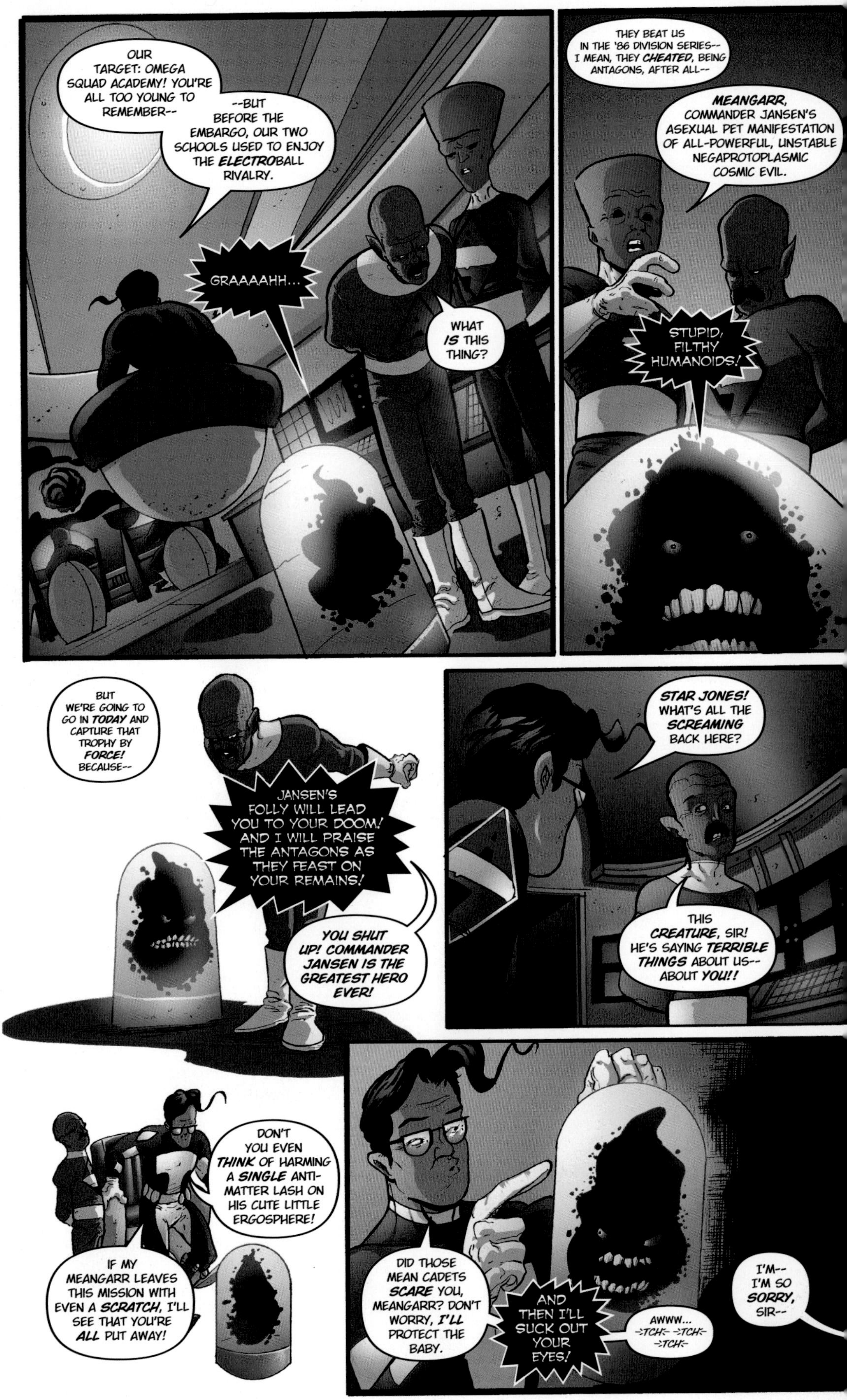
OUR TARGET: OMEGA SQUAD ACADEMY! YOU'RE ALL TOO YOUNG TO REMEMBER--
--BUT BEFORE THE EMBARGO, OUR TWO SCHOOLS USED TO ENJOY THE ELECTROBALL RIVALRY.
GRAAAAHH...
WHAT IS THIS THING?
THEY BEAT US IN THE '86 DIVISION SERIES-- I MEAN, THEY CHEATED, BEING ANTAGONS, AFTER ALL--
MEANGARR, COMMANDER JANSEN'S ASEXUAL PET MANIFESTATION OF ALL-POWERFUL, UNSTABLE NEGAPROTOPLASMIC COSMIC EVIL.
STUPID, FILTHY HUMANOIDS!
BUT WE'RE GOING TO GO IN TODAY AND CAPTURE THAT TROPHY BY FORCE! BECAUSE--
JANSEN'S FOLLY WILL LEAD YOU TO YOUR DOOM! AND I WILL PRAISE THE ANTAGONS AS THEY FEAST ON YOUR REMAINS!
YOU SHUT UP! COMMANDER JANSEN IS THE GREATEST HERO EVER!
STAR JONES! WHAT'S ALL THE SCREAMING BACK HERE?
THIS CREATURE, SIR! HE'S SAYING TERRIBLE THINGS ABOUT US-- ABOUT YOU!!
DON'T YOU EVEN THINK OF HARMING A SINGLE ANTI-MATTER LASH ON HIS CUTE LITTLE ERGOSPHERE!
IF MY MEANGARR LEAVES THIS MISSION WITH EVEN A SCRATCH, I'LL SEE THAT YOU'RE ALL PUT AWAY!
DID THOSE MEAN CADETS SCARE YOU, MEANGARR? DON'T WORRY, I'LL PROTECT THE BABY.
AND THEN I'LL SUCK OUT YOUR EYES!
AWWW... TCH TCH TCH
I'M-- I'M SO SORRY, SIR--

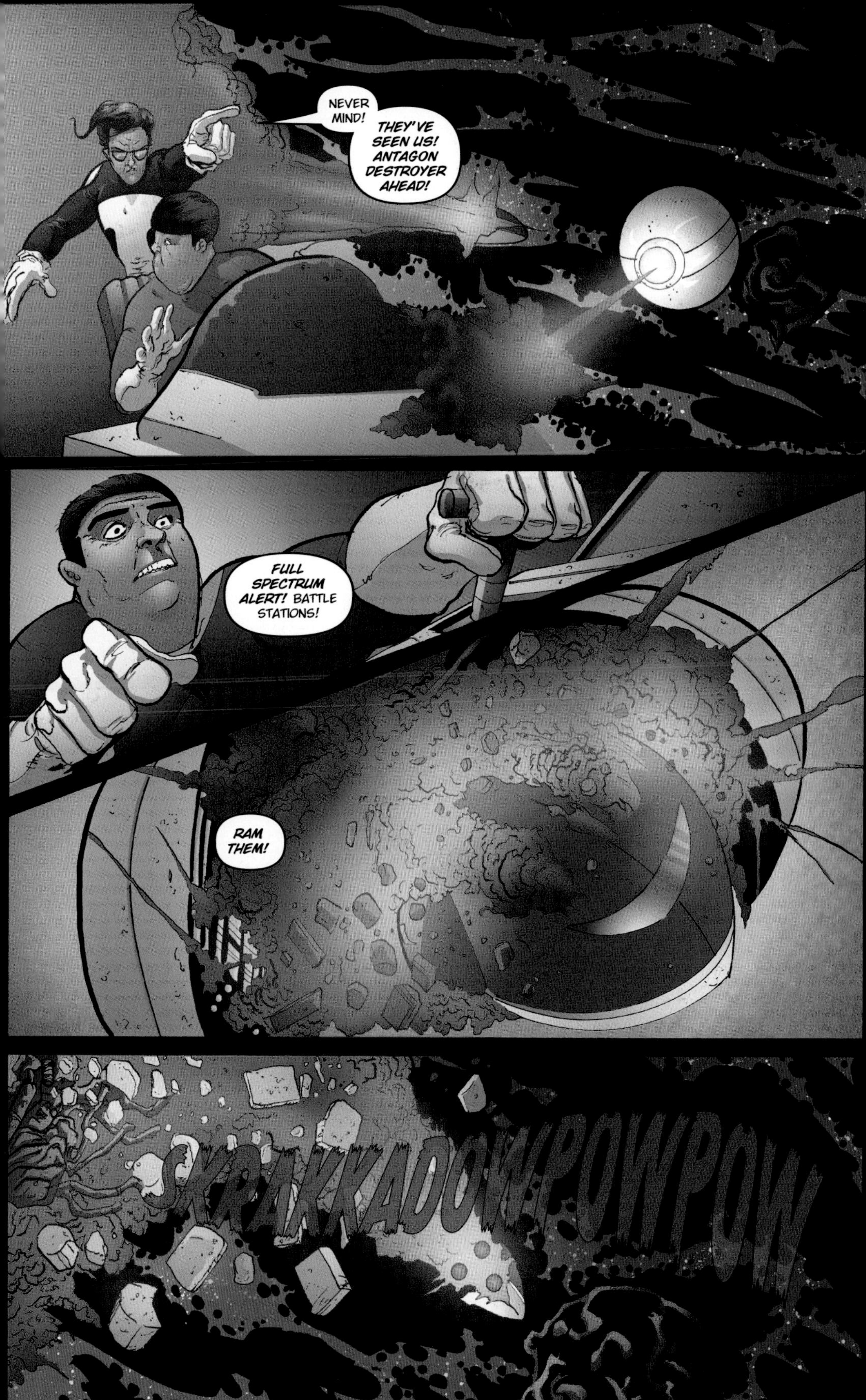
NEVER MIND!
THEY'VE SEEN US! ANTAGON DESTROYER AHEAD!
FULL SPECTRUM ALERT! BATTLE STATIONS!
RAM THEM!
SKRAKKADOWPOWPOWPOW

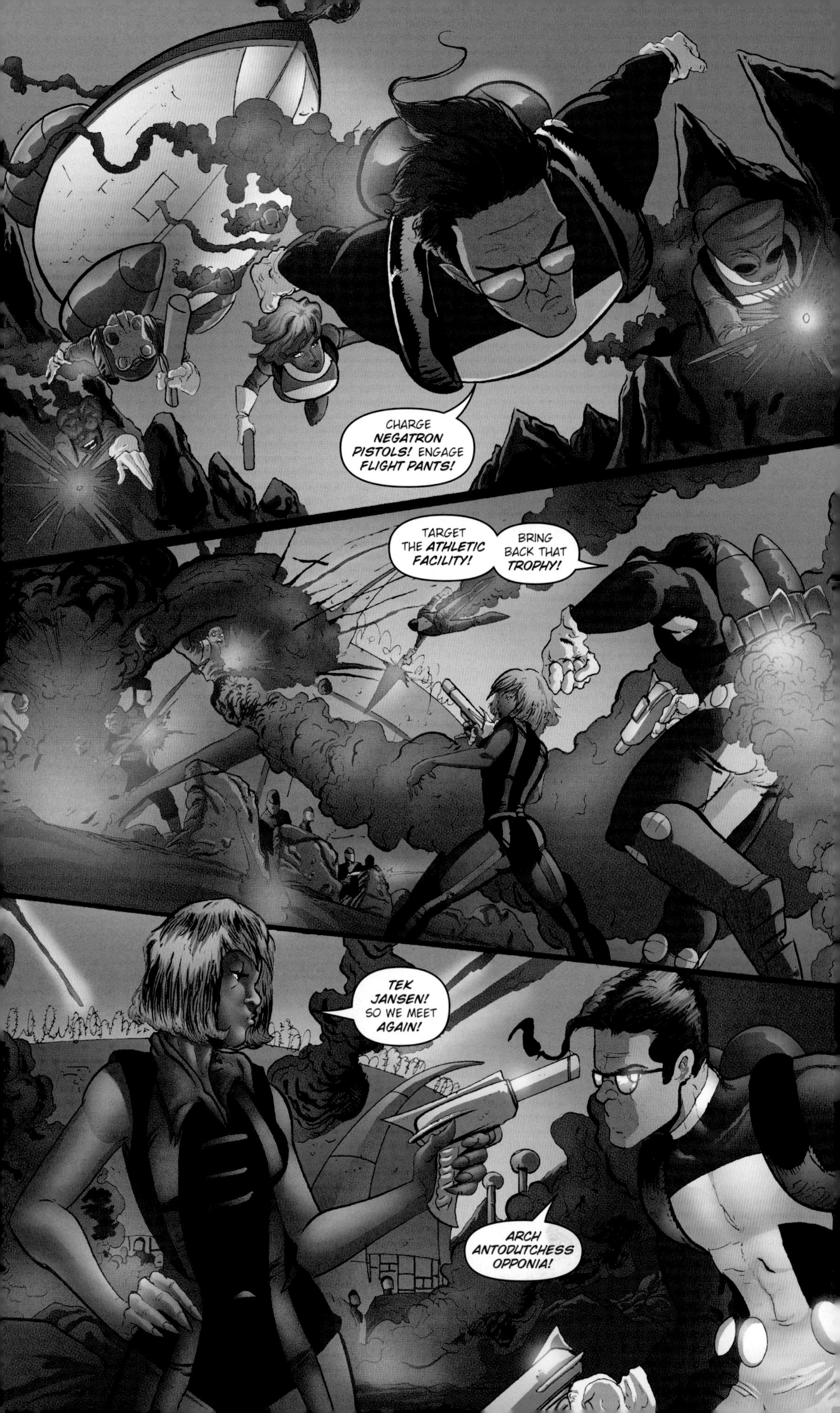
CHARGE NEGATRON PISTOLS! ENGAGE FLIGHT PANTS!
TARGET THE ATHLETIC FACILITY!
BRING BACK THAT TROPHY!
TEK JANSEN! SO WE MEET AGAIN!
ARCH ANTODUTCHESS OPPONIA!

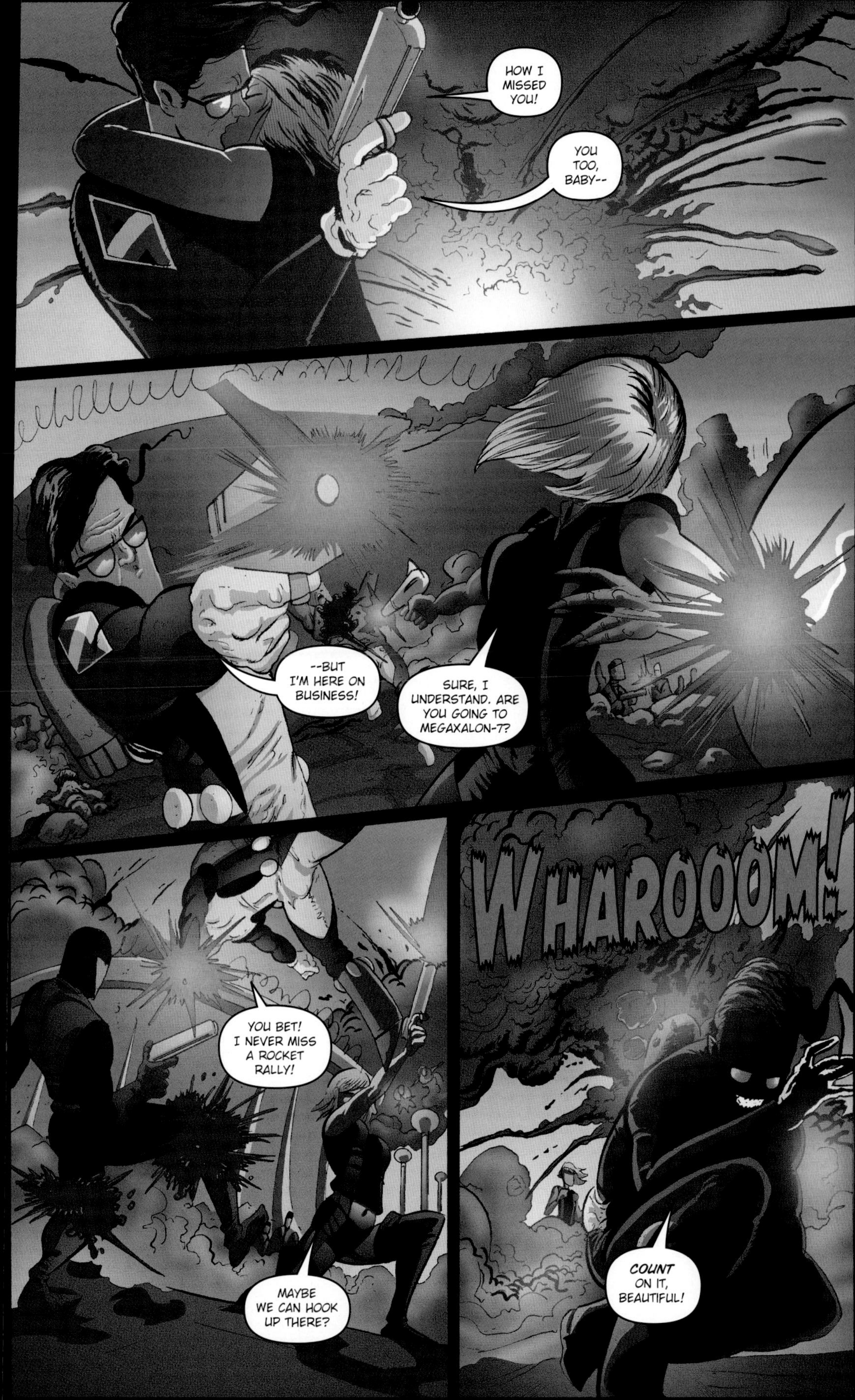
HOW I MISSED YOU!
YOU TOO, BABY--
--BUT I'M HERE ON BUSINESS!
SURE, I UNDERSTAND. ARE YOU GOING TO MEGAXALON-7?
YOU BET! I NEVER MISS A ROCKET RALLY!
MAYBE WE CAN HOOK UP THERE?
WHAROOOM!
COUNT ON IT, BEAUTIFUL!

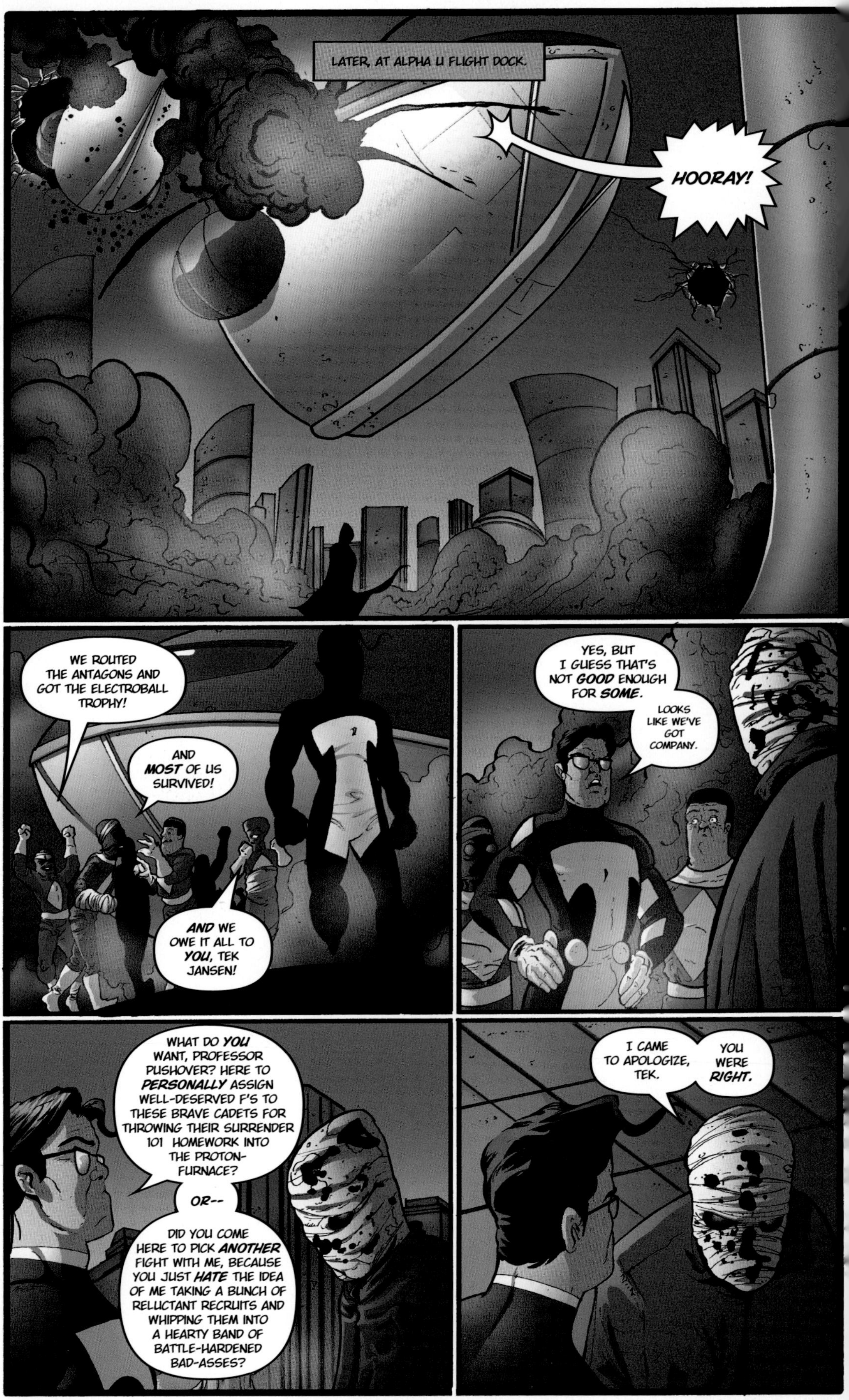
LATER, AT ALPHA U FLIGHT DOCK.
HOORAY!
WE ROUTED THE ANTAGONS AND GOT THE ELECTROBALL TROPHY!
AND MOST OF US SURVIVED!
AND WE OWE IT ALL TO YOU, TEK JANSEN!
YES, BUT I GUESS THAT'S NOT GOOD ENOUGH FOR SOME.
LOOKS LIKE WE'VE GOT COMPANY.
WHAT DO YOU WANT, PROFESSOR PUSHOVER? HERE TO PERSONALLY ASSIGN WELL-DESERVED F'S TO THESE BRAVE CADETS FOR THROWING THEIR SURRENDER 101 HOMEWORK INTO THE PROTON-FURNACE?
OR--
DID YOU COME HERE TO PICK ANOTHER FIGHT WITH ME, BECAUSE YOU JUST HATE THE IDEA OF ME TAKING A BUNCH OF RELUCTANT RECRUITS AND WHIPPING THEM INTO A HEARTY BAND OF BATTLE-HARDENED BAD-ASSES?
I CAME TO APOLOGIZE, TEK.
YOU WERE RIGHT.

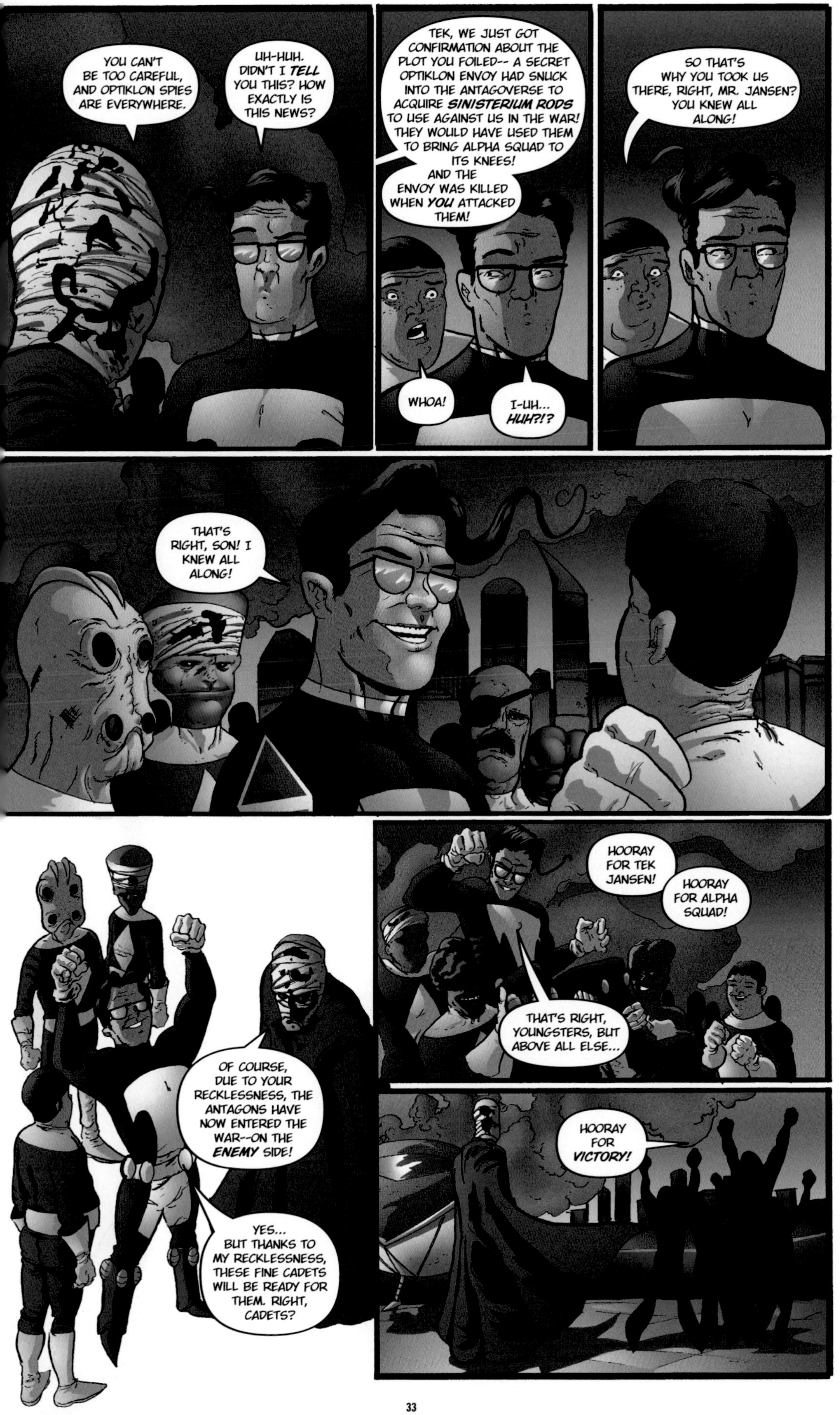
YOU CAN'T BE TOO CAREFUL, AND OPTIKLON SPIES ARE EVERYWHERE.
UH-HUH. DIDN'T I TELL YOU THIS? HOW EXACTLY IS THIS NEWS?
TEK, WE JUST GOT CONFIRMATION ABOUT THE PLOT YOU FOILED-- A SECRET OPTIKLON ENVOY HAD SNUCK INTO THE ANTAGOVERSE TO ACQUIRE SINISTERIUM RODS TO USE AGAINST US IN THE WAR! THEY WOULD HAVE USED THEM TO BRING ALPHA SQUAD TO ITS KNEES!
AND THE ENVOY WAS KILLED WHEN YOU ATTACKED THEM!
WHOA!
I-UH... HUH?!?
SO THAT'S WHY YOU TOOK US THERE, RIGHT, MR. JANSEN? YOU KNEW ALL ALONG!
THAT'S RIGHT, SON! I KNEW ALL ALONG!
OF COURSE, DUE TO YOUR RECKLESSNESS, THE ANTAGONS HAVE NOW ENTERED THE WAR--ON THE ENEMY SIDE!
YES... BUT THANKS TO MY RECKLESSNESS, THESE FINE CADETS WILL BE READY FOR THEM. RIGHT, CADETS?
HOORAY FOR TEK JANSEN!
HOORAY FOR ALPHA SQUAD!
THAT'S RIGHT, YOUNGSTERS, BUT ABOVE ALL ELSE...
HOORAY FOR VICTORY!

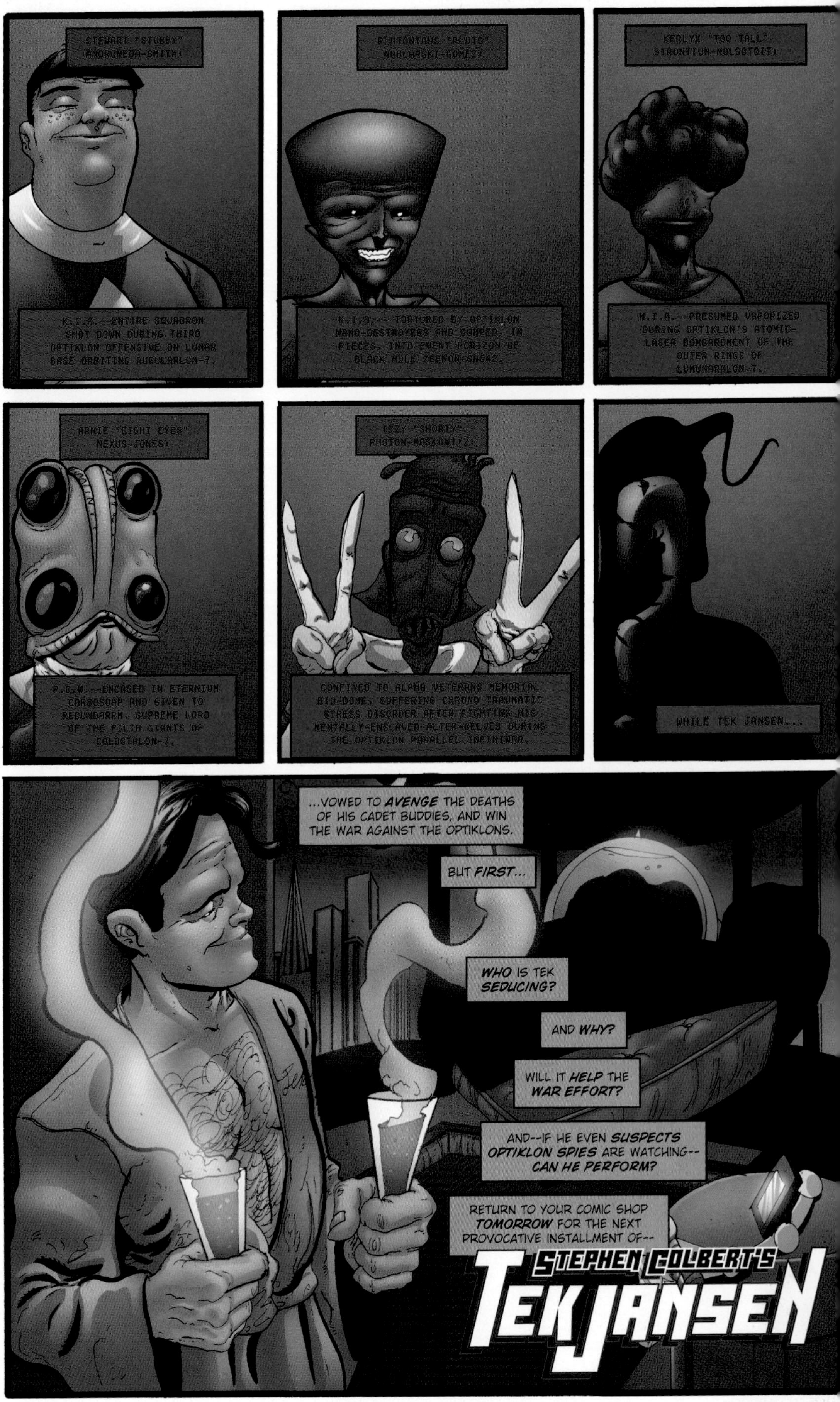
STEWART "STUBBY" ANDROMEDA-SMITH:
K.I.A.--ENTIRE SQUADRON SHOT DOWN DURING THIRD OPTIKLON OFFENSIVE ON LUNAR BASE ORBITING RUGULARLON-7.
PLUTONIOUS "PLUTO" NUBLARSKI-GOMEZ:
K.I.A.-- TORTURED BY OPTIKLON NANO-DESTROYERS AND DUMPED, IN PIECES, INTO EVENT HORIZON OF BLACK HOLE ZEENON-GAG42.
KERLYX "TOO TALL" STRONTIUM-MOLGOTOIT:
M.I.A.--PRESUMED VAPORIZED DURING OPTIKLON'S ATOMIC-LASER BOMBARDMENT OF THE OUTER RINGS OF LUMUNARALON-7.
ARNIE "EIGHT EYES" NEXUS-JONES:
P.O.W.--ENCASED IN ETERNIUM CARBOSOAP AND GIVEN TO RECUNDARRM, SUPREME LORD OF THE FILTH GIANTS OF COLOSTRALON-7.
IZZY "SHORTY" PHOTON-MOSKOWITZ:
CONFINED TO ALPHA VETERANS MEMORIAL BIO-DOME, SUFFERING CHRONO TRAUMATIC STRESS DISORDER AFTER FIGHTING HIS MENTALLY-ENSLAVED ALTER-SELVES DURING THE OPTIKLON PARALLEL INFINIWAR.
WHILE TEK JANSEN...
...VOWED TO AVENGE THE DEATHS OF HIS CADET BUDDIES, AND WIN THE WAR AGAINST THE OPTIKLONS.
BUT FIRST...
WHO IS TEK SEDUCING?
AND WHY?
WILL IT HELP THE WAR EFFORT?
AND--IF HE EVEN SUSPECTS OPTIKLON SPIES ARE WATCHING--CAN HE PERFORM?
RETURN TO YOUR COMIC SHOP TOMORROW FOR THE NEXT PROVOCATIVE INSTALLMENT OF--
STEPHEN COLBERT'S TEK JANSEN

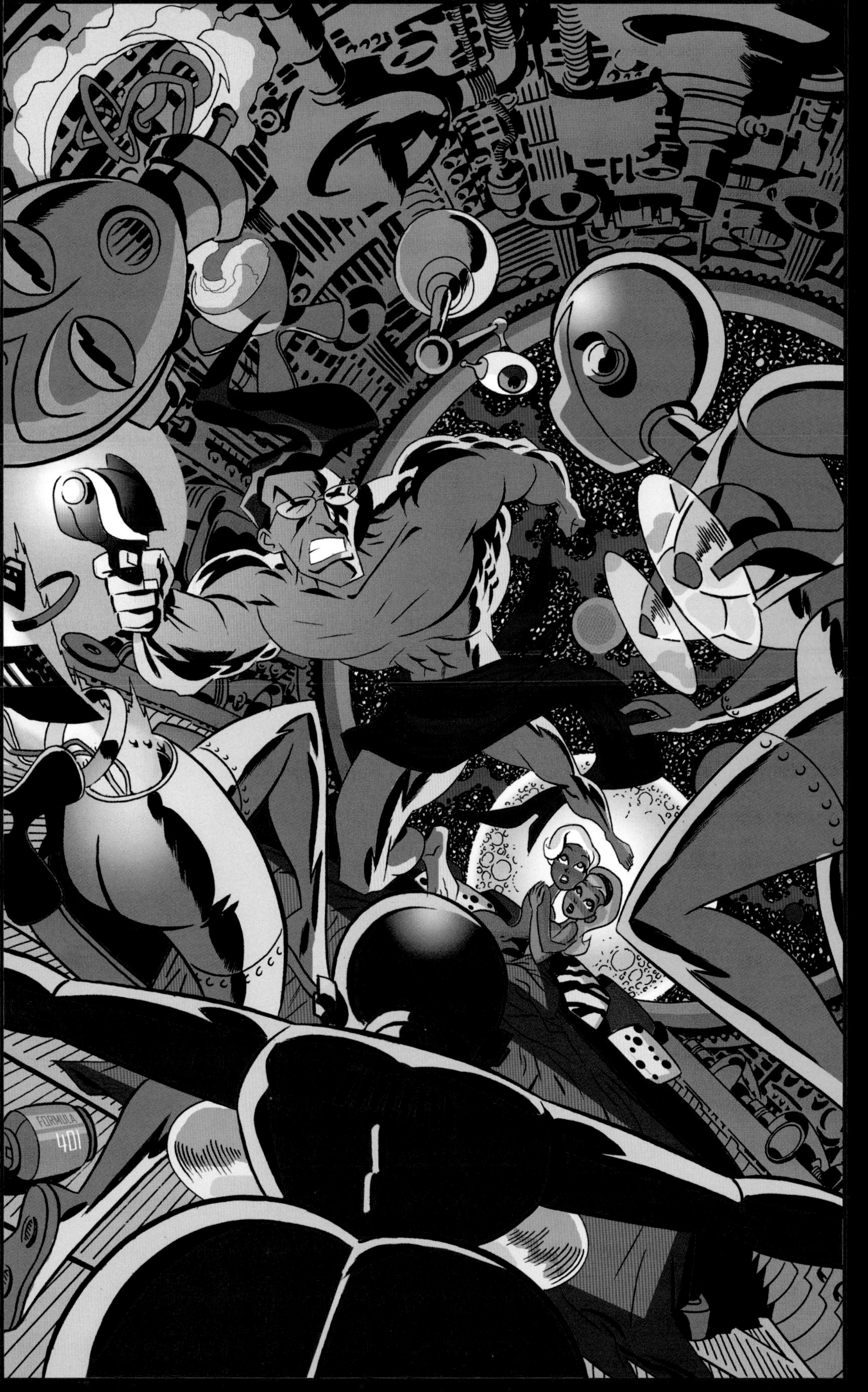
FORMULA
401

DARWYN COOKE

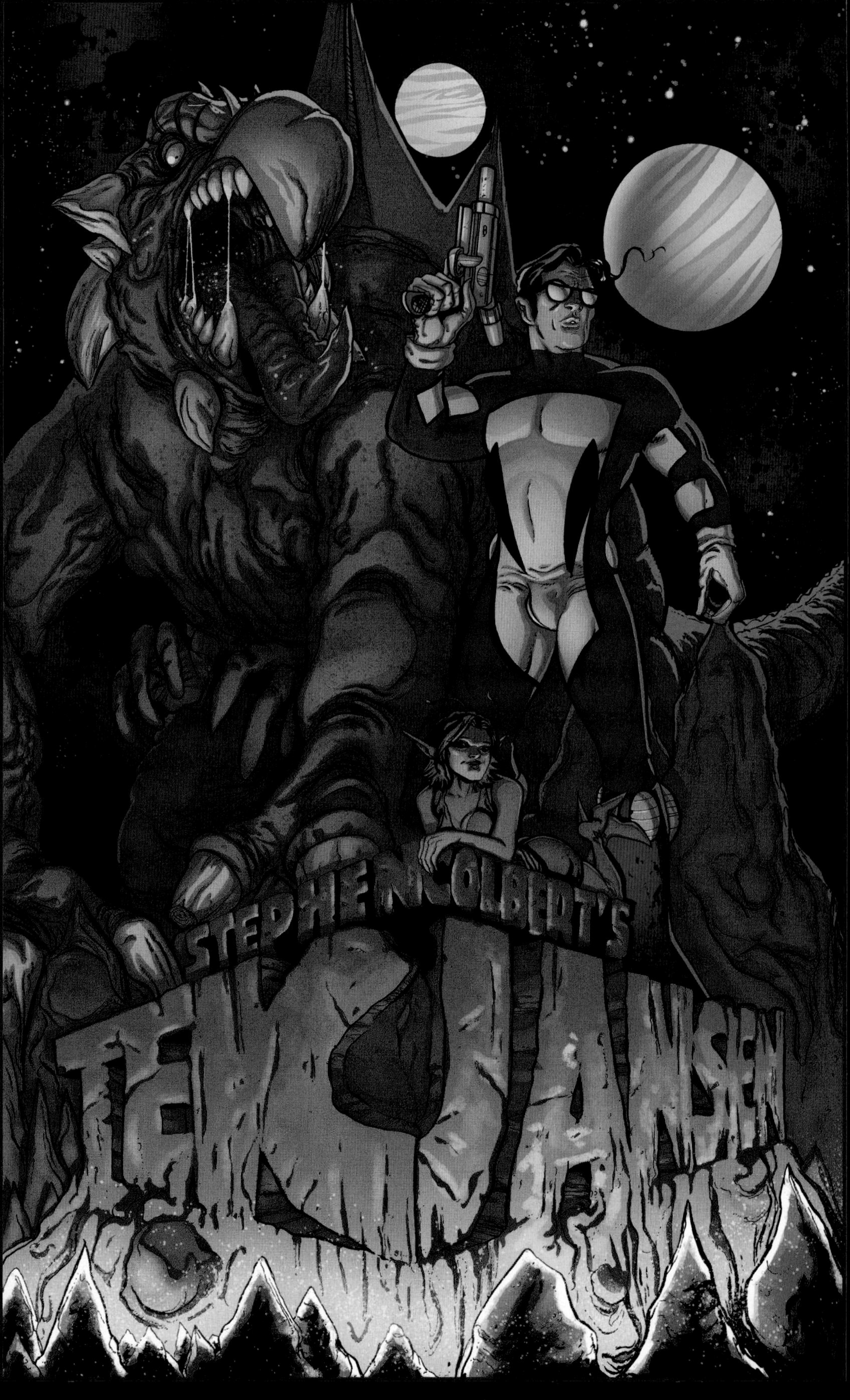
STEPHEN COLBERT'S
TEK JANSEN

art by ROBBI RODRIGUEZ with NATHAN FAIRBAIRN

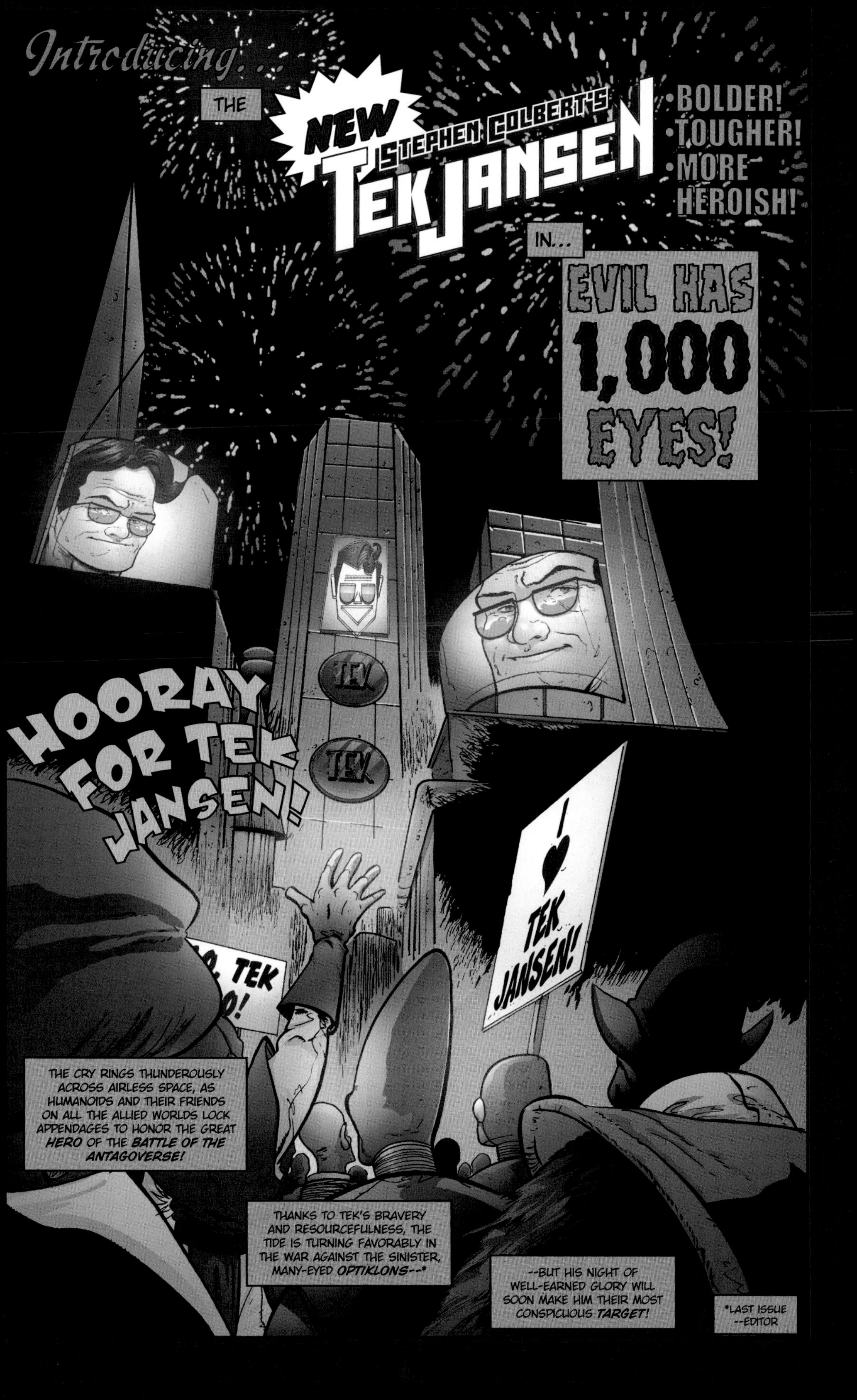
Introducing...
THE
NEW
STEPHEN COLBERT'S
TEK JANSEN
•BOLDER!
•TOUGHER!
•MORE HEROISH!
IN...
EVIL HAS 1,000 EYES!
HOORAY FOR TEK JANSEN!
TEK
TEK
I ♥ TEK JANSEN!
THE CRY RINGS THUNDEROUSLY ACROSS AIRLESS SPACE, AS HUMANOIDS AND THEIR FRIENDS ON ALL THE ALLIED WORLDS LOCK APPENDAGES TO HONOR THE GREAT HERO OF THE BATTLE OF THE ANTAGOVERSE!
THANKS TO TEK'S BRAVERY AND RESOURCEFULNESS, THE TIDE IS TURNING FAVORABLY IN THE WAR AGAINST THE SINISTER, MANY-EYED OPTIKLONS--*
--BUT HIS NIGHT OF WELL-EARNED GLORY WILL SOON MAKE HIM THEIR MOST CONSPICUOUS TARGET!
*LAST ISSUE --EDITOR

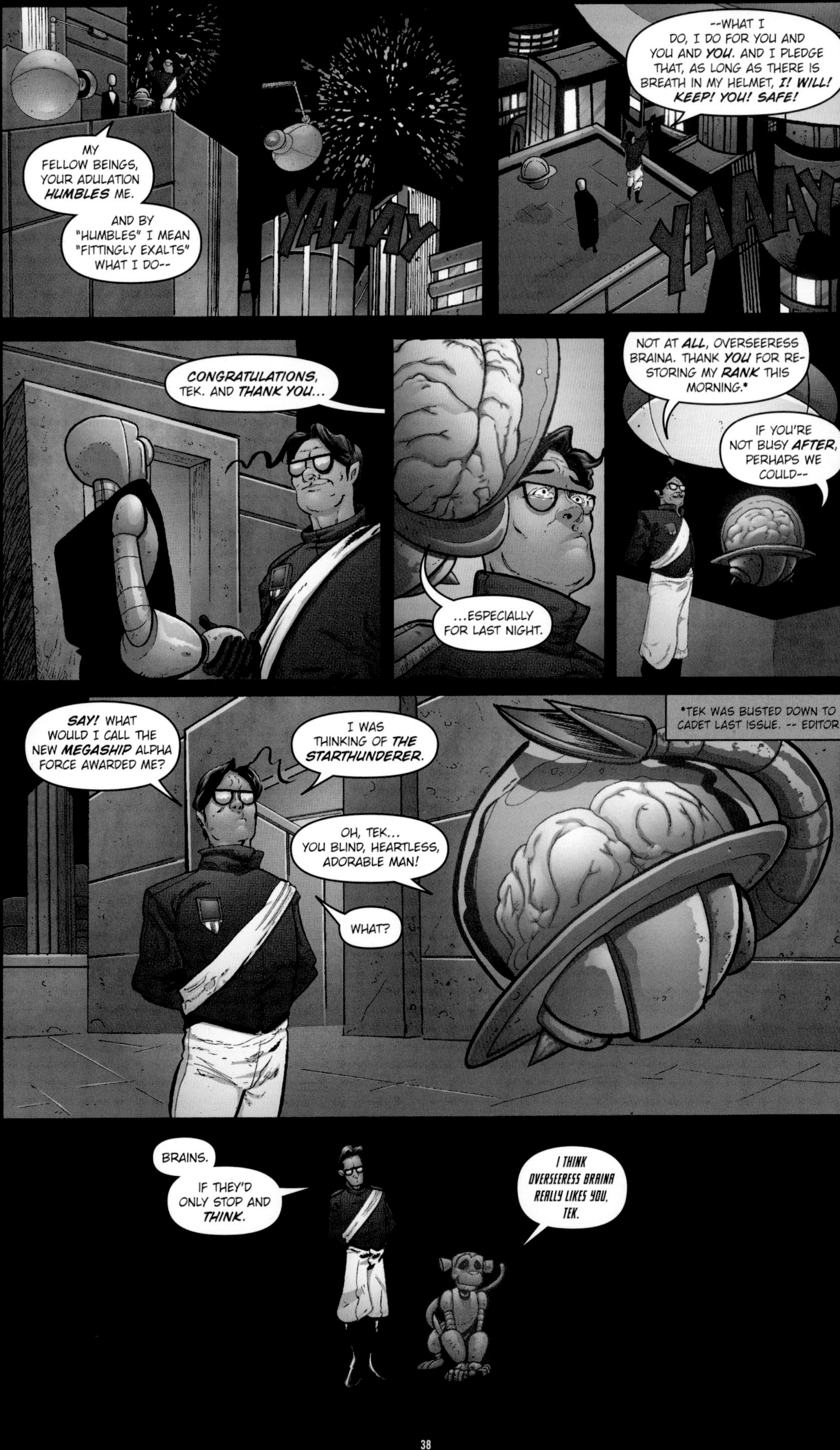
MY FELLOW BEINGS, YOUR ADULATION HUMBLES ME.
AND BY "HUMBLES" I MEAN "FITTINGLY EXALTS" WHAT I DO--
YAAAY
--WHAT I DO, I DO FOR YOU AND YOU AND YOU. AND I PLEDGE THAT, AS LONG AS THERE IS BREATH IN MY HELMET, I! WILL! KEEP! YOU! SAFE!
YAAAY
CONGRATULATIONS, TEK. AND THANK YOU...
...ESPECIALLY FOR LAST NIGHT.
NOT AT ALL, OVERSEERESS BRAINA. THANK YOU FOR RESTORING MY RANK THIS MORNING.*
IF YOU'RE NOT BUSY AFTER, PERHAPS WE COULD--
SAY! WHAT WOULD I CALL THE NEW MEGASHIP ALPHA FORCE AWARDED ME?
I WAS THINKING OF THE STARTHUNDERER.
*TEK WAS BUSTED DOWN TO CADET LAST ISSUE. -- EDITOR
OH, TEK... YOU BLIND, HEARTLESS, ADORABLE MAN!
WHAT?
BRAINS.
IF THEY'D ONLY STOP AND THINK.
I THINK OVERSEERESS BRAINA REALLY LIKES YOU, TEK.

EVERYONE LIKES ME, C.A.S.E.Y.*-- AND I LIKE EVERYONE. NOW GET THE QUARK AWAY BEFORE YOU GIVE ME RADIATION POISONING.

YOU BET, SKIPPER!

*C.A.S.E.Y.: COMPUTERIZED AUTOMATED SIMIANOID ENGINEERING UNIT. -- EDITOR

I DON'T LIKE YOU, JANSEN-- EXCEPT MAYBE WITH A BIG SIDE ORDER OF VELTHOOBIAN PINKBEANS!

OH, BUT YOU'LL LEARN TO, MEANGARR. MARK MY WORDS.

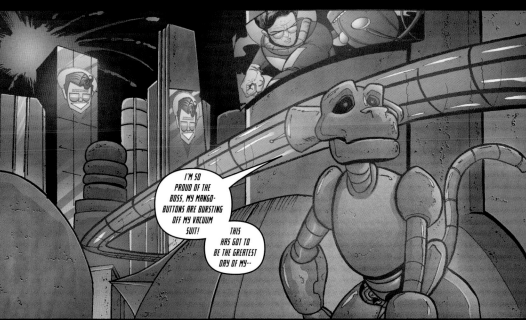

I'M SO PROUD OF THE BOSS, MY MANGO-BUTTONS ARE BURSTING OFF MY VACUUM SUIT!

THIS HAS GOT TO BE THE GREATEST DAY OF MY--

AAAH!

HELP!

TEH! HELP!

BUT C.A.S.E.Y.'S CRIES ARE SUFFOCATED...

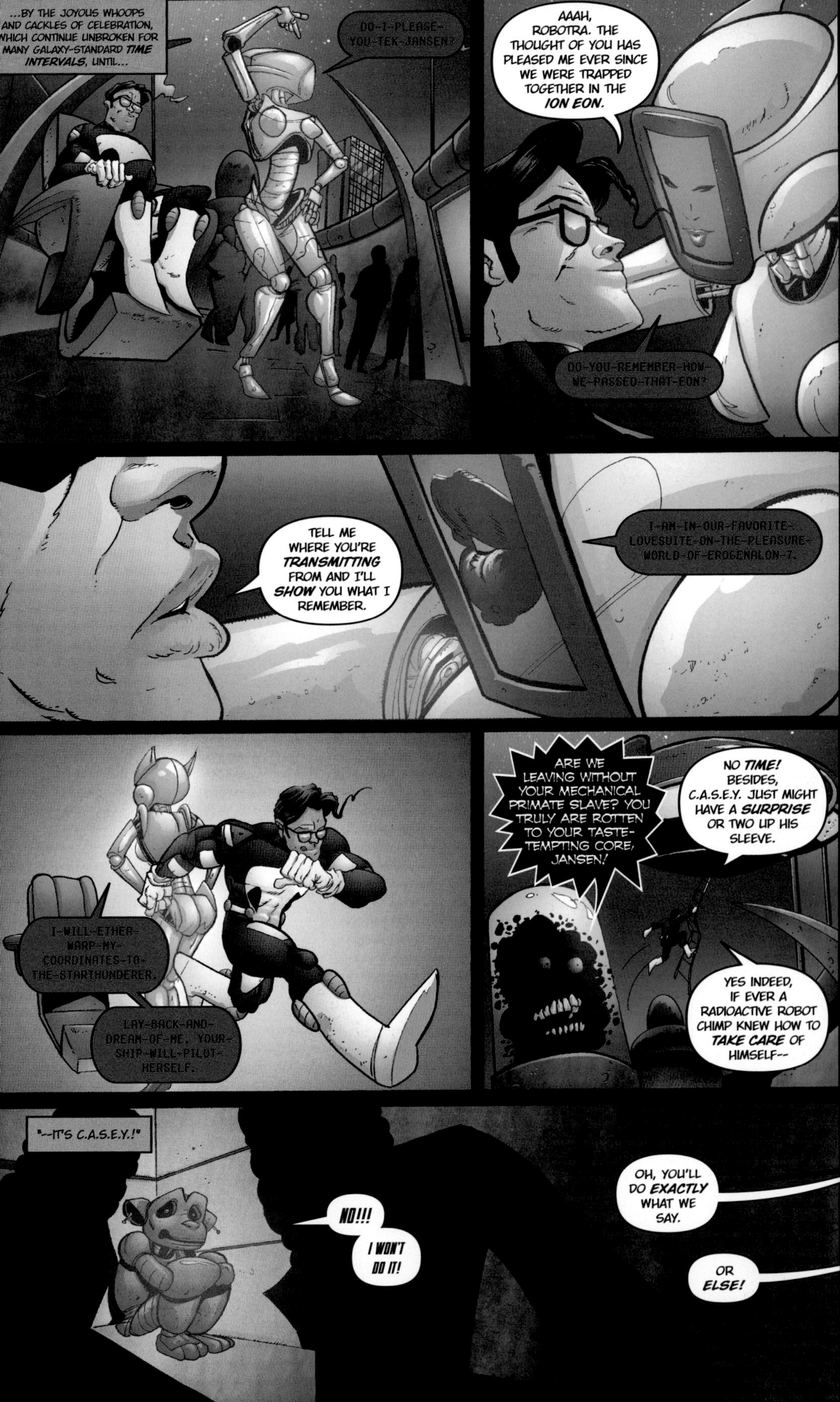
...BY THE JOYOUS WHOOPS AND CACKLES OF CELEBRATION, WHICH CONTINUE UNBROKEN FOR MANY GALAXY-STANDARD TIME INTERVALS, UNTIL...
DO-I-PLEASE-YOU-TEK-JANSEN?
AAAH, ROBOTRA. THE THOUGHT OF YOU HAS PLEASED ME EVER SINCE WE WERE TRAPPED TOGETHER IN THE ION EON.
DO-YOU-REMEMBER-HOW-WE-PASSED-THAT-EON?
TELL ME WHERE YOU'RE TRANSMITTING FROM AND I'LL SHOW YOU WHAT I REMEMBER.
I-AM-IN-OUR-FAVORITE-LOVESUITE-ON-THE-PLEASURE-WORLD-OF-EROGENALON-7.
I-WILL-ETHER-WARP-MY-COORDINATES-TO-THE-STARTHUNDERER.
LAY-BACK-AND-DREAM-OF-ME. YOUR-SHIP-WILL-PILOT-HERSELF.
ARE WE LEAVING WITHOUT YOUR MECHANICAL PRIMATE SLAVE? YOU TRULY ARE ROTTEN TO YOUR TASTE-TEMPTING CORE, JANSEN!
NO TIME! BESIDES, C.A.S.E.Y. JUST MIGHT HAVE A SURPRISE OR TWO UP HIS SLEEVE.
YES INDEED, IF EVER A RADIOACTIVE ROBOT CHIMP KNEW HOW TO TAKE CARE OF HIMSELF--
"--IT'S C.A.S.E.Y.!"
NO!!!
I WON'T DO IT!
OH, YOU'LL DO EXACTLY WHAT WE SAY.
OR ELSE!

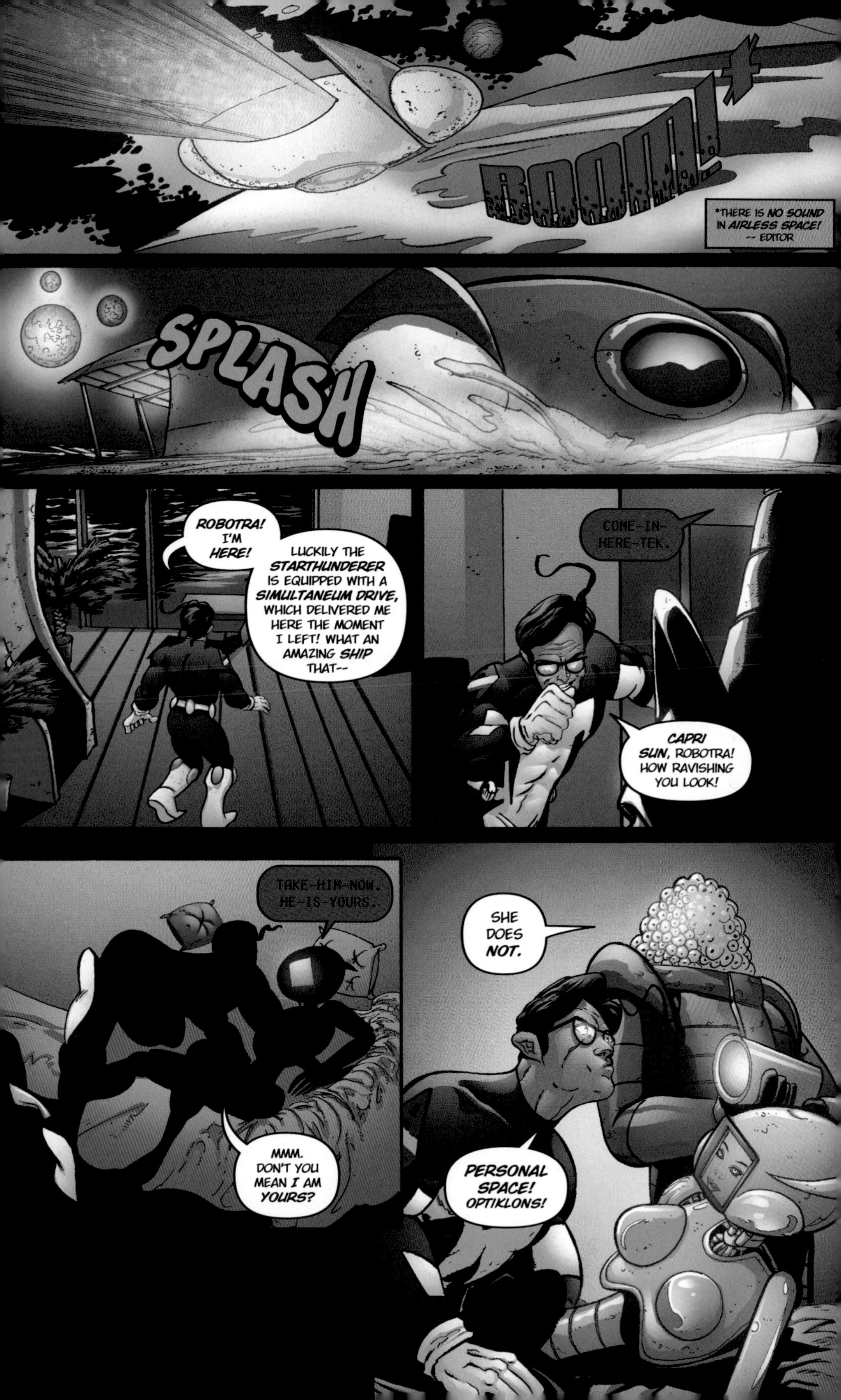
BOOM!*
*THERE IS NO SOUND IN AIRLESS SPACE! -- EDITOR
SPLASH
ROBOTRA! I'M HERE!
LUCKILY THE STARTHUNDERER IS EQUIPPED WITH A SIMULTANEUM DRIVE, WHICH DELIVERED ME HERE THE MOMENT I LEFT! WHAT AN AMAZING SHIP THAT--
COME-IN-HERE-TEK.
CAPRI SUN, ROBOTRA! HOW RAVISHING YOU LOOK!
TAKE-HIM-NOW. HE-IS-YOURS.
MMM. DON'T YOU MEAN I AM YOURS?
SHE DOES NOT.
PERSONAL SPACE! OPTIKLONS!

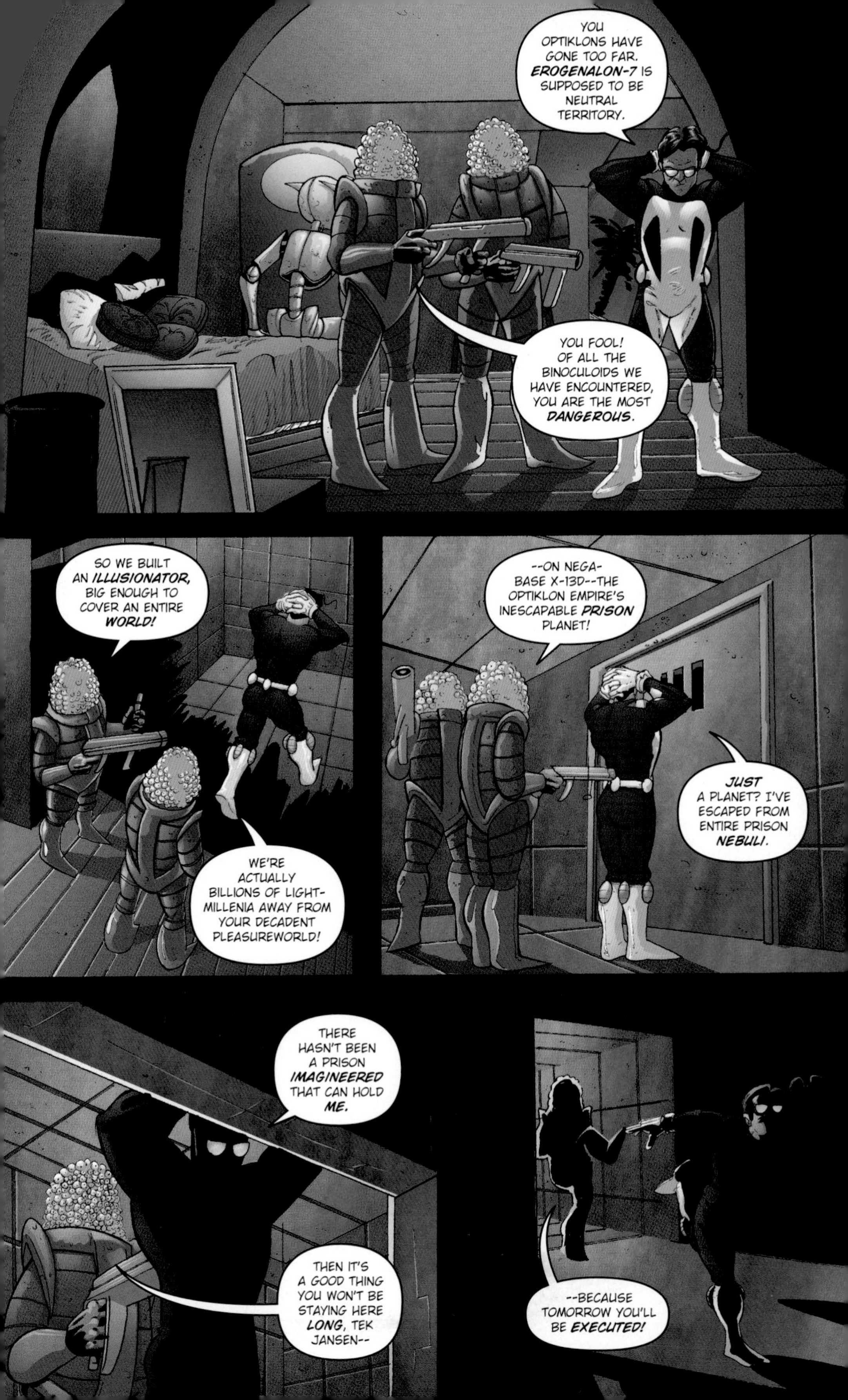
YOU OPTIKLONS HAVE GONE TOO FAR. EROGENALON-7 IS SUPPOSED TO BE NEUTRAL TERRITORY.
YOU FOOL! OF ALL THE BINOCULOIDS WE HAVE ENCOUNTERED, YOU ARE THE MOST DANGEROUS.
SO WE BUILT AN ILLUSIONATOR, BIG ENOUGH TO COVER AN ENTIRE WORLD!
WE'RE ACTUALLY BILLIONS OF LIGHT-MILLENIA AWAY FROM YOUR DECADENT PLEASUREWORLD!
--ON NEGA-BASE X-13D--THE OPTIKLON EMPIRE'S INESCAPABLE PRISON PLANET!
JUST A PLANET? I'VE ESCAPED FROM ENTIRE PRISON NEBULI.
THERE HASN'T BEEN A PRISON IMAGINEERED THAT CAN HOLD ME.
THEN IT'S A GOOD THING YOU WON'T BE STAYING HERE LONG, TEK JANSEN--
--BECAUSE TOMORROW YOU'LL BE EXECUTED!

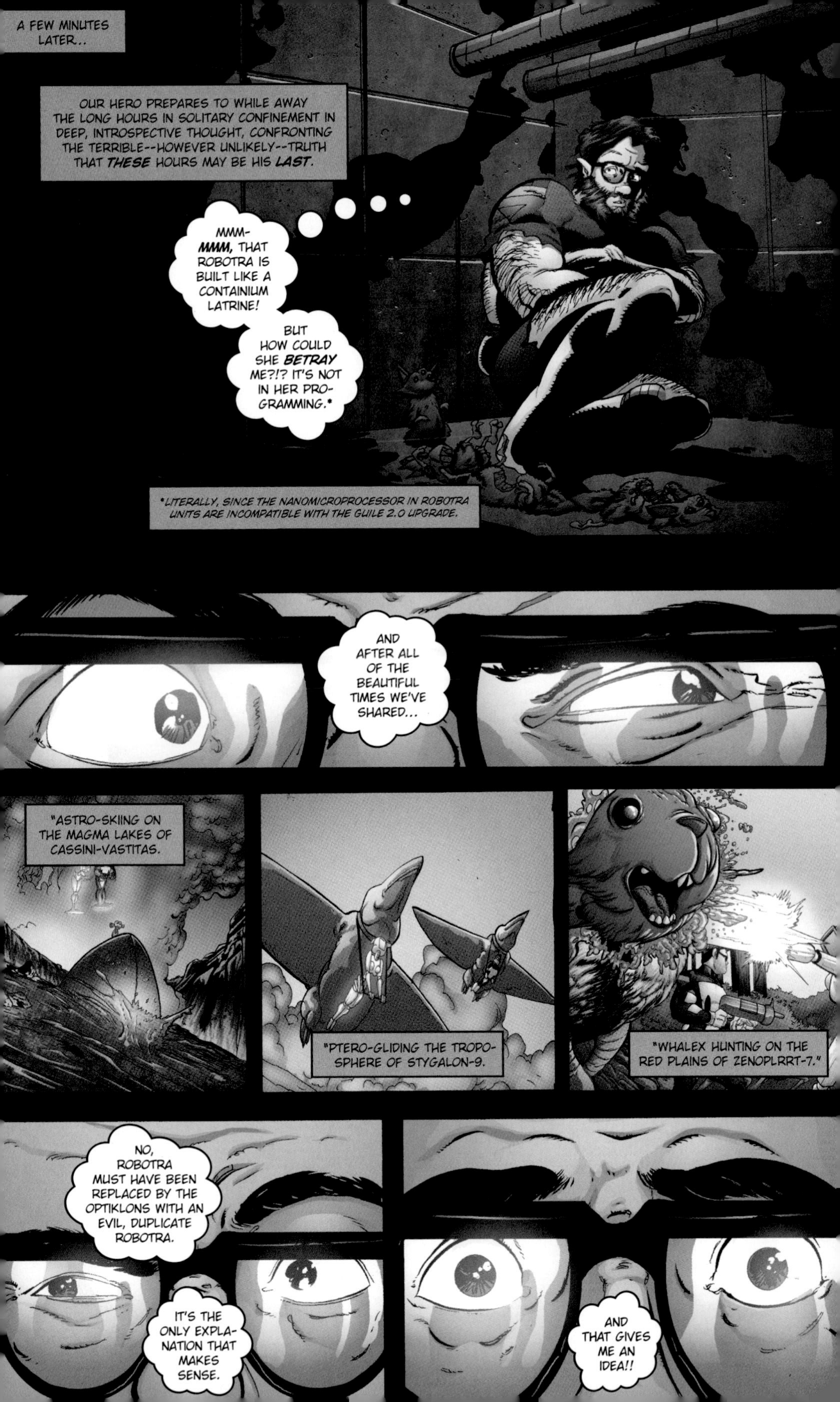
A FEW MINUTES LATER..
OUR HERO PREPARES TO WHILE AWAY THE LONG HOURS IN SOLITARY CONFINEMENT IN DEEP, INTROSPECTIVE THOUGHT, CONFRONTING THE TERRIBLE--HOWEVER UNLIKELY--TRUTH THAT ***THESE*** HOURS MAY BE HIS ***LAST***.
MMM-***MMM,*** THAT ROBOTRA IS BUILT LIKE A CONTAINIUM LATRINE!
BUT HOW COULD SHE ***BETRAY*** ME?!? IT'S NOT IN HER PRO-GRAMMING.*
*LITERALLY, SINCE THE NANOMICROPROCESSOR IN ROBOTRA UNITS ARE INCOMPATIBLE WITH THE GUILE 2.0 UPGRADE.
AND AFTER ALL OF THE BEAUTIFUL TIMES WE'VE SHARED...
"ASTRO-SKIING ON THE MAGMA LAKES OF CASSINI-VASTITAS.
"PTERO-GLIDING THE TROPO-SPHERE OF STYGALON-9.
"WHALEX HUNTING ON THE RED PLAINS OF ZENOPLRRT-7."
NO, ROBOTRA MUST HAVE BEEN REPLACED BY THE OPTIKLONS WITH AN EVIL, DUPLICATE ROBOTRA.
IT'S THE ONLY EXPLA-NATION THAT MAKES SENSE.
AND THAT GIVES ME AN IDEA!!

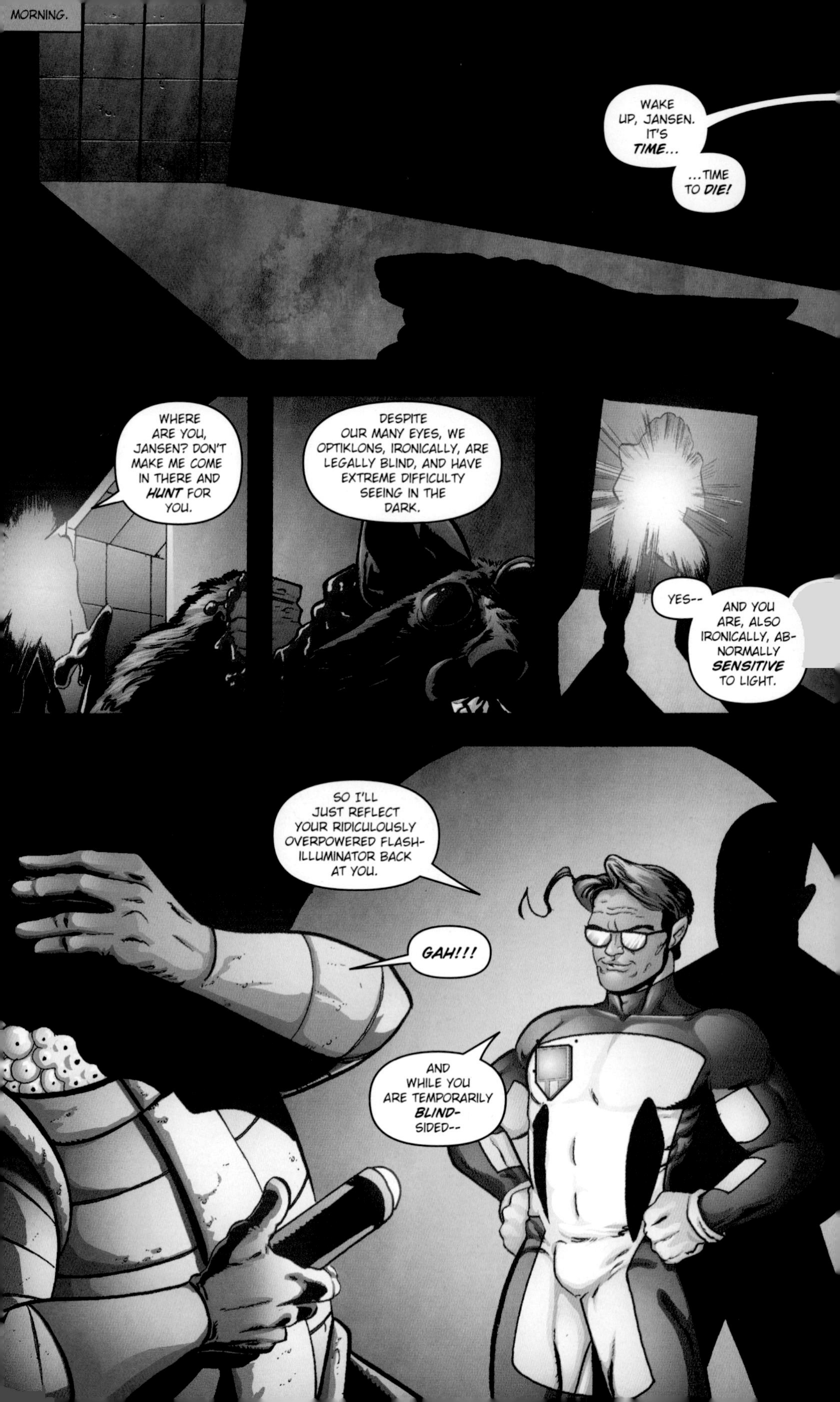
MORNING.
WAKE UP, JANSEN. IT'S TIME...
...TIME TO DIE!
WHERE ARE YOU, JANSEN? DON'T MAKE ME COME IN THERE AND HUNT FOR YOU.
DESPITE OUR MANY EYES, WE OPTIKLONS, IRONICALLY, ARE LEGALLY BLIND, AND HAVE EXTREME DIFFICULTY SEEING IN THE DARK.
YES--
AND YOU ARE, ALSO IRONICALLY, AB-NORMALLY SENSITIVE TO LIGHT.
SO I'LL JUST REFLECT YOUR RIDICULOUSLY OVERPOWERED FLASH-ILLUMINATOR BACK AT YOU.
GAH!!!
AND WHILE YOU ARE TEMPORARILY BLIND-SIDED--

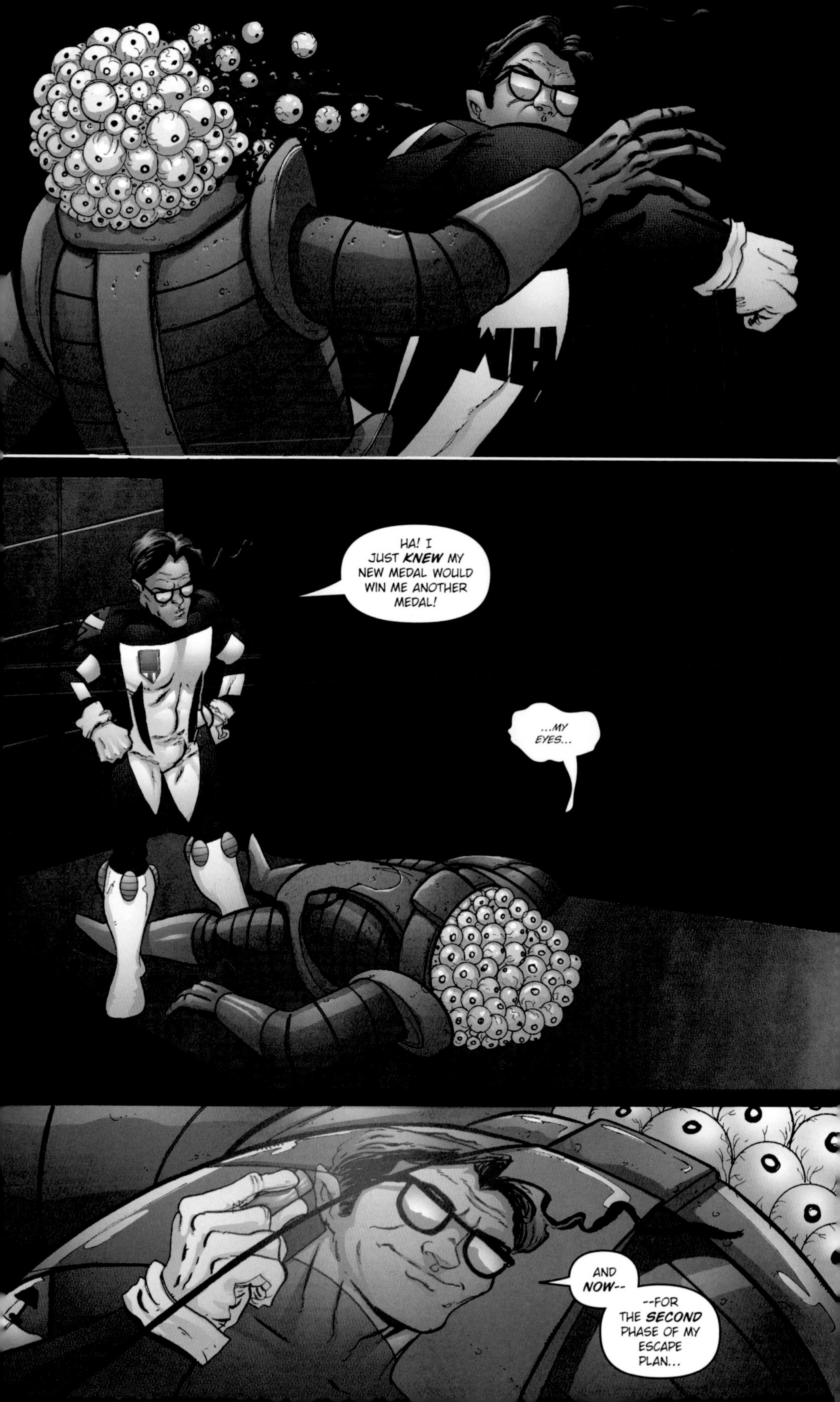
HA! I JUST **KNEW** MY NEW MEDAL WOULD WIN ME ANOTHER MEDAL!
...MY EYES...
AND **NOW**--
--FOR THE **SECOND** PHASE OF MY ESCAPE PLAN...

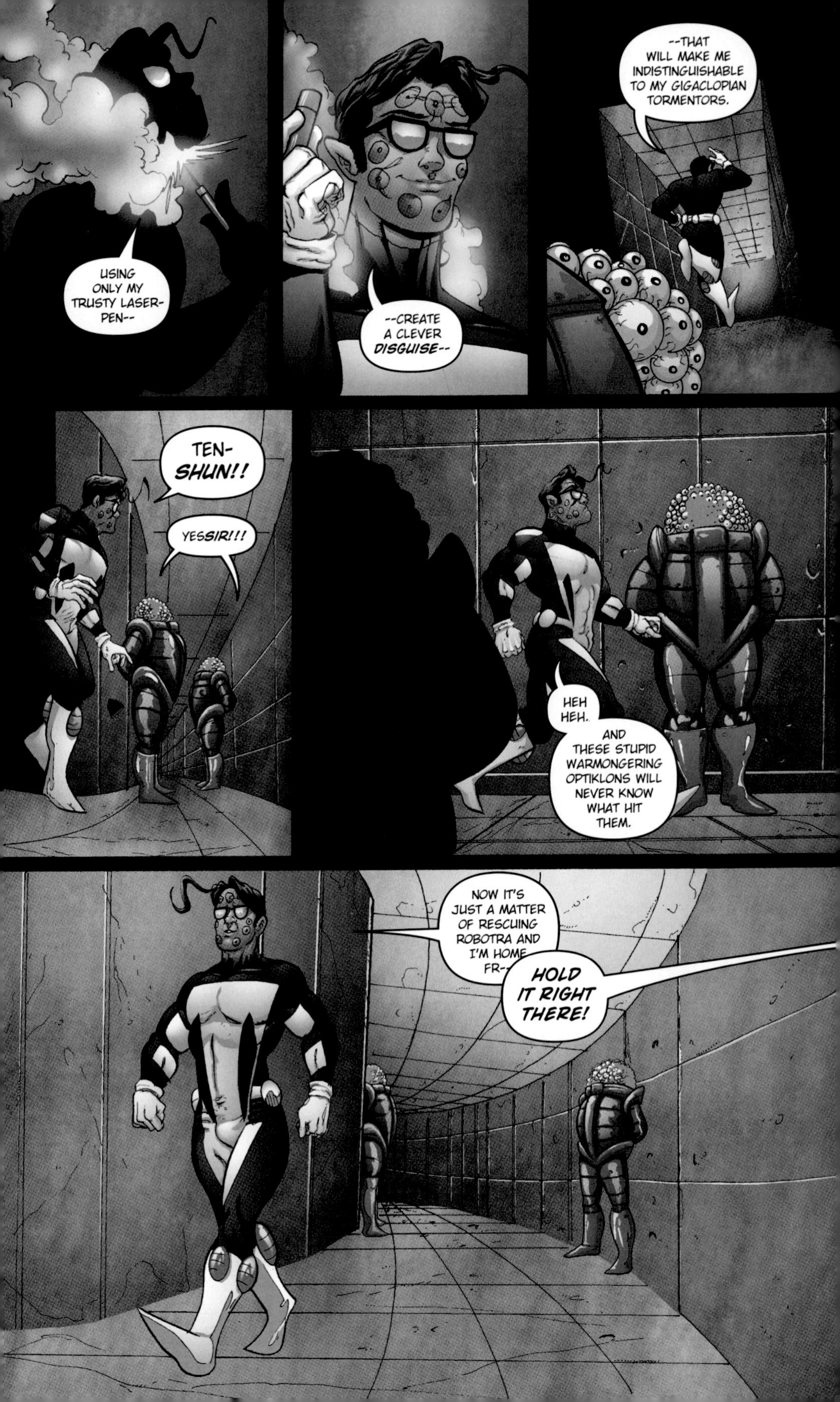
USING ONLY MY TRUSTY LASER-PEN--
--CREATE A CLEVER *DISGUISE*--
--THAT WILL MAKE ME INDISTINGUISHABLE TO MY GIGACLOPIAN TORMENTORS.
TEN-*SHUN!!*
YES*SIR!!!*
HEH HEH.
AND THESE STUPID WARMONGERING OPTIKLONS WILL NEVER KNOW WHAT HIT THEM.
NOW IT'S JUST A MATTER OF RESCUING ROBOTRA AND I'M HOME FR--
HOLD IT RIGHT THERE!

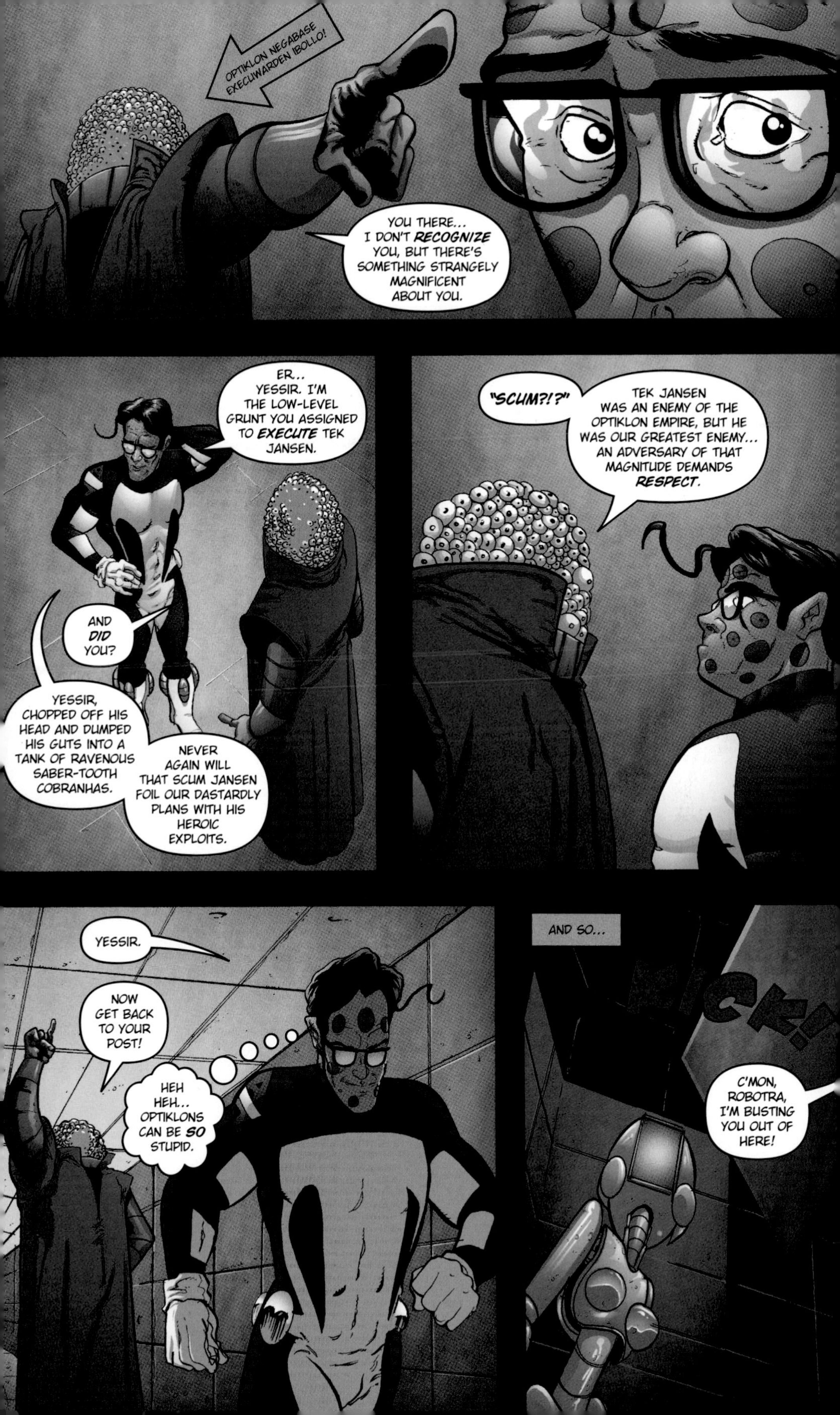
OPTIKLON NEGABASE EXECUWARDEN IBOLLO!
YOU THERE... I DON'T RECOGNIZE YOU, BUT THERE'S SOMETHING STRANGELY MAGNIFICENT ABOUT YOU.
ER... YESSIR. I'M THE LOW-LEVEL GRUNT YOU ASSIGNED TO EXECUTE TEK JANSEN.
AND DID YOU?
YESSIR, CHOPPED OFF HIS HEAD AND DUMPED HIS GUTS INTO A TANK OF RAVENOUS SABER-TOOTH COBRANHAS.
NEVER AGAIN WILL THAT SCUM JANSEN FOIL OUR DASTARDLY PLANS WITH HIS HEROIC EXPLOITS.
"SCUM?!?"
TEK JANSEN WAS AN ENEMY OF THE OPTIKLON EMPIRE, BUT HE WAS OUR GREATEST ENEMY... AN ADVERSARY OF THAT MAGNITUDE DEMANDS RESPECT.
YESSIR.
NOW GET BACK TO YOUR POST!
HEH HEH... OPTIKLONS CAN BE SO STUPID.
AND SO...
C'MON, ROBOTRA, I'M BUSTING YOU OUT OF HERE!

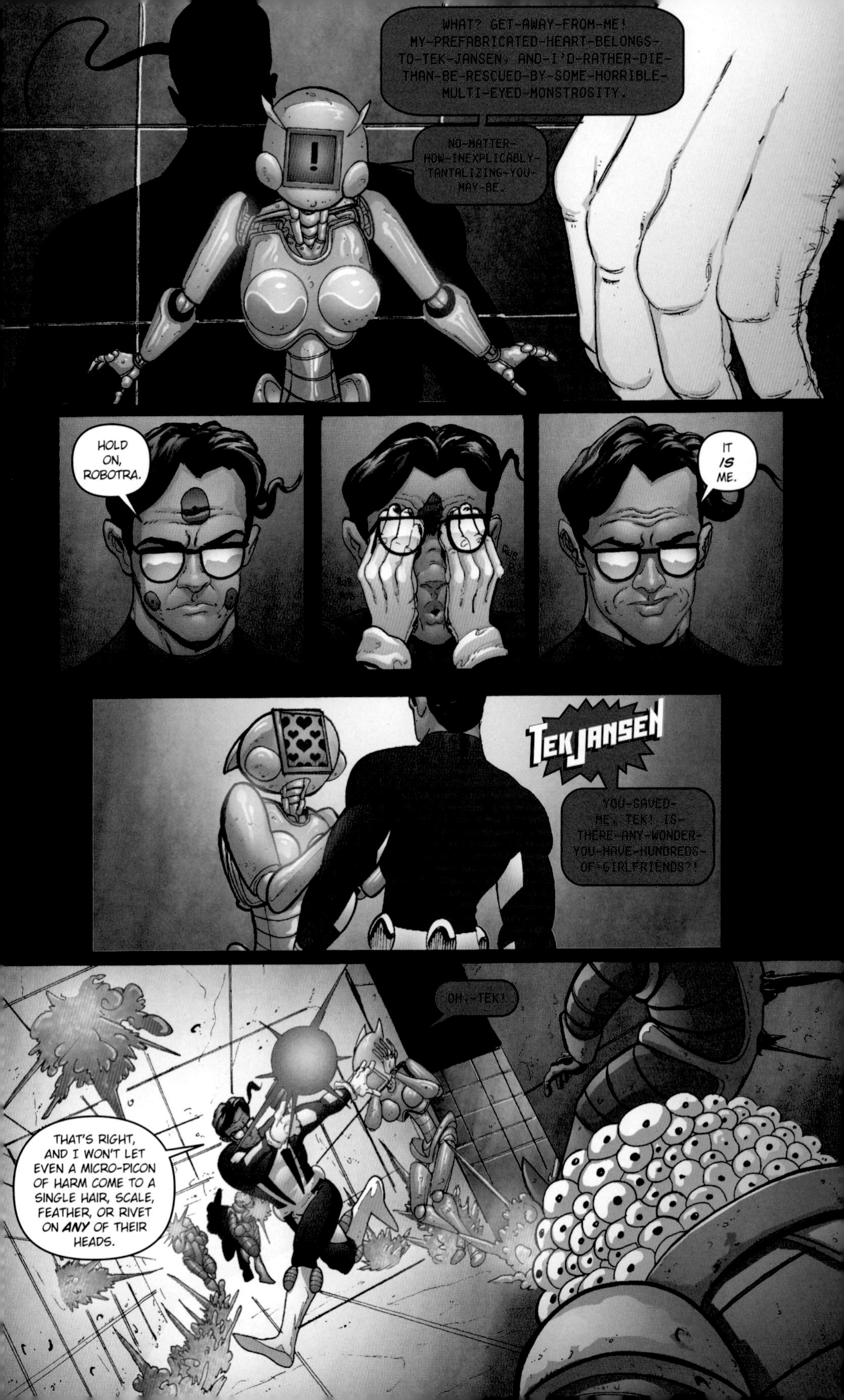
WHAT? GET-AWAY-FROM-ME! MY-PREFABRICATED-HEART-BELONGS-TO-TEK-JANSEN, AND-I'D-RATHER-DIE-THAN-BE-RESCUED-BY-SOME-HORRIBLE-MULTI-EYED-MONSTROSITY.
NO-MATTER-HOW-INEXPLICABLY-TANTALIZING-YOU-MAY-BE.
HOLD ON, ROBOTRA.
IT *IS* ME.
TEKJANSEN
YOU-SAVED-ME, TEK! IS-THERE-ANY-WONDER-YOU-HAVE-HUNDREDS-OF-GIRLFRIENDS?!
OH, TEK!
THAT'S RIGHT, AND I WON'T LET EVEN A MICRO-PICON OF HARM COME TO A SINGLE HAIR, SCALE, FEATHER, OR RIVET ON *ANY* OF THEIR HEADS.

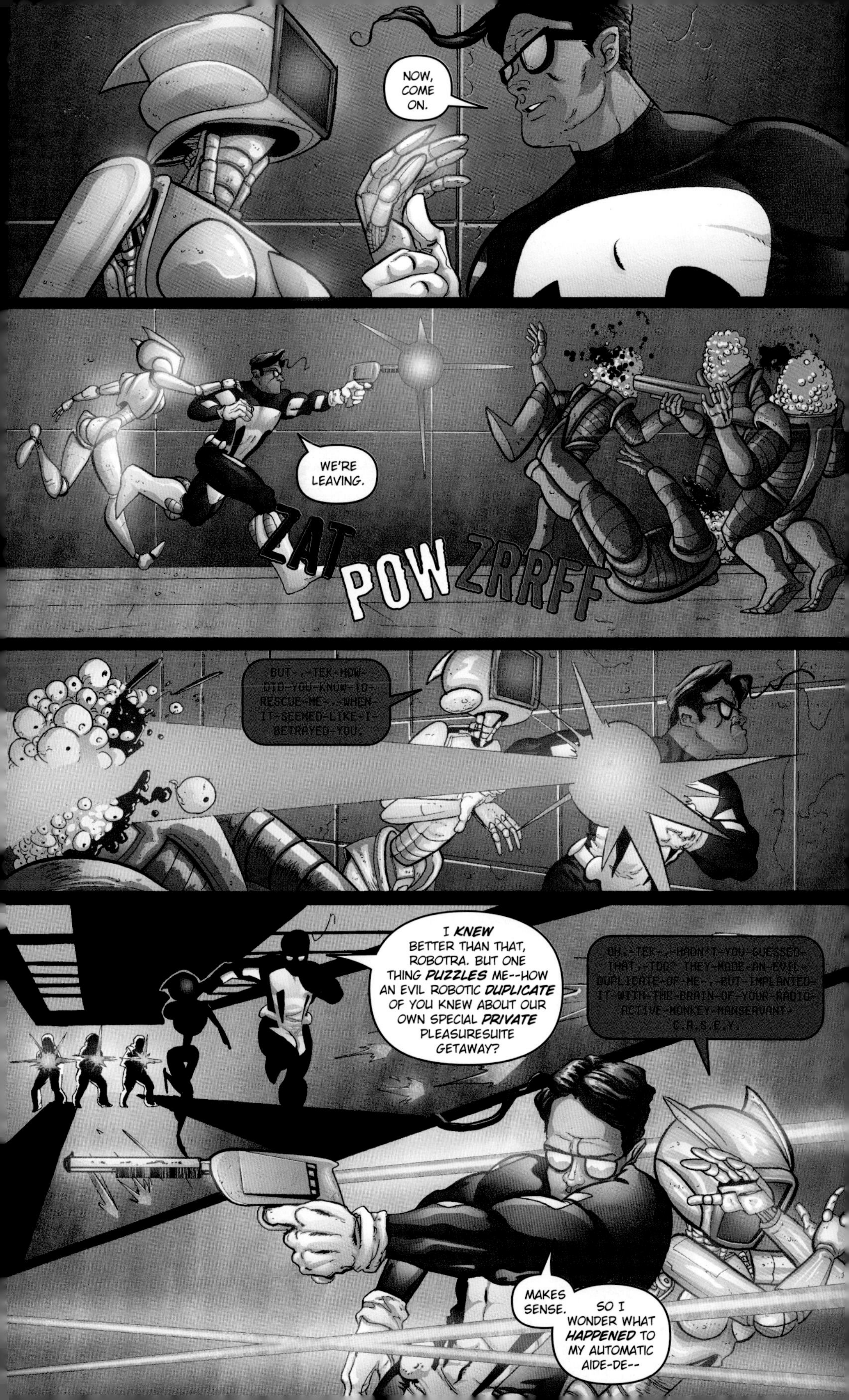

NOW, COME ON.
WE'RE LEAVING.
ZAT
POW
ZRRFF
BUT-,-TEK-HOW-DID-YOU-KNOW-TO-RESCUE-ME-,-WHEN-IT-SEEMED-LIKE-I-BETRAYED-YOU.
I *KNEW* BETTER THAN THAT, ROBOTRA. BUT ONE THING *PUZZLES* ME--HOW AN EVIL ROBOTIC *DUPLICATE* OF YOU KNEW ABOUT OUR OWN SPECIAL *PRIVATE* PLEASURESUITE GETAWAY?
OH,-TEK-,-HADN'T-YOU-GUESSED-THAT,-TOO? THEY-MADE-AN-EVIL-DUPLICATE-OF-ME-,-BUT-IMPLANTED-IT-WITH-THE-BRAIN-OF-YOUR-RADIO-ACTIVE-MONKEY-MANSERVANT-C.A.S.E.Y.
MAKES SENSE.
SO I WONDER WHAT *HAPPENED* TO MY AUTOMATIC AIDE-DE--

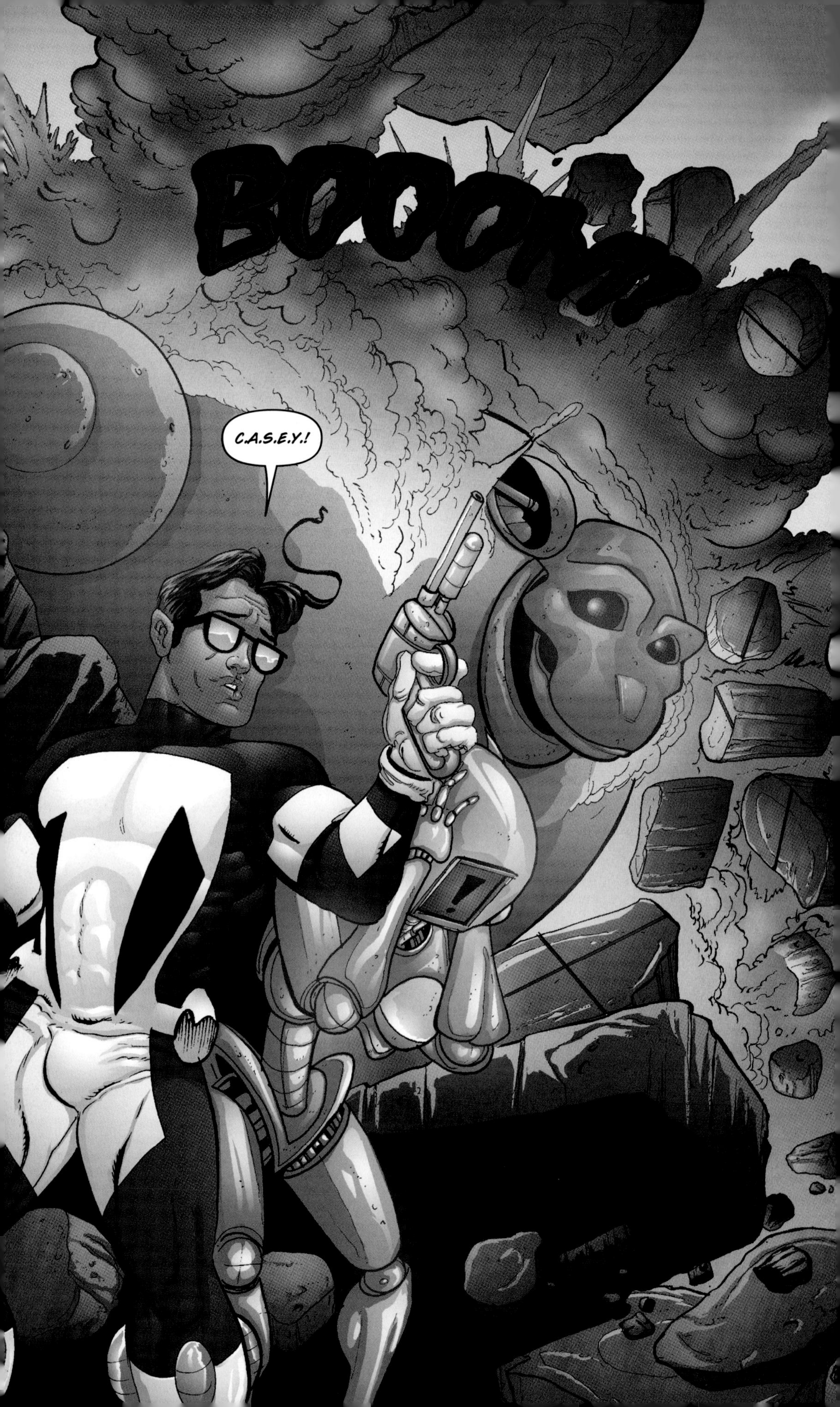
BOOOM!
C.A.S.E.Y.!

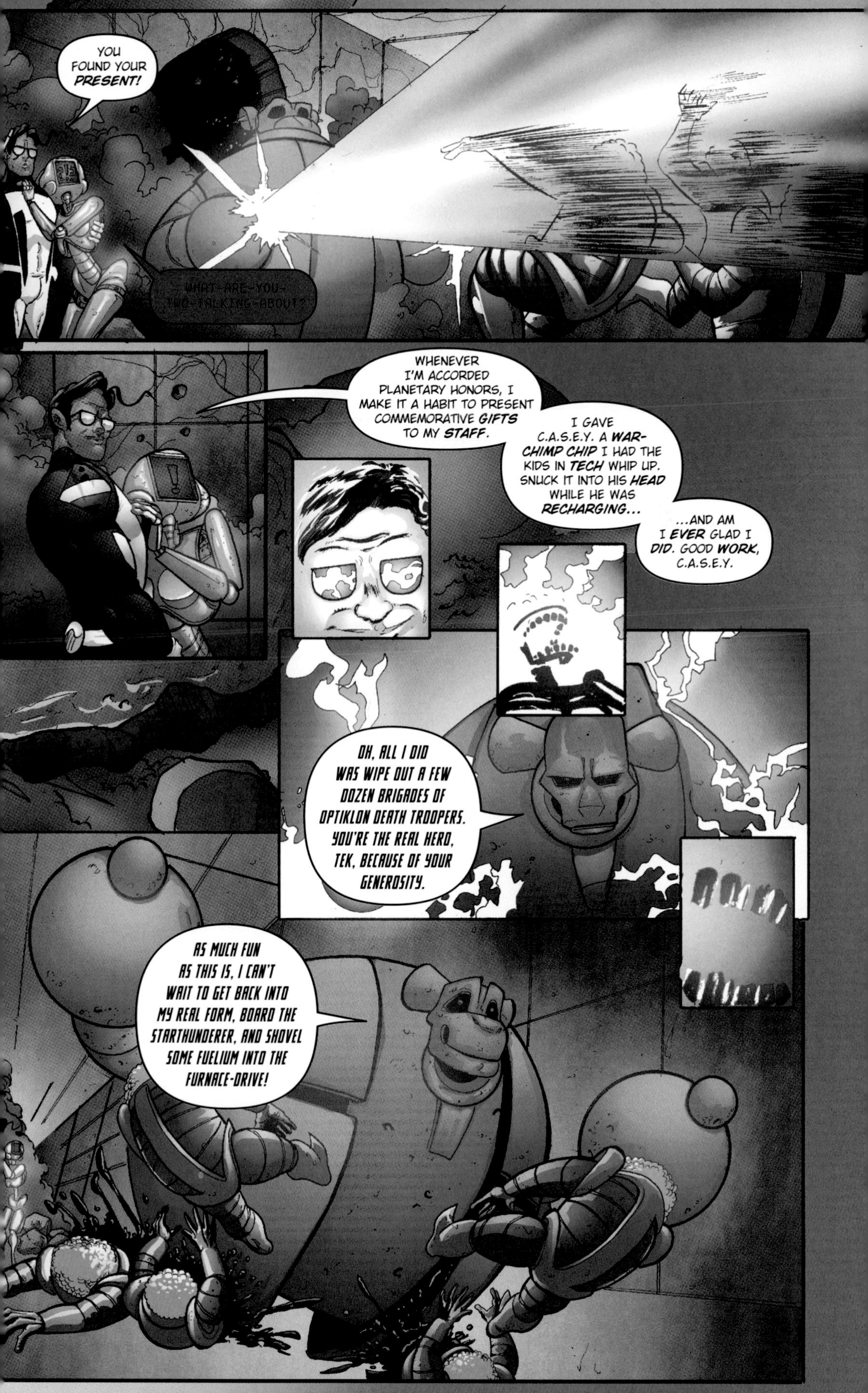
YOU FOUND YOUR PRESENT!
WHAT-ARE-YOU-TWO-TALKING-ABOUT?
WHENEVER I'M ACCORDED PLANETARY HONORS, I MAKE IT A HABIT TO PRESENT COMMEMORATIVE GIFTS TO MY STAFF.
I GAVE C.A.S.E.Y. A WAR-CHIMP CHIP I HAD THE KIDS IN TECH WHIP UP. SNUCK IT INTO HIS HEAD WHILE HE WAS RECHARGING...
...AND AM I EVER GLAD I DID. GOOD WORK, C.A.S.E.Y.
OH, ALL I DID WAS WIPE OUT A FEW DOZEN BRIGADES OF OPTIKLON DEATH TROOPERS. YOU'RE THE REAL HERO, TEK, BECAUSE OF YOUR GENEROSITY.
AS MUCH FUN AS THIS IS, I CAN'T WAIT TO GET BACK INTO MY REAL FORM, BOARD THE STARTHUNDERER, AND SHOVEL SOME FUELIUM INTO THE FURNACE-DRIVE!

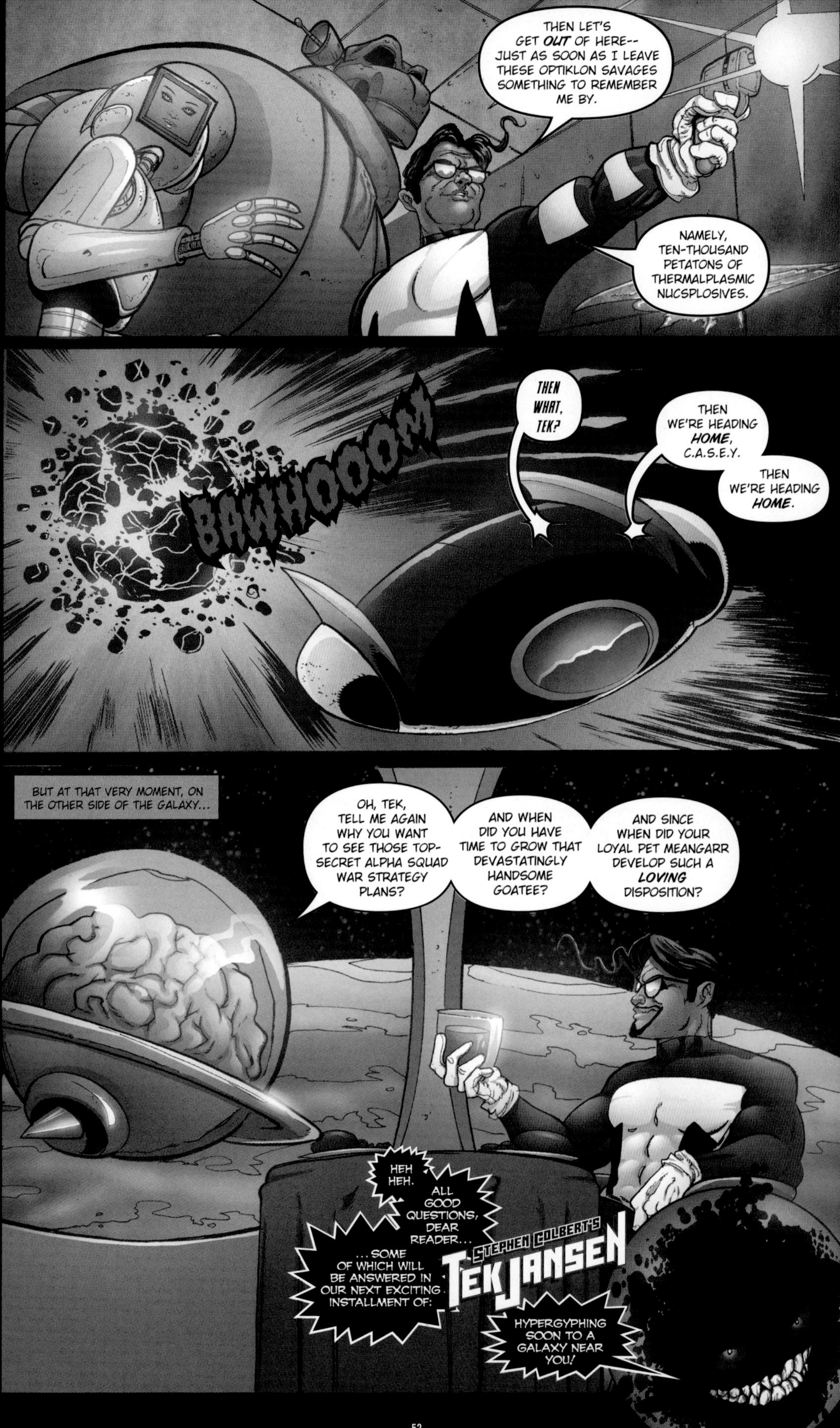
THEN LET'S GET OUT OF HERE-- JUST AS SOON AS I LEAVE THESE OPTIKLON SAVAGES SOMETHING TO REMEMBER ME BY.
NAMELY, TEN-THOUSAND PETATONS OF THERMALPLASMIC NUCSPLOSIVES.
BAWHOOOM
THEN WHAT, TEK?
THEN WE'RE HEADING HOME, C.A.S.E.Y.
THEN WE'RE HEADING HOME.
BUT AT THAT VERY MOMENT, ON THE OTHER SIDE OF THE GALAXY...
OH, TEK, TELL ME AGAIN WHY YOU WANT TO SEE THOSE TOP-SECRET ALPHA SQUAD WAR STRATEGY PLANS?
AND WHEN DID YOU HAVE TIME TO GROW THAT DEVASTATINGLY HANDSOME GOATEE?
AND SINCE WHEN DID YOUR LOYAL PET MEANGARR DEVELOP SUCH A LOVING DISPOSITION?
HEH HEH.
ALL GOOD QUESTIONS, DEAR READER...
...SOME OF WHICH WILL BE ANSWERED IN OUR NEXT EXCITING INSTALLMENT OF:
STEPHEN COLBERT'S TEK JANSEN
HYPERGYPHING SOON TO A GALAXY NEAR YOU!

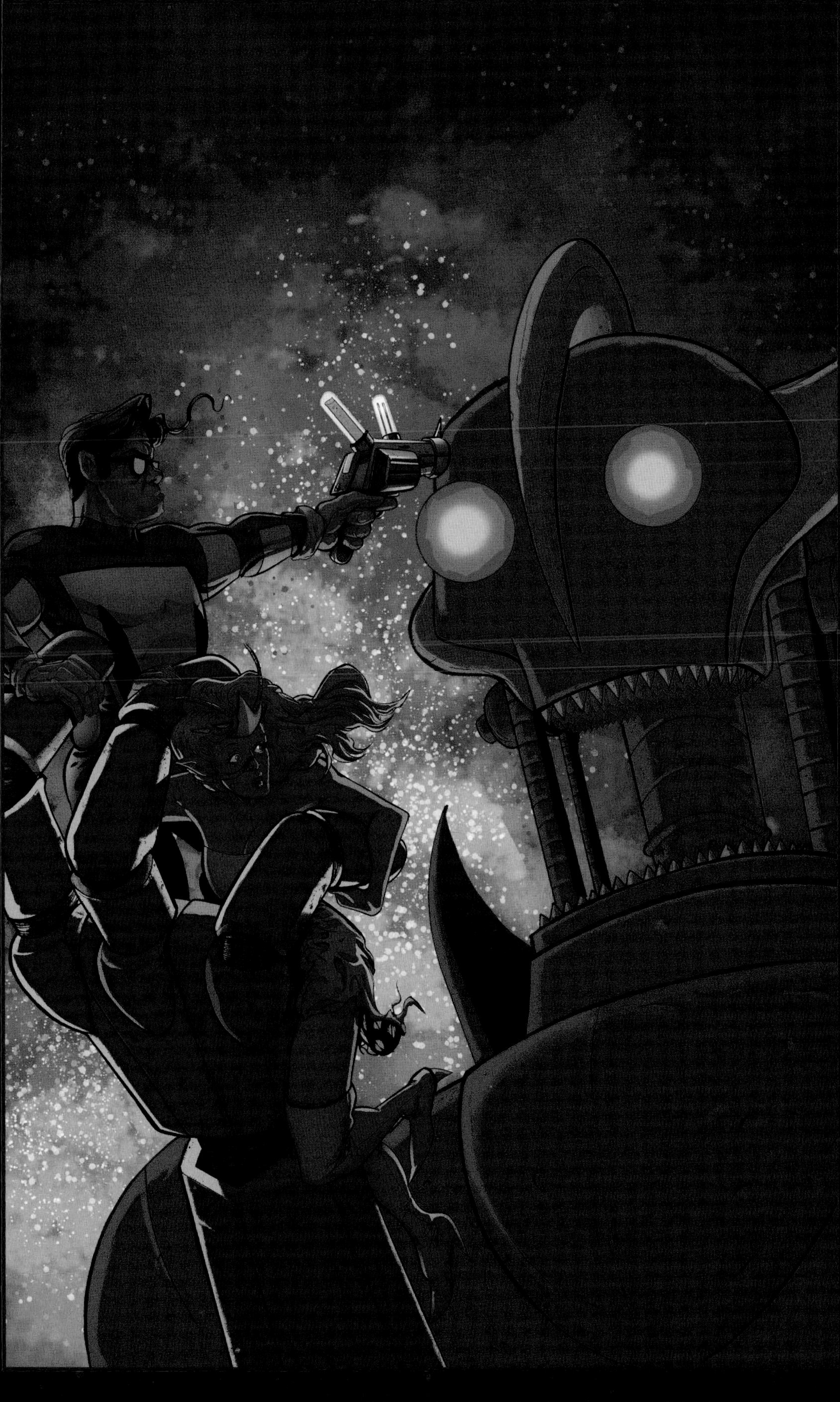

art by ROBBI RODRIGUEZ with NATHAN FAIRBAIRN

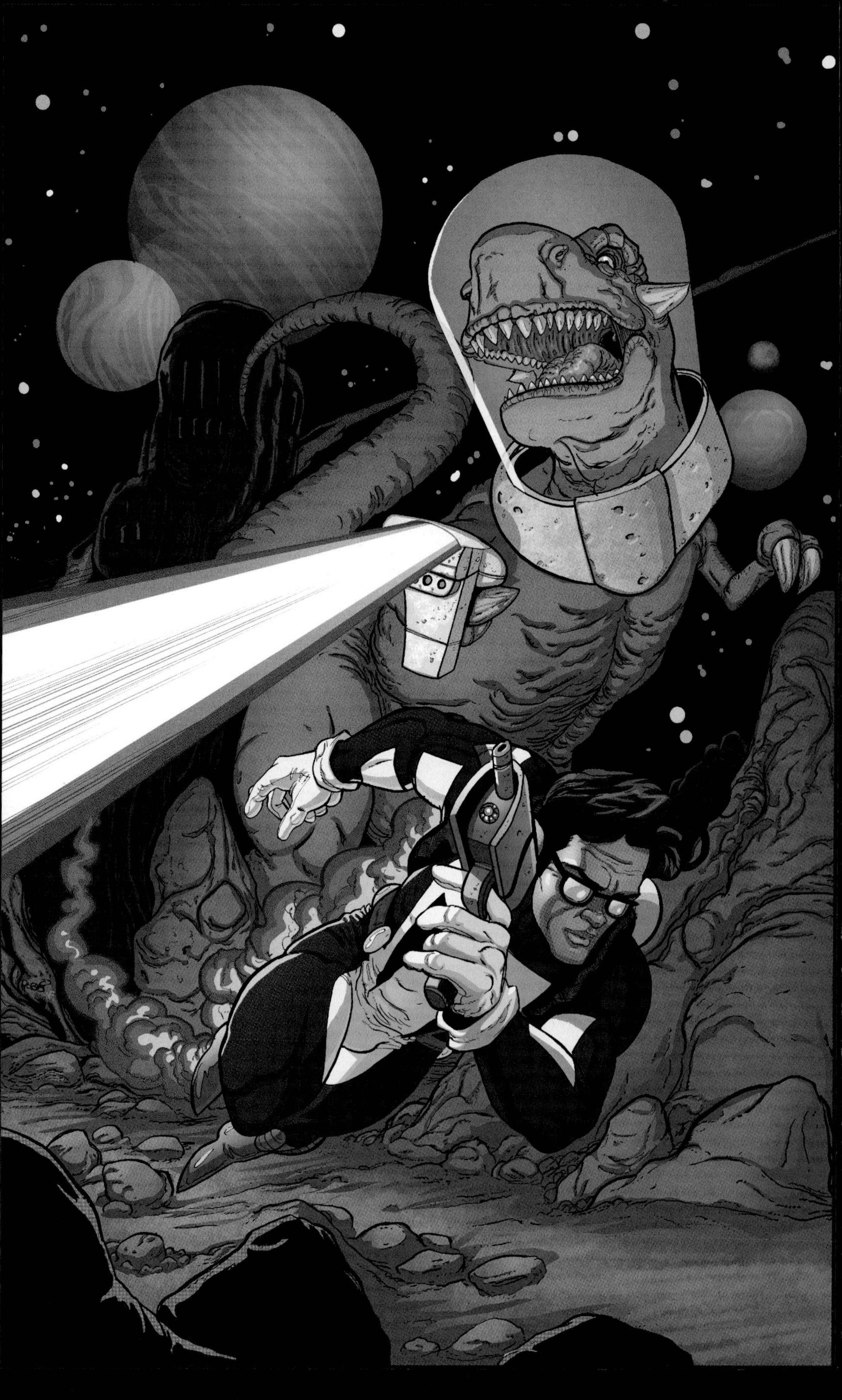

ROBBI RODRIGUEZ NATHAN FAIRBAIRN

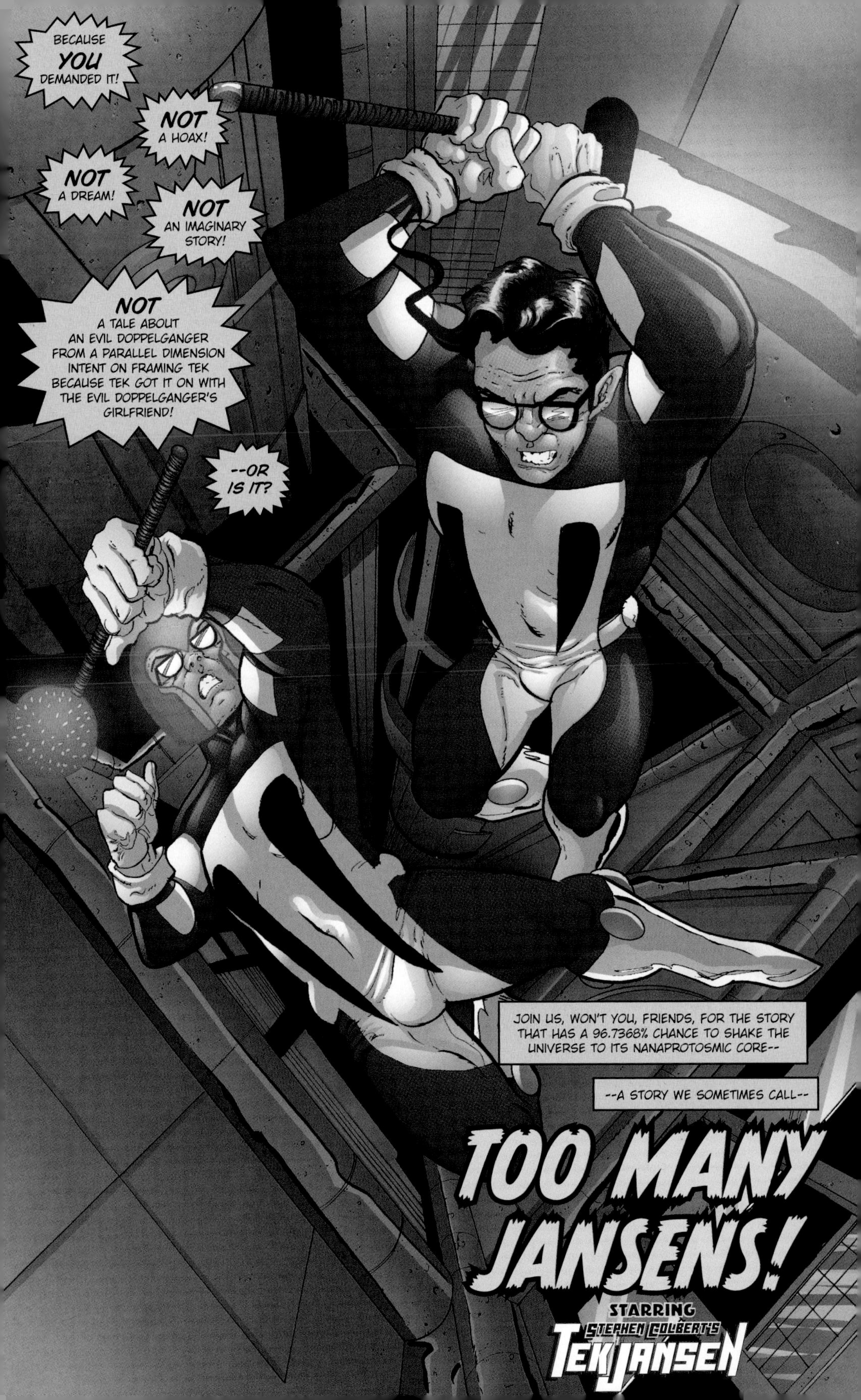

BECAUSE YOU DEMANDED IT!
NOT A HOAX!
NOT A DREAM!
NOT AN IMAGINARY STORY!
NOT A TALE ABOUT AN EVIL DOPPELGANGER FROM A PARALLEL DIMENSION INTENT ON FRAMING TEK BECAUSE TEK GOT IT ON WITH THE EVIL DOPPELGANGER'S GIRLFRIEND!
--OR IS IT?
JOIN US, WON'T YOU, FRIENDS, FOR THE STORY THAT HAS A 96.7368% CHANCE TO SHAKE THE UNIVERSE TO ITS NANAPROTOSMIC CORE--
--A STORY WE SOMETIMES CALL--
TOO MANY JANSENS!
STARRING
STEPHEN COLBERT'S
TEK JANSEN

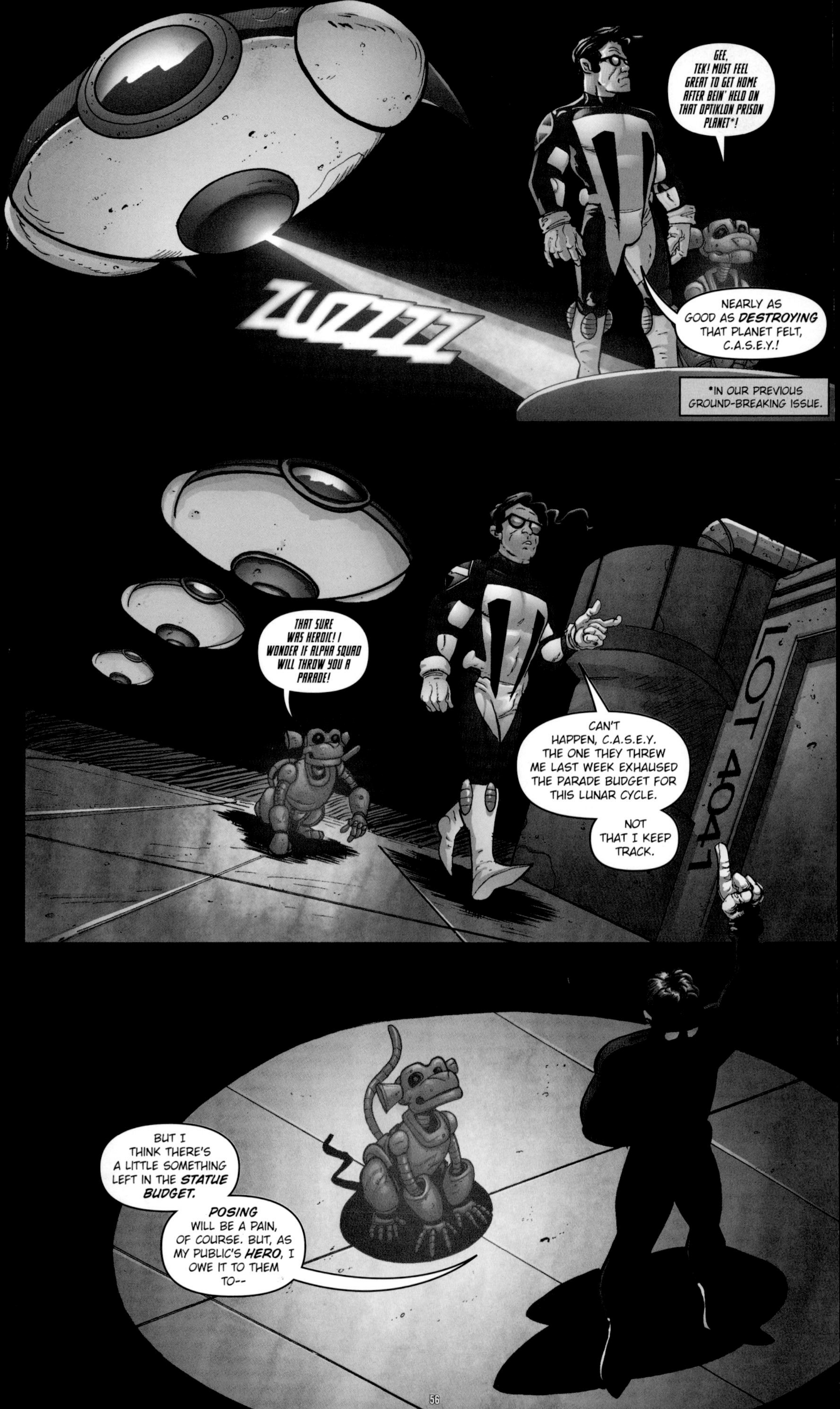
GEE, TEK! MUST FEEL GREAT TO GET HOME AFTER BEIN' HELD ON THAT OPTIKLON PRISON PLANET*!
ZWOOZZ
NEARLY AS GOOD AS **DESTROYING** THAT PLANET FELT, C.A.S.E.Y.!
*IN OUR PREVIOUS GROUND-BREAKING ISSUE.
THAT SURE WAS HEROIC! I WONDER IF ALPHA SQUAD WILL THROW YOU A PARADE!
CAN'T HAPPEN, C.A.S.E.Y. THE ONE THEY THREW ME LAST WEEK EXHAUSED THE PARADE BUDGET FOR THIS LUNAR CYCLE.
NOT THAT I KEEP TRACK.
LOT 4041
BUT I THINK THERE'S A LITTLE SOMETHING LEFT IN THE ***STATUE BUDGET.***
POSING WILL BE A PAIN, OF COURSE. BUT, AS MY PUBLIC'S ***HERO***, I OWE IT TO THEM TO--

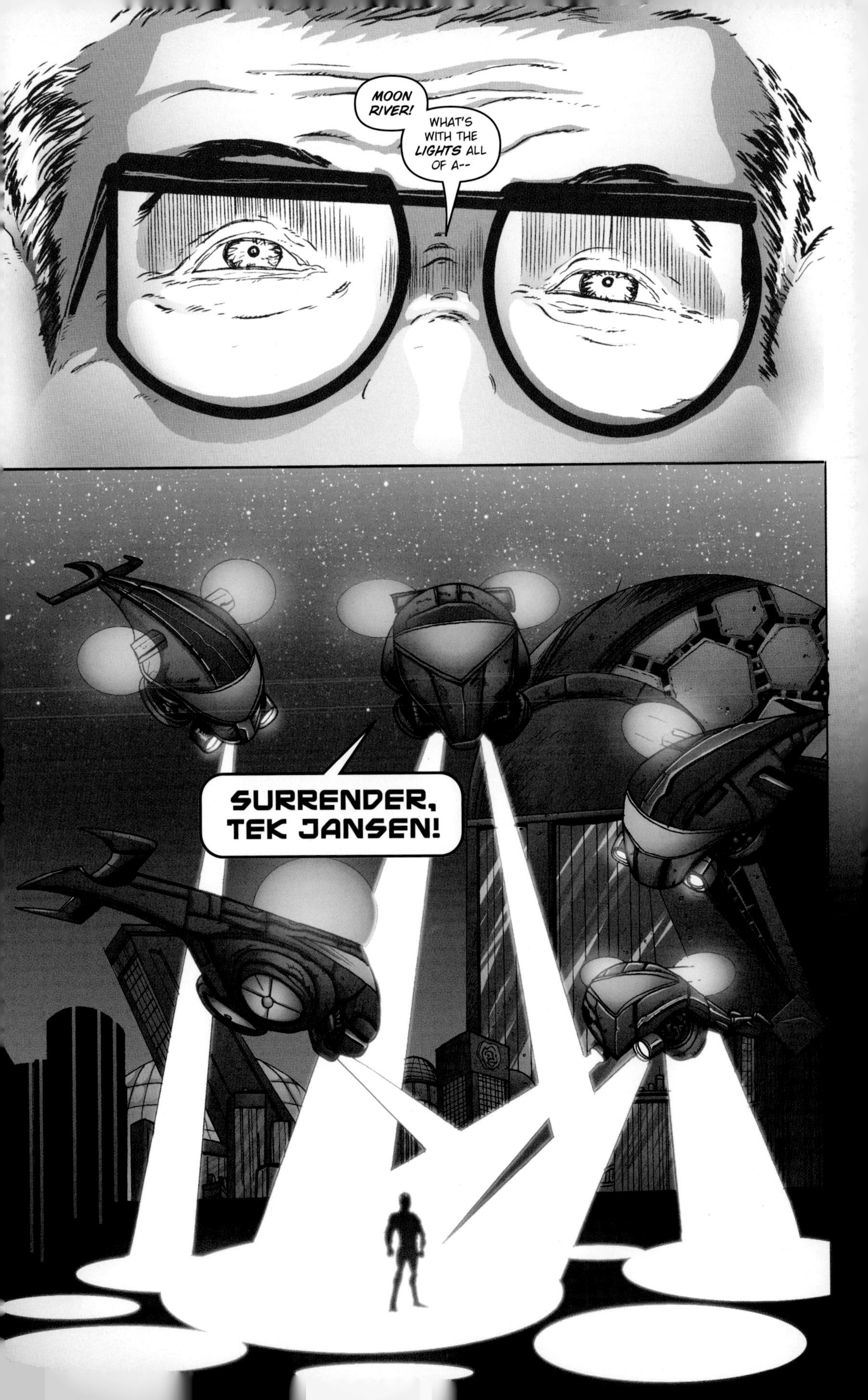
MOON RIVER!
WHAT'S WITH THE LIGHTS ALL OF A--
SURRENDER, TEK JANSEN!

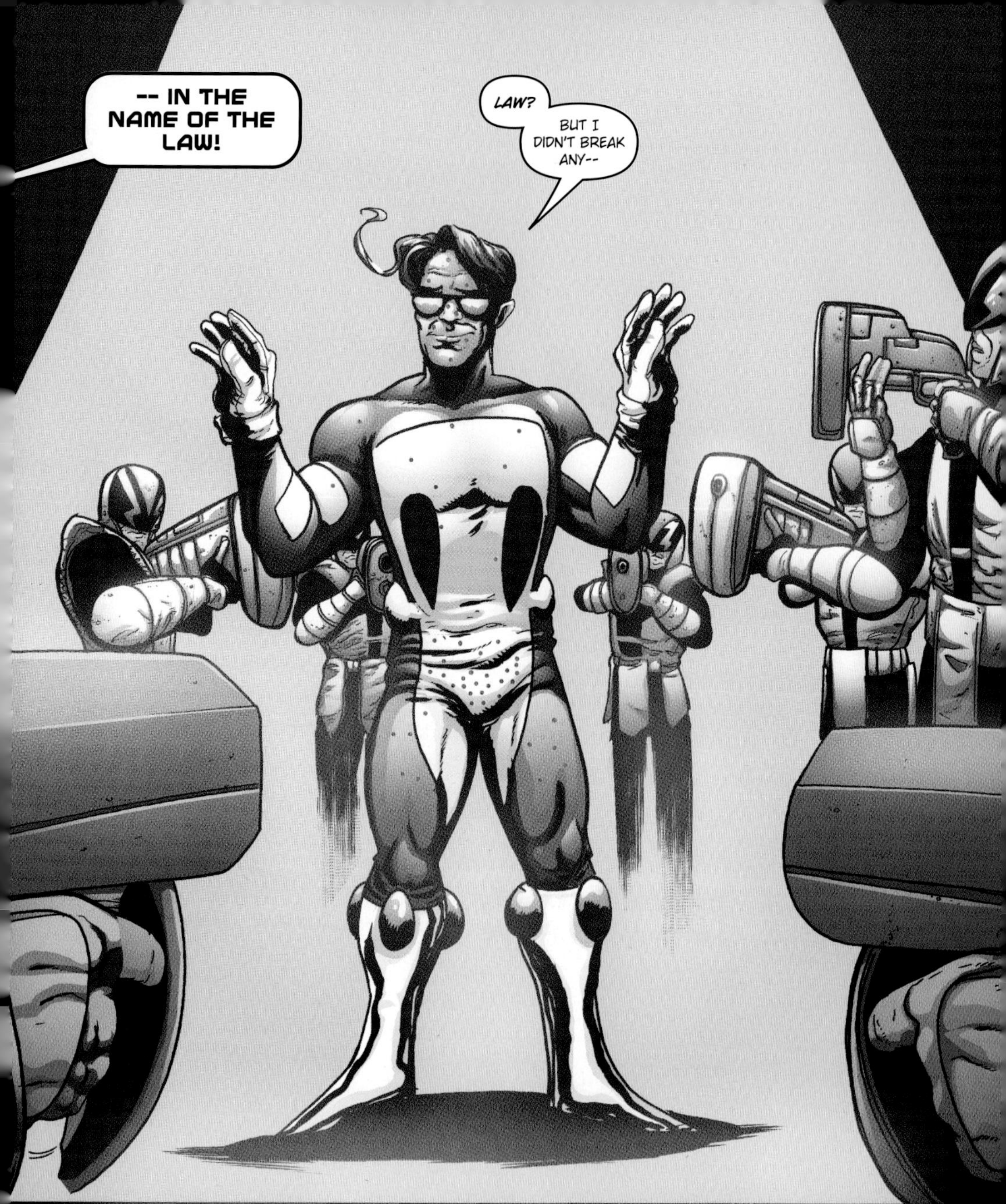
-- IN THE NAME OF THE LAW!
LAW? BUT I DIDN'T BREAK ANY--
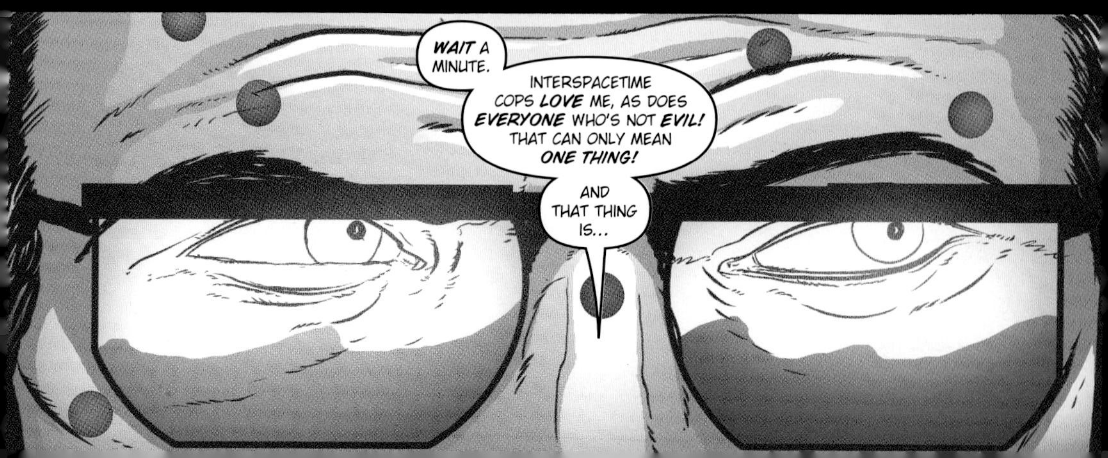
WAIT A MINUTE.
INTERSPACETIME COPS LOVE ME, AS DOES EVERYONE WHO'S NOT EVIL! THAT CAN ONLY MEAN ONE THING!
AND THAT THING IS...

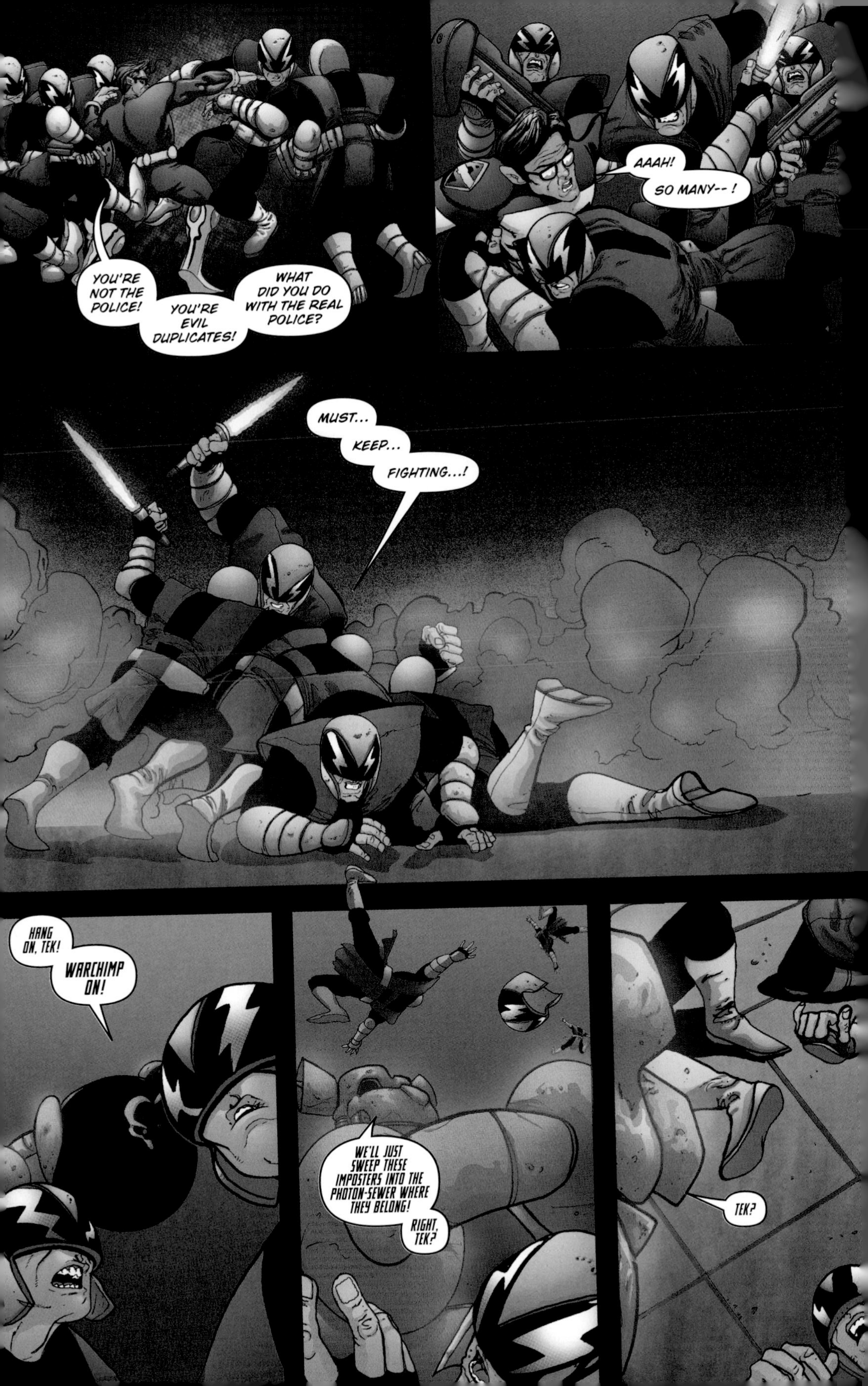
YOU'RE NOT THE POLICE!
YOU'RE EVIL DUPLICATES!
WHAT DID YOU DO WITH THE REAL POLICE?
AAAH!
SO MANY-- !
MUST...
KEEP...
FIGHTING...!
HANG ON, TEK!
WARCHIMP ON!
WE'LL JUST SWEEP THESE IMPOSTERS INTO THE PHOTON-SEWER WHERE THEY BELONG!
RIGHT, TEK?
TEK?

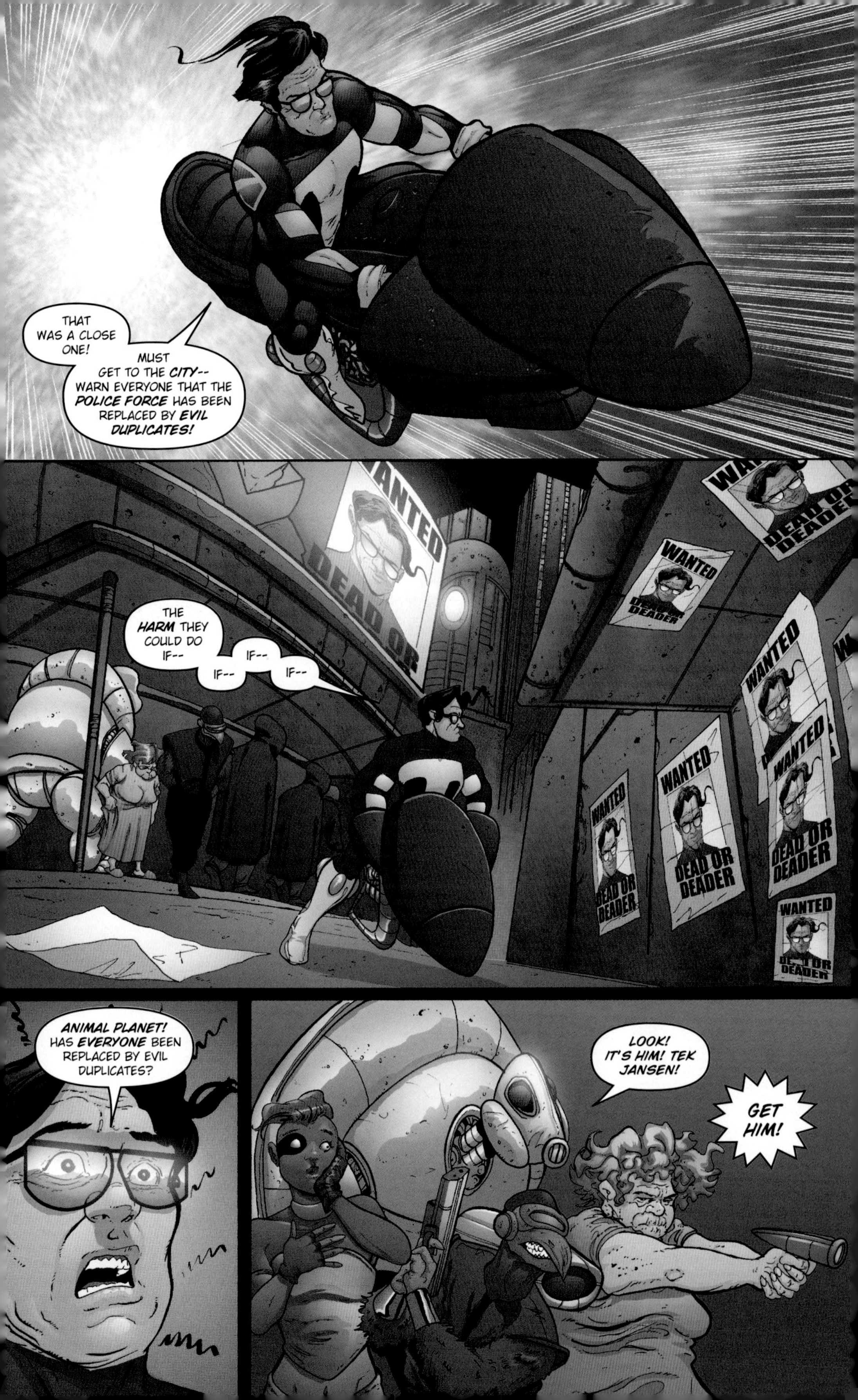
THAT WAS A CLOSE ONE!
MUST GET TO THE *CITY*-- WARN EVERYONE THAT THE ***POLICE FORCE*** HAS BEEN REPLACED BY ***EVIL DUPLICATES!***
WANTED
DEAD OR DEADER
THE *HARM* THEY COULD DO IF--
IF--
IF--
IF--
ANIMAL PLANET! HAS ***EVERYONE*** BEEN REPLACED BY EVIL DUPLICATES?
LOOK! IT'S HIM! TEK JANSEN!
GET HIM!

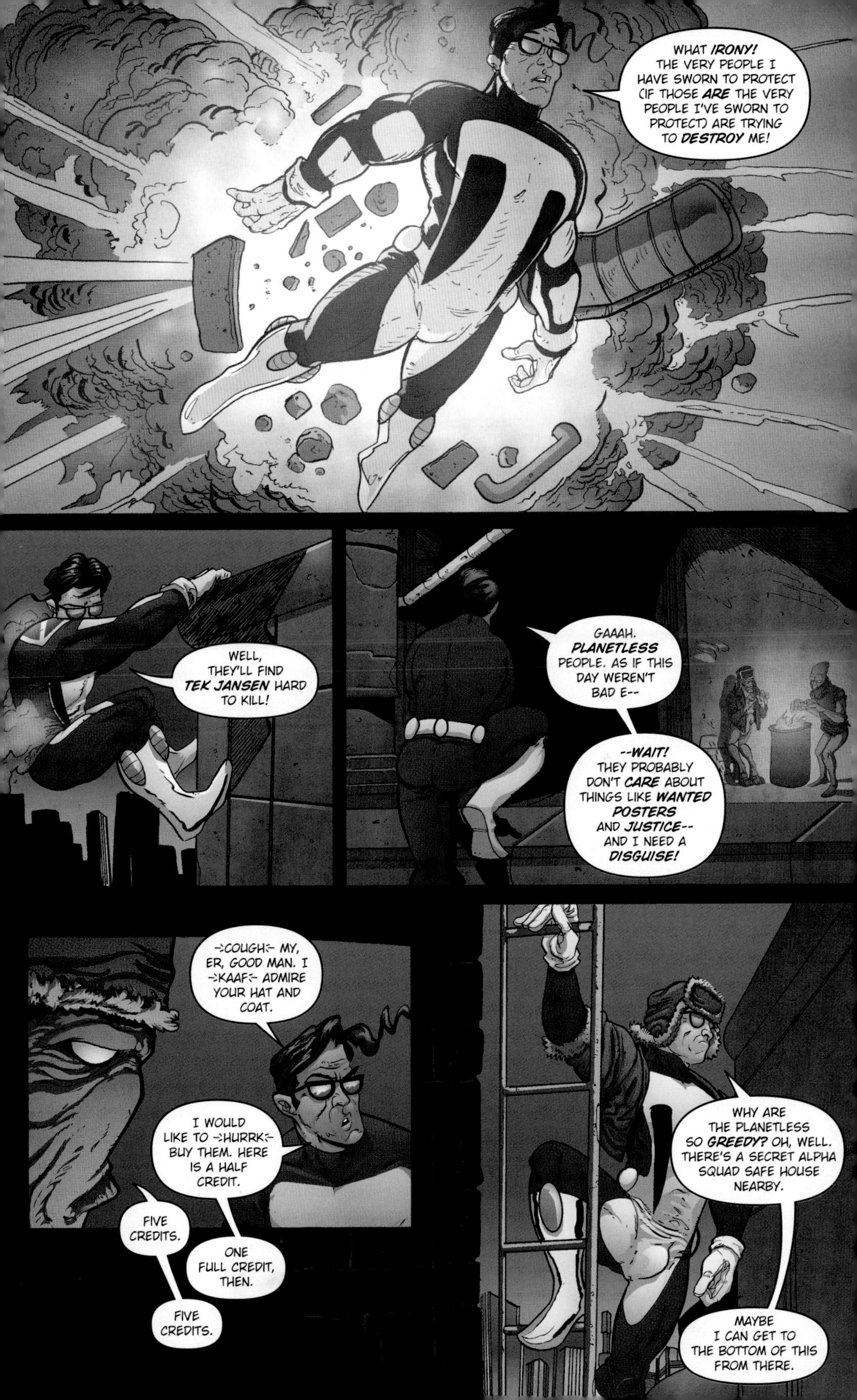
WHAT IRONY! THE VERY PEOPLE I HAVE SWORN TO PROTECT (IF THOSE ARE THE VERY PEOPLE I'VE SWORN TO PROTECT) ARE TRYING TO DESTROY ME!
WELL, THEY'LL FIND TEK JANSEN HARD TO KILL!
GAAAH. PLANETLESS PEOPLE. AS IF THIS DAY WEREN'T BAD E--
--WAIT! THEY PROBABLY DON'T CARE ABOUT THINGS LIKE WANTED POSTERS AND JUSTICE-- AND I NEED A DISGUISE!
-COUGH- MY, ER, GOOD MAN. I -KAAF- ADMIRE YOUR HAT AND COAT.
I WOULD LIKE TO -HURRK- BUY THEM. HERE IS A HALF CREDIT.
FIVE CREDITS.
ONE FULL CREDIT, THEN.
FIVE CREDITS.
WHY ARE THE PLANETLESS SO GREEDY? OH, WELL. THERE'S A SECRET ALPHA SQUAD SAFE HOUSE NEARBY.
MAYBE I CAN GET TO THE BOTTOM OF THIS FROM THERE.

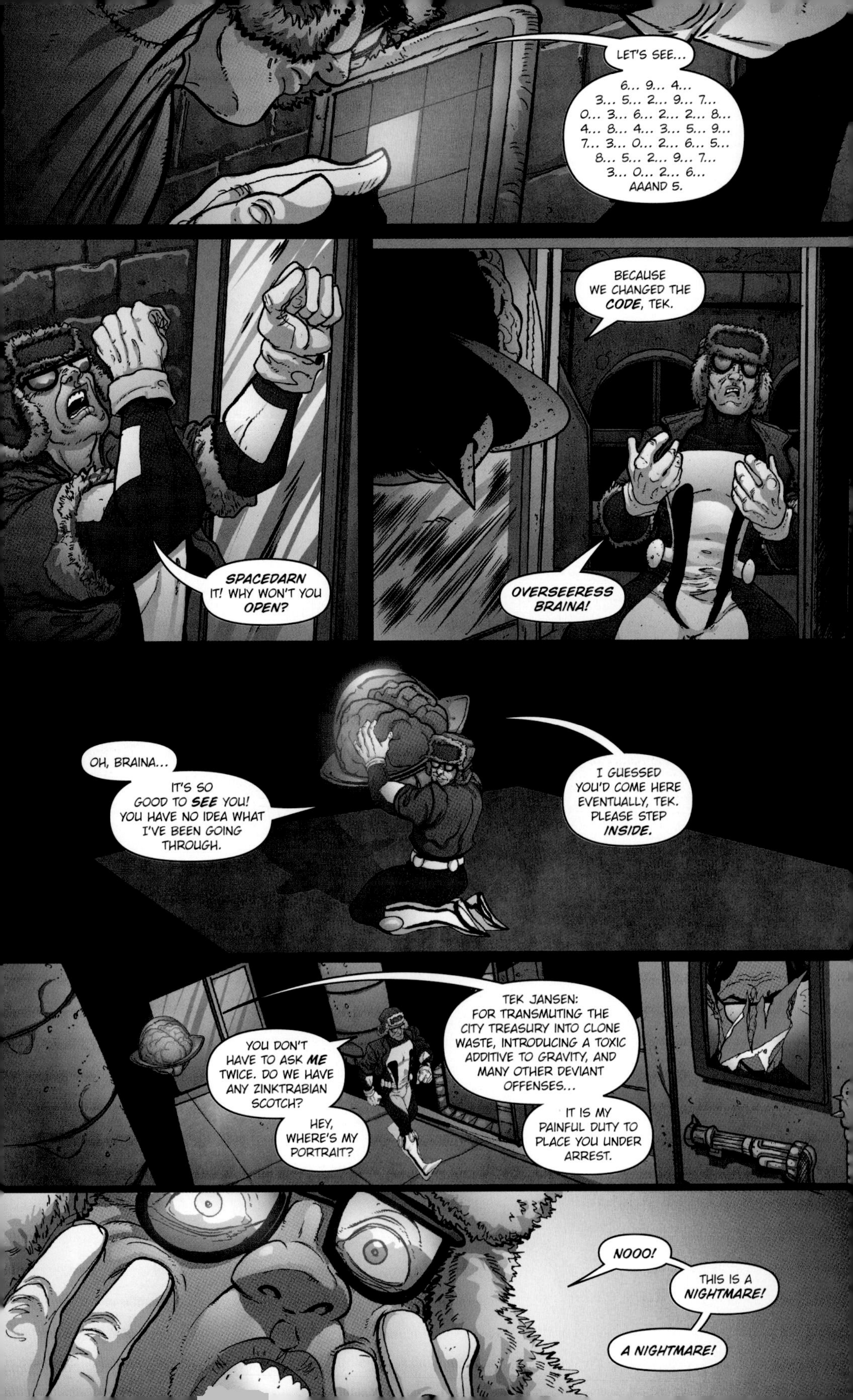
LET'S SEE...
6... 9... 4... 3... 5... 2... 9... 7... 0... 3... 6... 2... 2... 8... 4... 8... 4... 3... 5... 9... 7... 3... 0... 2... 6... 5... 8... 5... 2... 9... 7... 3... 0... 2... 6... AAAND 5.
SPACEDARN IT! WHY WON'T YOU OPEN?
BECAUSE WE CHANGED THE CODE, TEK.
OVERSEEERESS BRAINA!
OH, BRAINA...
IT'S SO GOOD TO SEE YOU! YOU HAVE NO IDEA WHAT I'VE BEEN GOING THROUGH.
I GUESSED YOU'D COME HERE EVENTUALLY, TEK. PLEASE STEP INSIDE.
YOU DON'T HAVE TO ASK ME TWICE. DO WE HAVE ANY ZINKTRABIAN SCOTCH?
HEY, WHERE'S MY PORTRAIT?
TEK JANSEN: FOR TRANSMUTING THE CITY TREASURY INTO CLONE WASTE, INTRODUCING A TOXIC ADDITIVE TO GRAVITY, AND MANY OTHER DEVIANT OFFENSES...
IT IS MY PAINFUL DUTY TO PLACE YOU UNDER ARREST.
NOOO!
THIS IS A NIGHTMARE!
A NIGHTMARE!

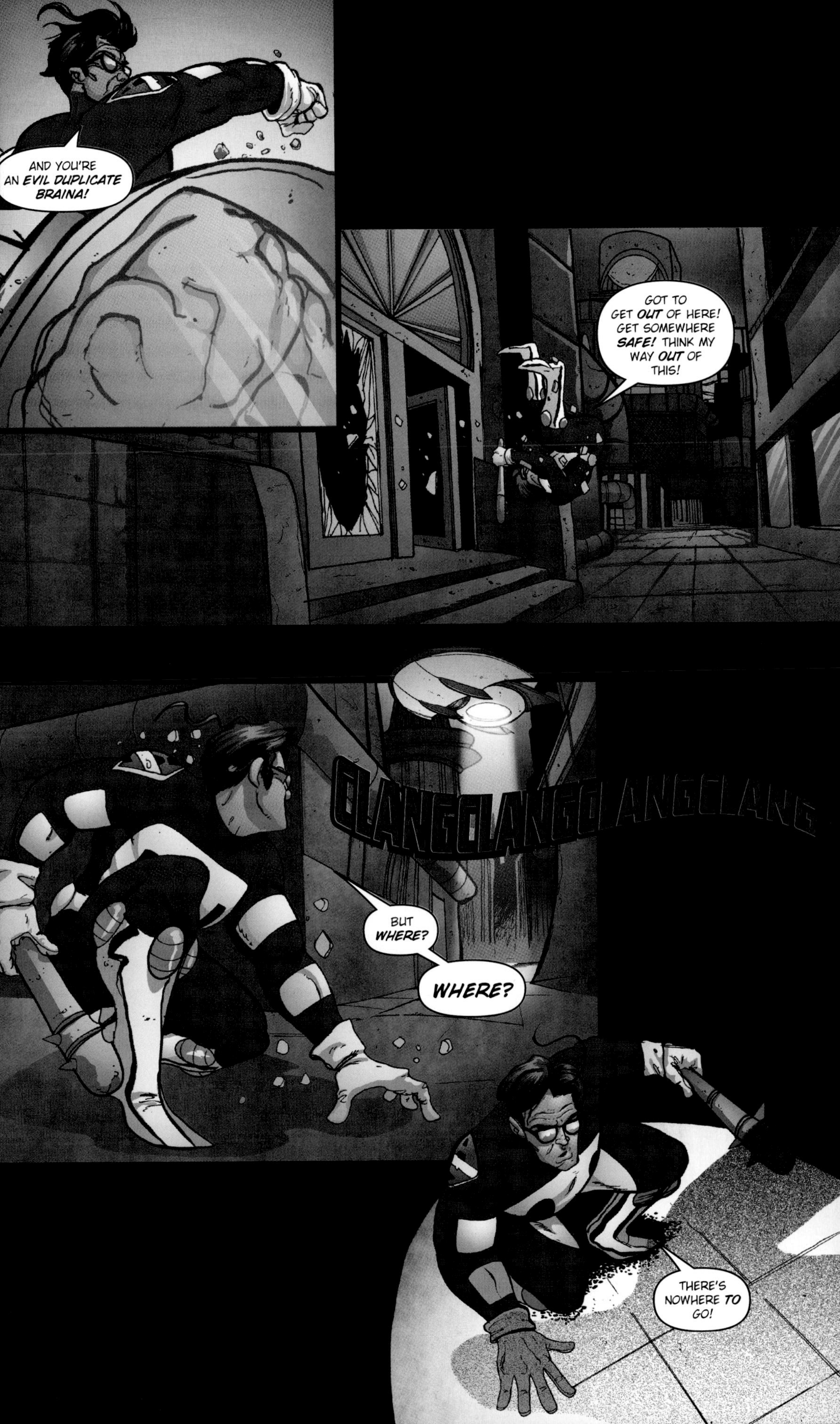
AND YOU'RE AN EVIL DUPLICATE BRAINA!
GOT TO GET OUT OF HERE! GET SOMEWHERE SAFE! THINK MY WAY OUT OF THIS!
CLANGCLANGCLANGCLANG
BUT WHERE?
WHERE?
THERE'S NOWHERE TO GO!

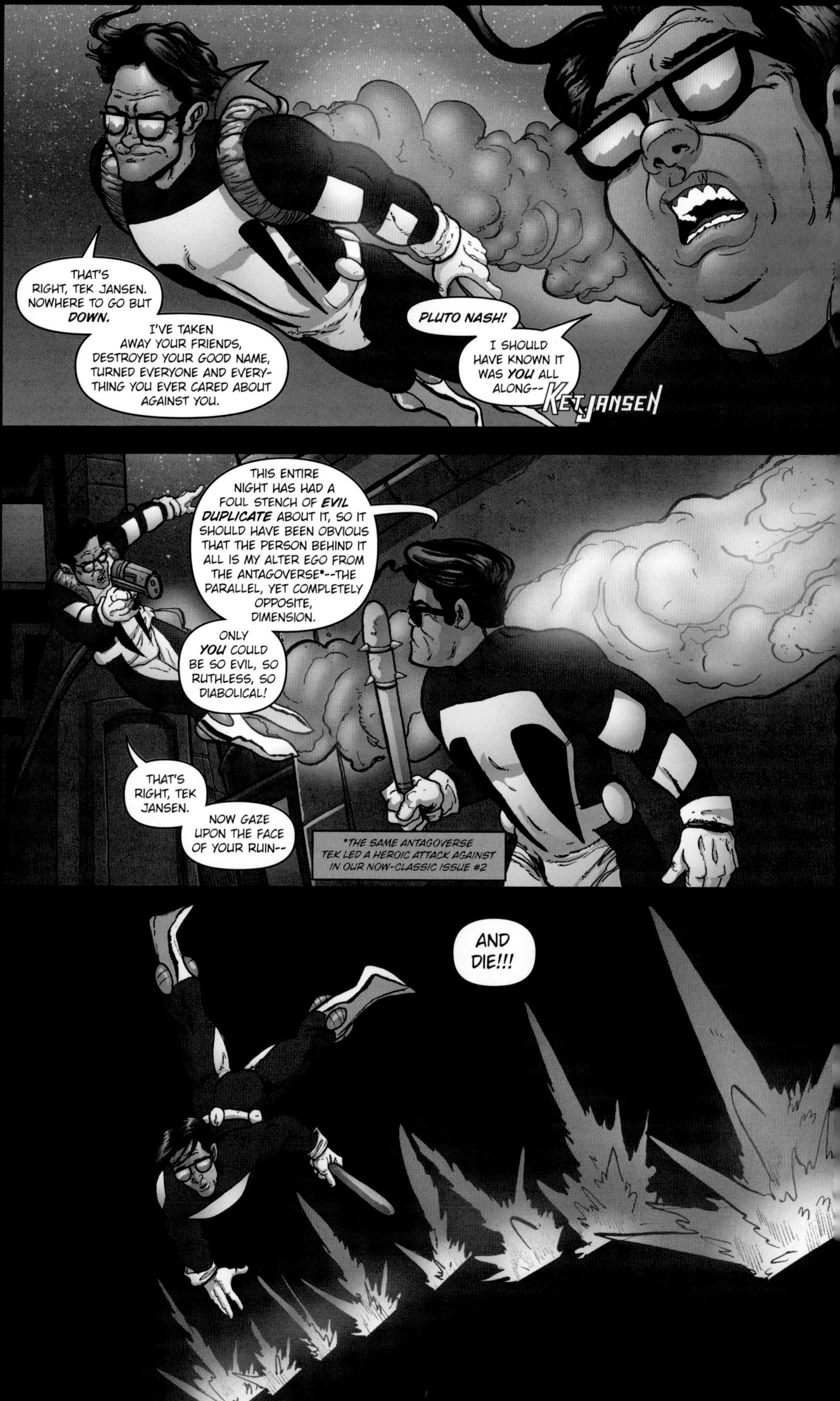
THAT'S RIGHT, TEK JANSEN. NOWHERE TO GO BUT **DOWN.**
I'VE TAKEN AWAY YOUR FRIENDS, DESTROYED YOUR GOOD NAME, TURNED EVERYONE AND EVERYTHING YOU EVER CARED ABOUT AGAINST YOU.
PLUTO NASH!
I SHOULD HAVE KNOWN IT WAS **YOU** ALL ALONG--
KET JANSEN
THIS ENTIRE NIGHT HAS HAD A FOUL STENCH OF **EVIL DUPLICATE** ABOUT IT, SO IT SHOULD HAVE BEEN OBVIOUS THAT THE PERSON BEHIND IT ALL IS MY ALTER EGO FROM THE ANTAGOVERSE*--THE PARALLEL, YET COMPLETELY OPPOSITE, DIMENSION.
ONLY **YOU** COULD BE SO EVIL, SO RUTHLESS, SO DIABOLICAL!
THAT'S RIGHT, TEK JANSEN.
NOW GAZE UPON THE FACE OF YOUR RUIN--
*THE SAME ANTAGOVERSE TEK LED A HEROIC ATTACK AGAINST IN OUR NOW-CLASSIC ISSUE #2
AND DIE!!!

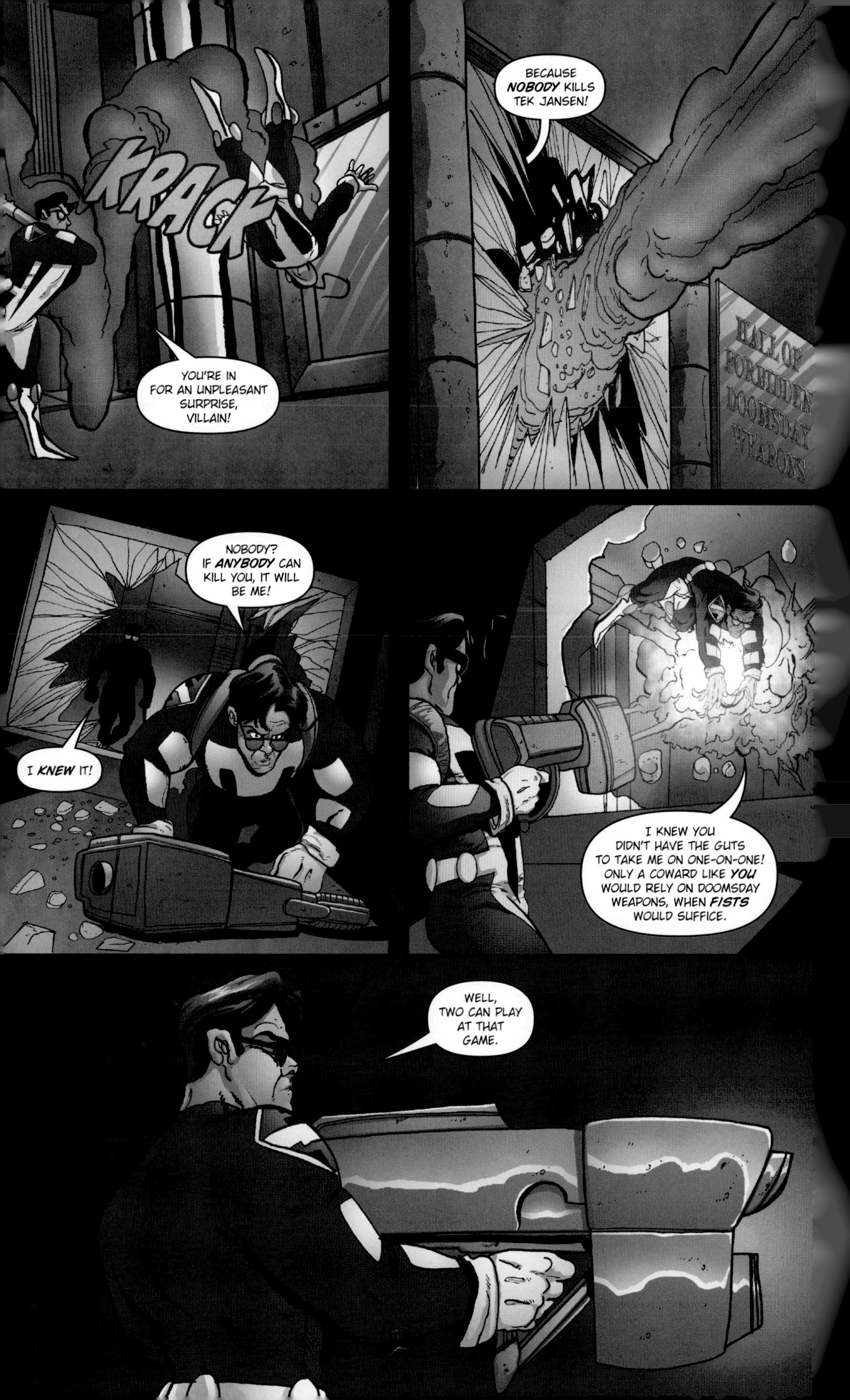
KRACK
YOU'RE IN FOR AN UNPLEASANT SURPRISE, VILLAIN!
BECAUSE ***NOBODY*** KILLS TEK JANSEN!
HALL OF FORBIDDEN DOOMSDAY WEAPONS
NOBODY? IF ***ANYBODY*** CAN KILL YOU, IT WILL BE ME!
I ***KNEW*** IT!
I KNEW YOU DIDN'T HAVE THE GUTS TO TAKE ME ON ONE-ON-ONE! ONLY A COWARD LIKE ***YOU*** WOULD RELY ON DOOMSDAY WEAPONS, WHEN ***FISTS*** WOULD SUFFICE.
WELL, TWO CAN PLAY AT THAT GAME.

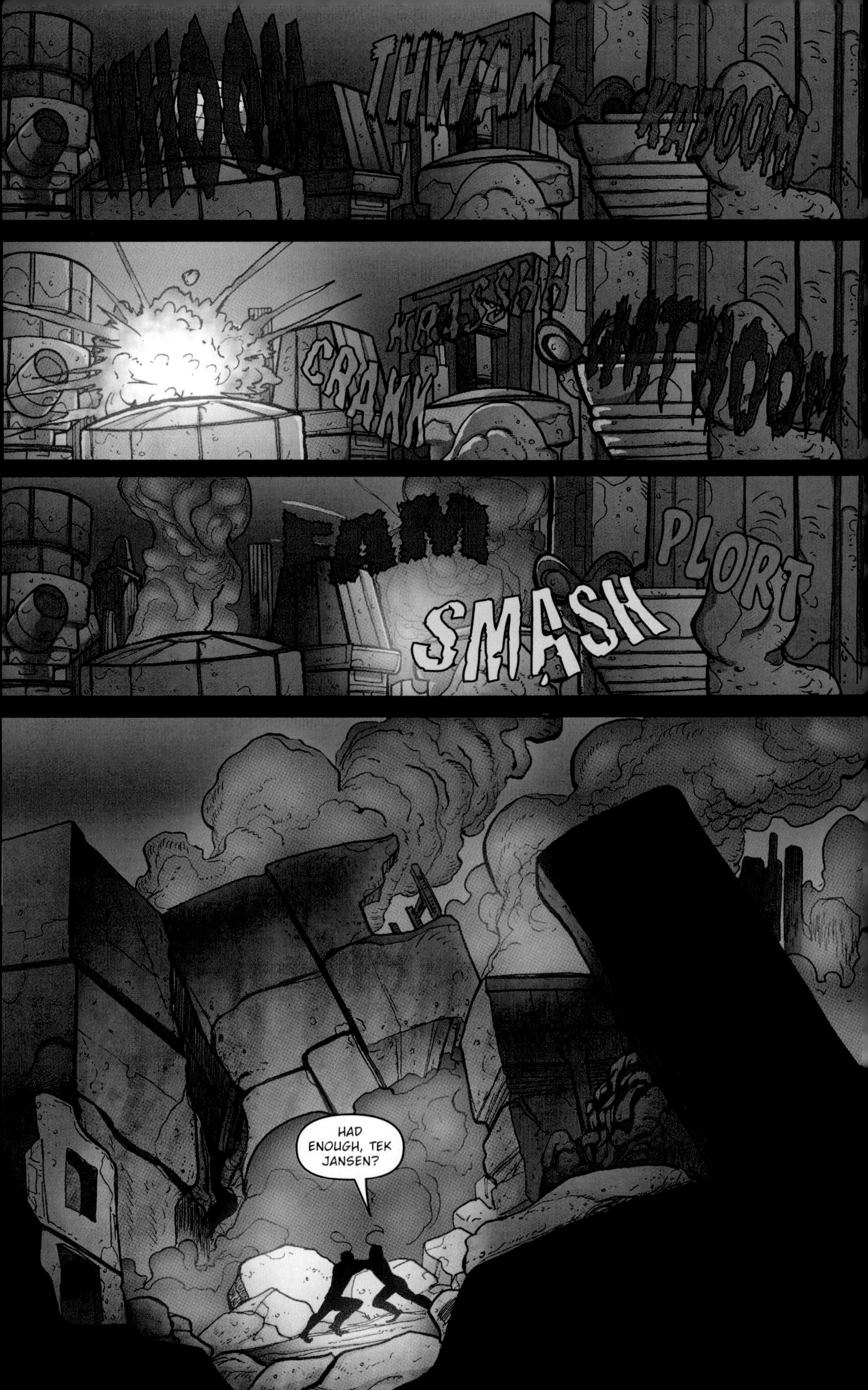
WHOOOM
THWAM
KABOOM
CRAKK
SMASH
PLORT
HAD ENOUGH, TEK JANSEN?

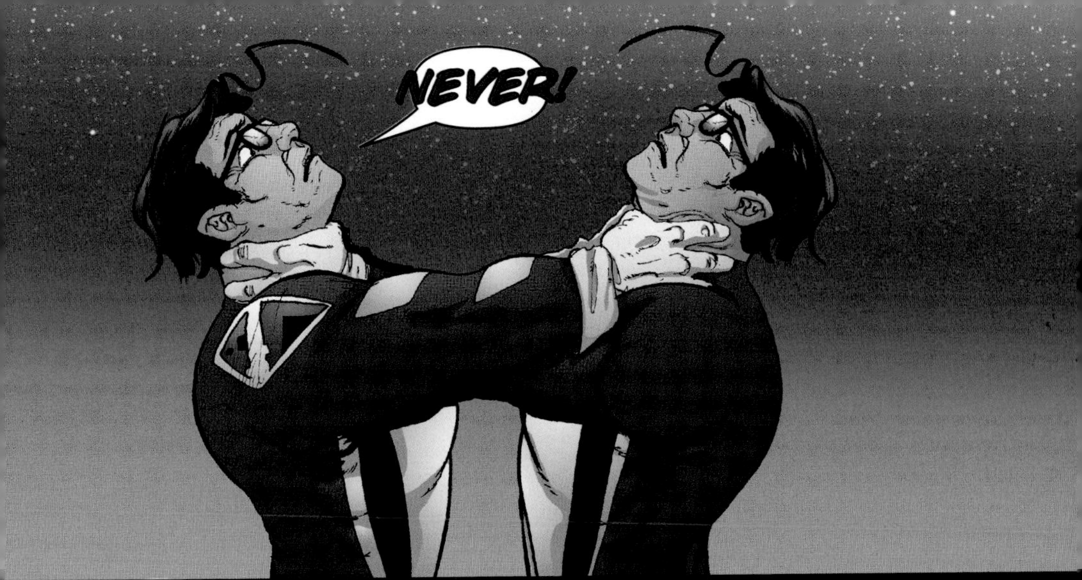
NEVER!

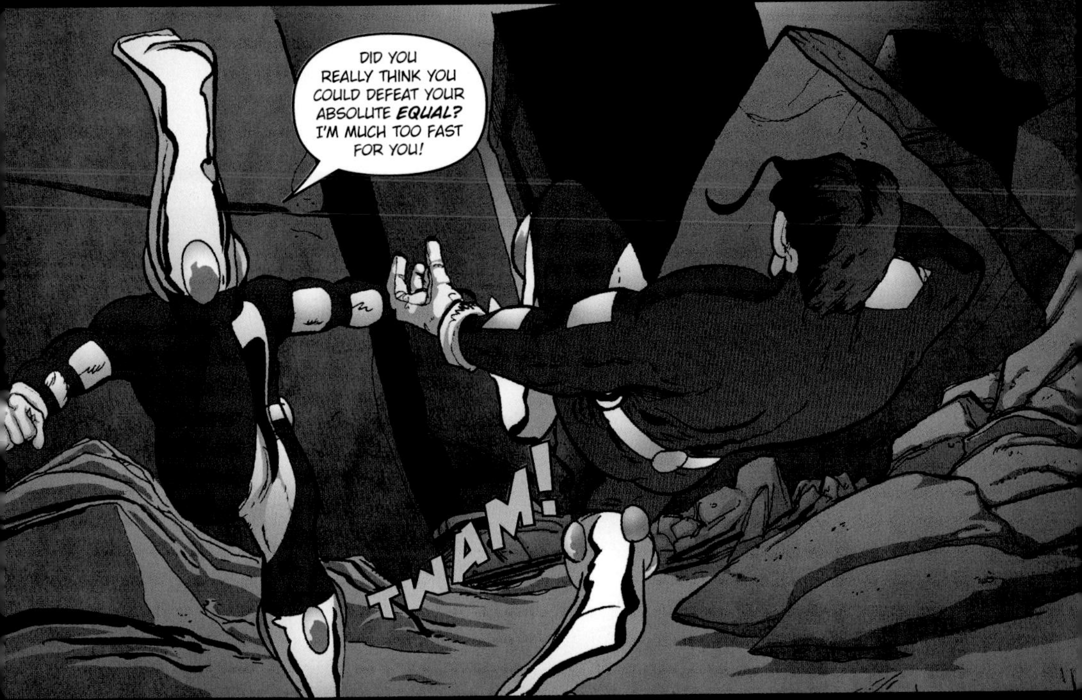
DID YOU REALLY THINK YOU COULD DEFEAT YOUR ABSOLUTE *EQUAL?* I'M MUCH TOO FAST FOR YOU!
TWAM!

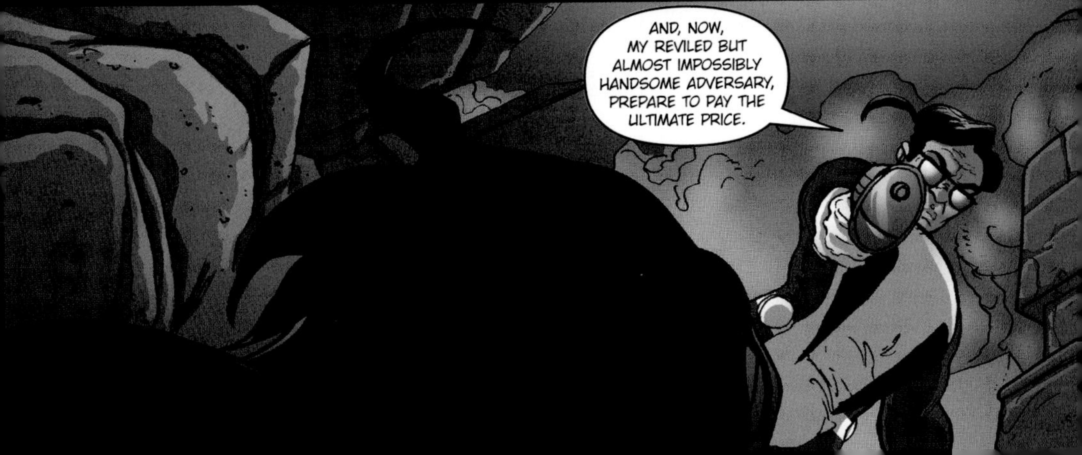
AND, NOW, MY REVILED BUT ALMOST IMPOSSIBLY HANDSOME ADVERSARY, PREPARE TO PAY THE ULTIMATE PRICE.

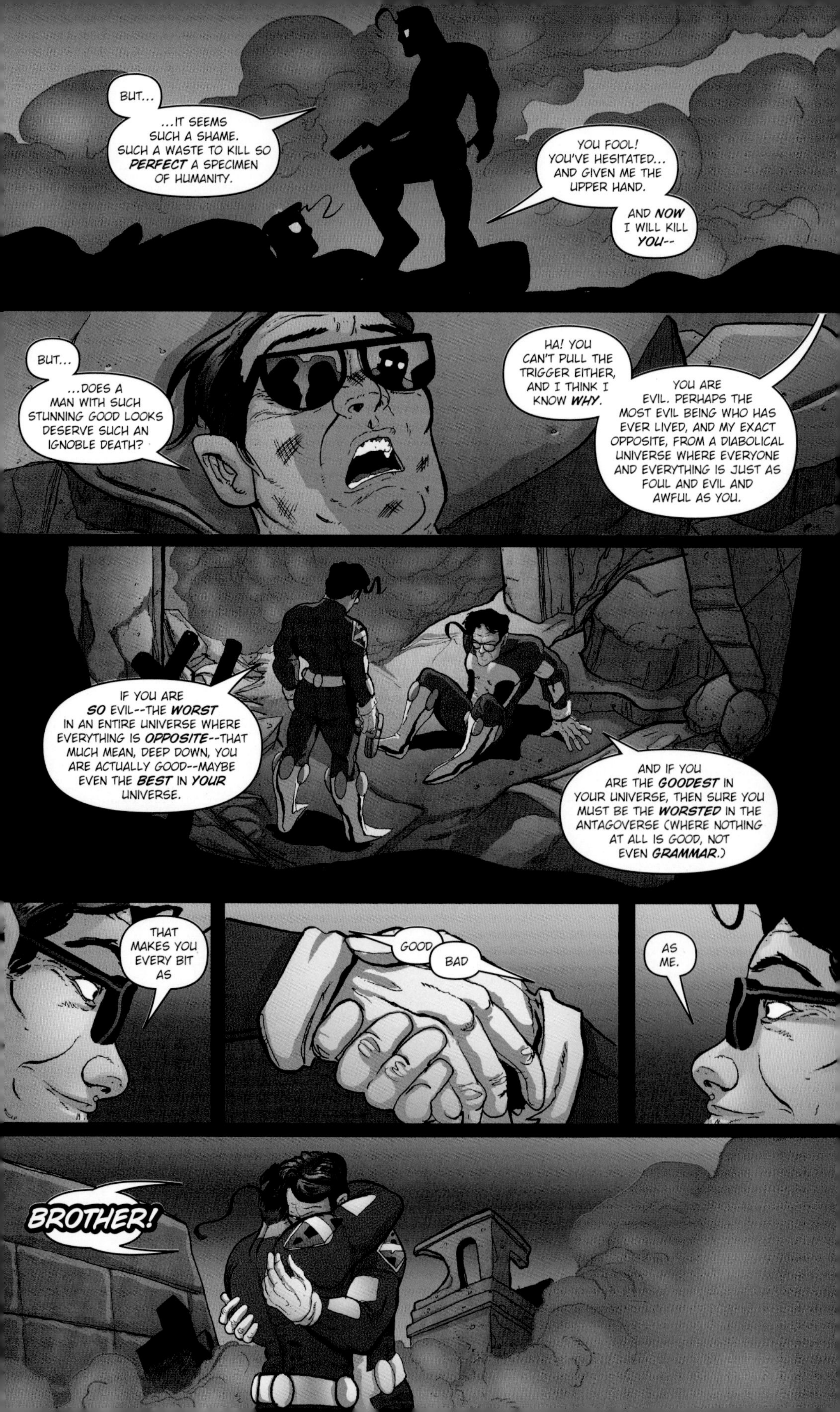
BUT...
...IT SEEMS SUCH A SHAME. SUCH A WASTE TO KILL SO PERFECT A SPECIMEN OF HUMANITY.
YOU FOOL! YOU'VE HESITATED... AND GIVEN ME THE UPPER HAND.
AND NOW I WILL KILL YOU--
BUT...
...DOES A MAN WITH SUCH STUNNING GOOD LOOKS DESERVE SUCH AN IGNOBLE DEATH?
HA! YOU CAN'T PULL THE TRIGGER EITHER, AND I THINK I KNOW WHY.
YOU ARE EVIL. PERHAPS THE MOST EVIL BEING WHO HAS EVER LIVED, AND MY EXACT OPPOSITE, FROM A DIABOLICAL UNIVERSE WHERE EVERYONE AND EVERYTHING IS JUST AS FOUL AND EVIL AND AWFUL AS YOU.
IF YOU ARE SO EVIL--THE WORST IN AN ENTIRE UNIVERSE WHERE EVERYTHING IS OPPOSITE--THAT MUCH MEAN, DEEP DOWN, YOU ARE ACTUALLY GOOD--MAYBE EVEN THE BEST IN YOUR UNIVERSE.
AND IF YOU ARE THE GOODEST IN YOUR UNIVERSE, THEN SURE YOU MUST BE THE WORSTED IN THE ANTAGOVERSE (WHERE NOTHING AT ALL IS GOOD, NOT EVEN GRAMMAR.)
THAT MAKES YOU EVERY BIT AS
GOOD
BAD
AS ME.
BROTHER!

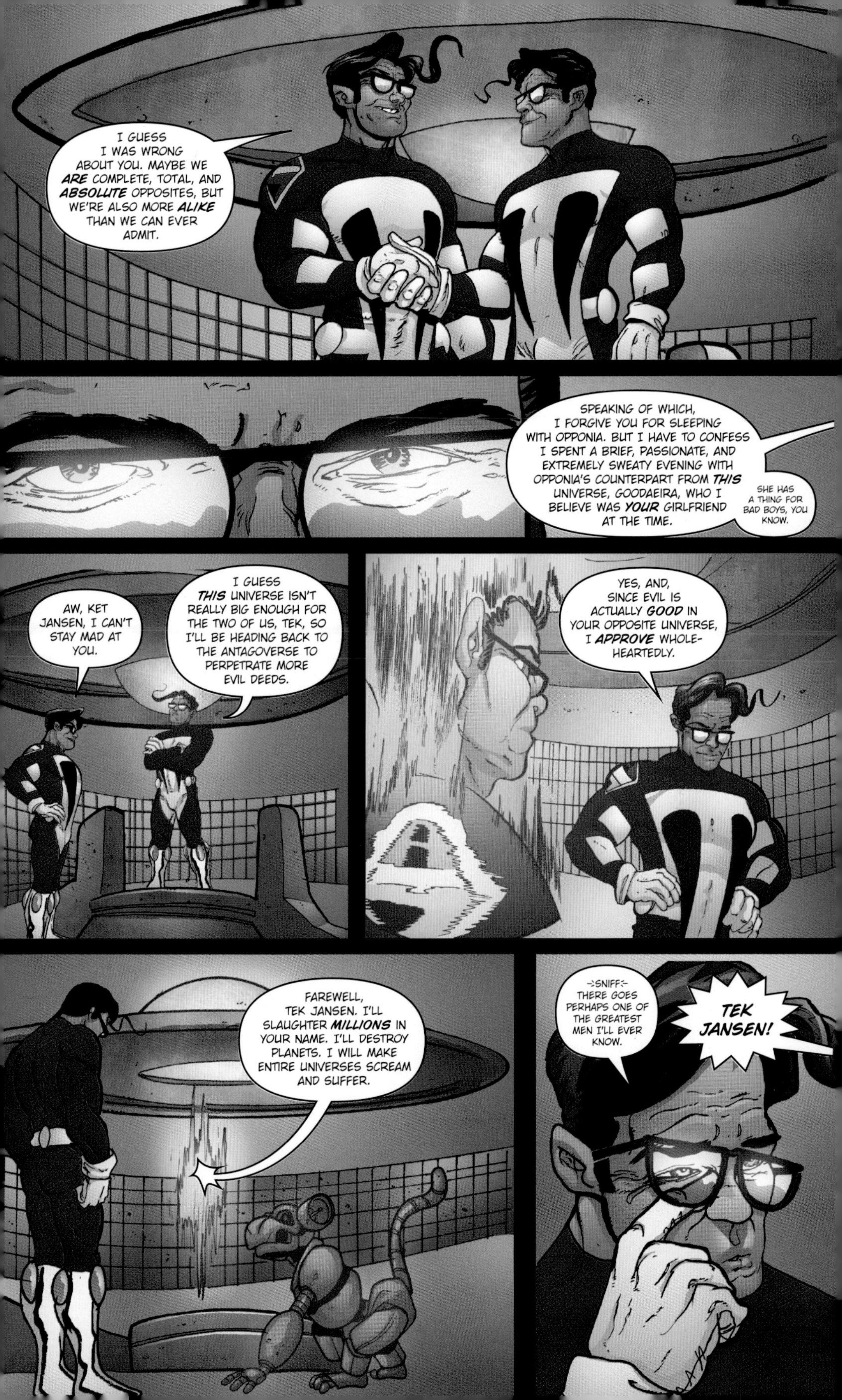

I GUESS I WAS WRONG ABOUT YOU. MAYBE WE ***ARE*** COMPLETE, TOTAL, AND ***ABSOLUTE*** OPPOSITES, BUT WE'RE ALSO MORE ***ALIKE*** THAN WE CAN EVER ADMIT.
SPEAKING OF WHICH, I FORGIVE YOU FOR SLEEPING WITH OPPONIA. BUT I HAVE TO CONFESS I SPENT A BRIEF, PASSIONATE, AND EXTREMELY SWEATY EVENING WITH OPPONIA'S COUNTERPART FROM ***THIS*** UNIVERSE, GOODAEIRA, WHO I BELIEVE WAS ***YOUR*** GIRLFRIEND AT THE TIME.
SHE HAS A THING FOR BAD BOYS, YOU KNOW.
AW, KET JANSEN, I CAN'T STAY MAD AT YOU.
I GUESS ***THIS*** UNIVERSE ISN'T REALLY BIG ENOUGH FOR THE TWO OF US, TEK, SO I'LL BE HEADING BACK TO THE ANTAGOVERSE TO PERPETRATE MORE EVIL DEEDS.
YES, AND, SINCE EVIL IS ACTUALLY ***GOOD*** IN YOUR OPPOSITE UNIVERSE, I ***APPROVE*** WHOLE-HEARTEDLY.
FAREWELL, TEK JANSEN. I'LL SLAUGHTER ***MILLIONS*** IN YOUR NAME. I'LL DESTROY PLANETS. I WILL MAKE ENTIRE UNIVERSES SCREAM AND SUFFER.
-SNIFF- THERE GOES PERHAPS ONE OF THE GREATEST MEN I'LL EVER KNOW.
TEK JANSEN!

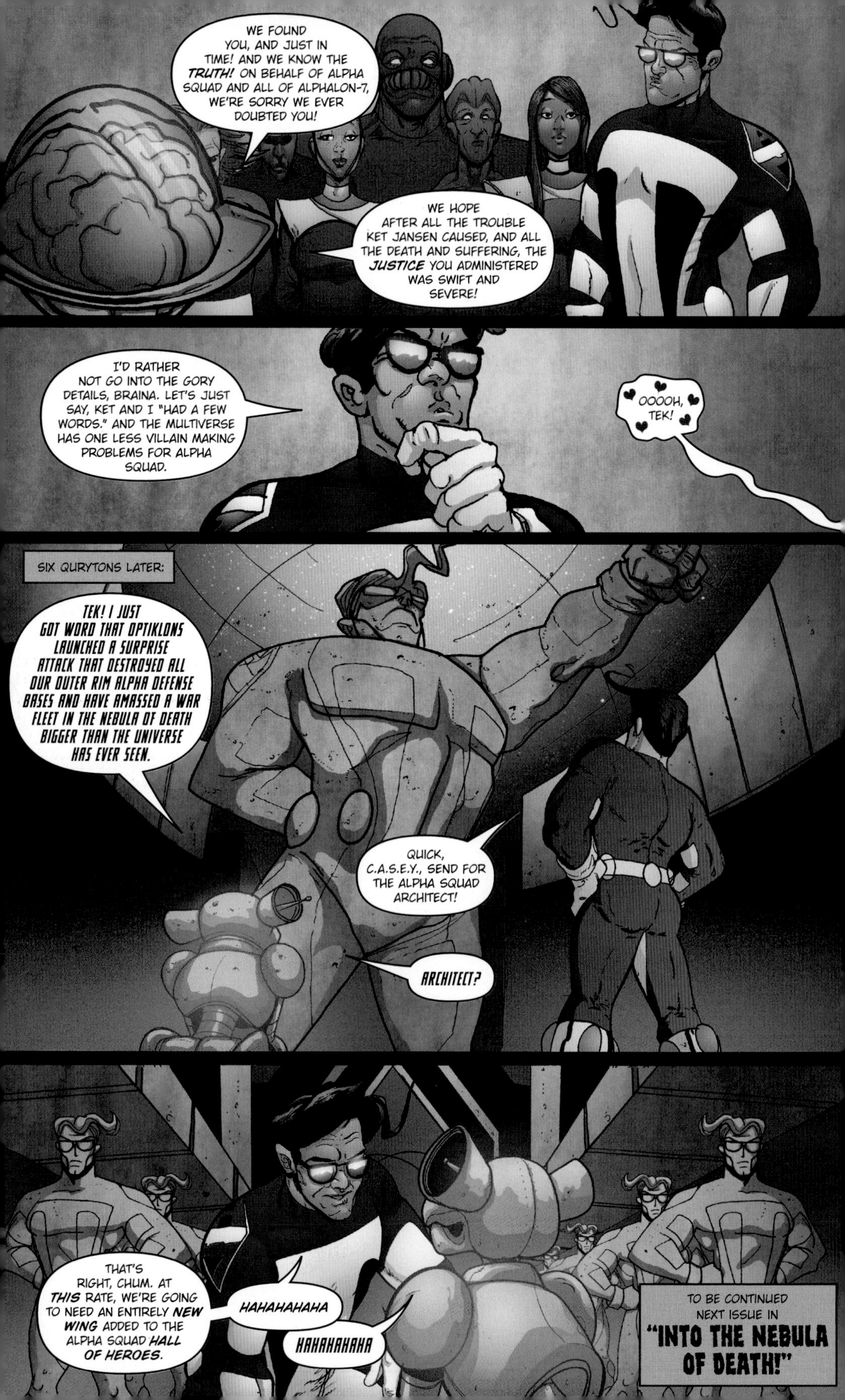
WE FOUND YOU, AND JUST IN TIME! AND WE KNOW THE *TRUTH!* ON BEHALF OF ALPHA SQUAD AND ALL OF ALPHALON-7, WE'RE SORRY WE EVER DOUBTED YOU!
WE HOPE AFTER ALL THE TROUBLE KET JANSEN CAUSED, AND ALL THE DEATH AND SUFFERING, THE *JUSTICE* YOU ADMINISTERED WAS SWIFT AND SEVERE!
I'D RATHER NOT GO INTO THE GORY DETAILS, BRAINA. LET'S JUST SAY, KET AND I "HAD A FEW WORDS." AND THE MULTIVERSE HAS ONE LESS VILLAIN MAKING PROBLEMS FOR ALPHA SQUAD.
OOOOH, TEK!
SIX QURYTONS LATER:
TEK! I JUST GOT WORD THAT OPTIKLONS LAUNCHED A SURPRISE ATTACK THAT DESTROYED ALL OUR OUTER RIM ALPHA DEFENSE BASES AND HAVE AMASSED A WAR FLEET IN THE NEBULA OF DEATH BIGGER THAN THE UNIVERSE HAS EVER SEEN.
QUICK, C.A.S.E.Y., SEND FOR THE ALPHA SQUAD ARCHITECT!
ARCHITECT?
THAT'S RIGHT, CHUM. AT *THIS* RATE, WE'RE GOING TO NEED AN ENTIRELY *NEW WING* ADDED TO THE ALPHA SQUAD *HALL OF HEROES*.
HAHAHAHAHA
HAHAHAHAHA
TO BE CONTINUED NEXT ISSUE IN
"INTO THE NEBULA OF DEATH!"

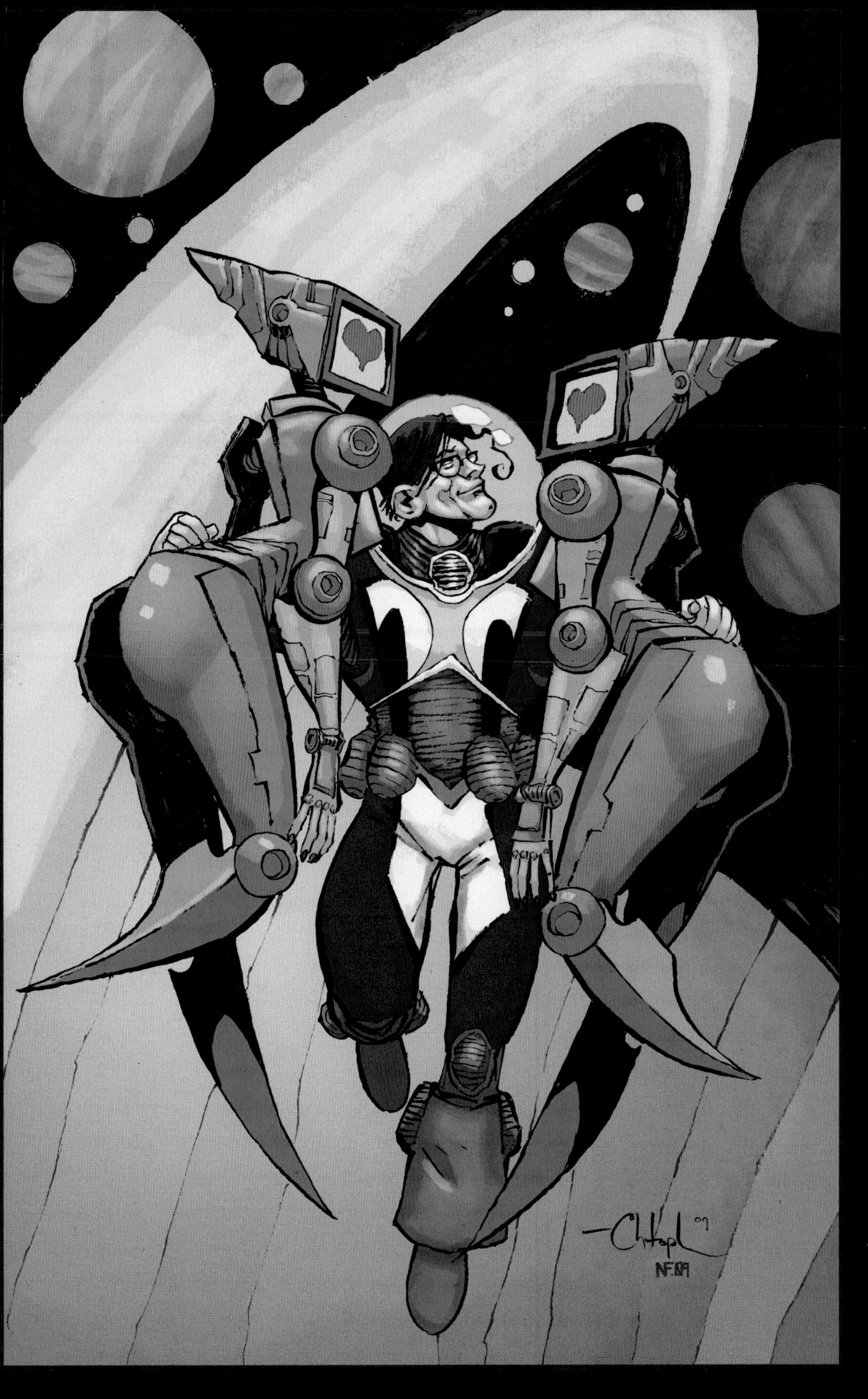

CHRISTOPHER MITTEN NATHAN FAIRBAIRN

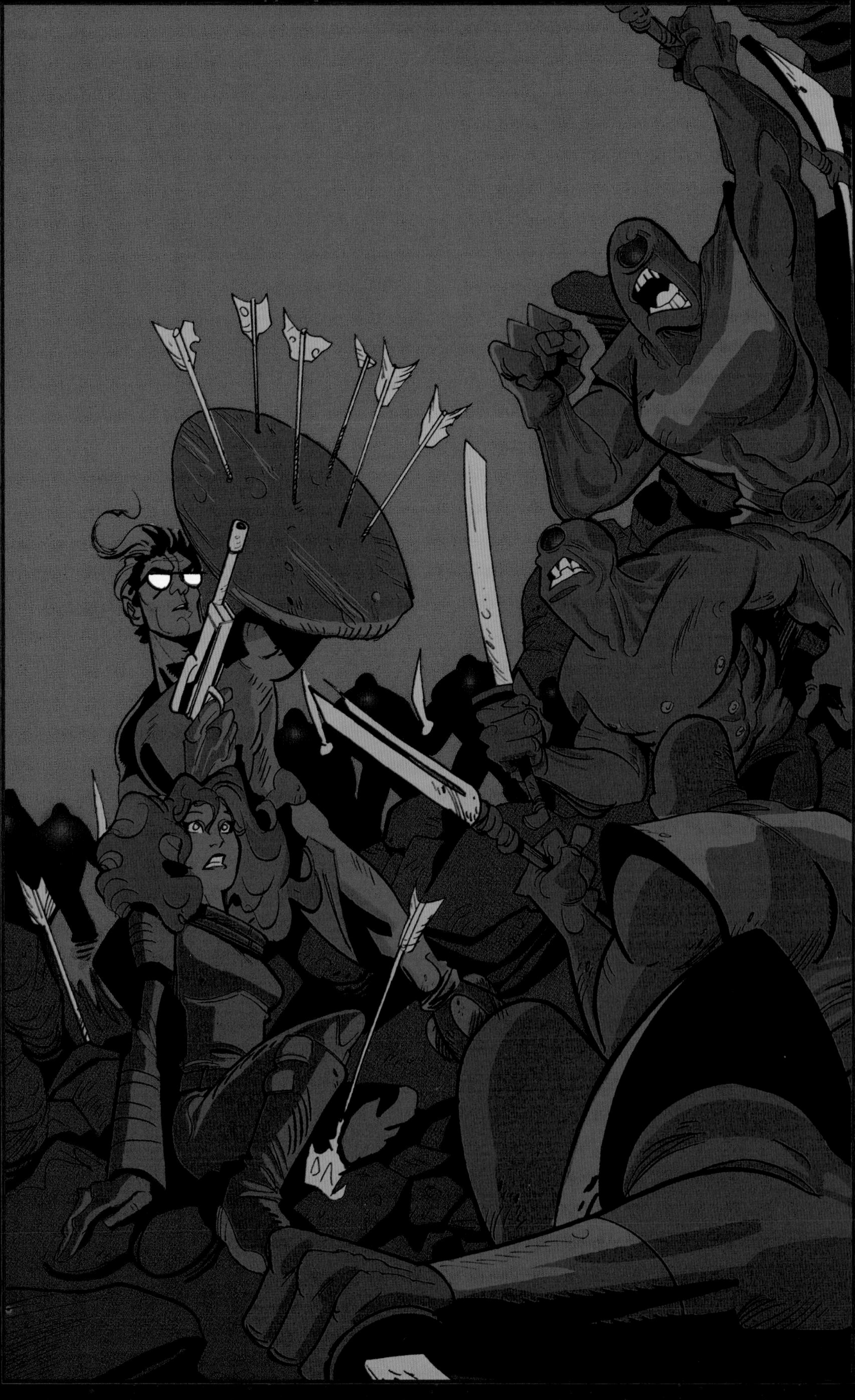

art by ROBBI RODRIGUEZ

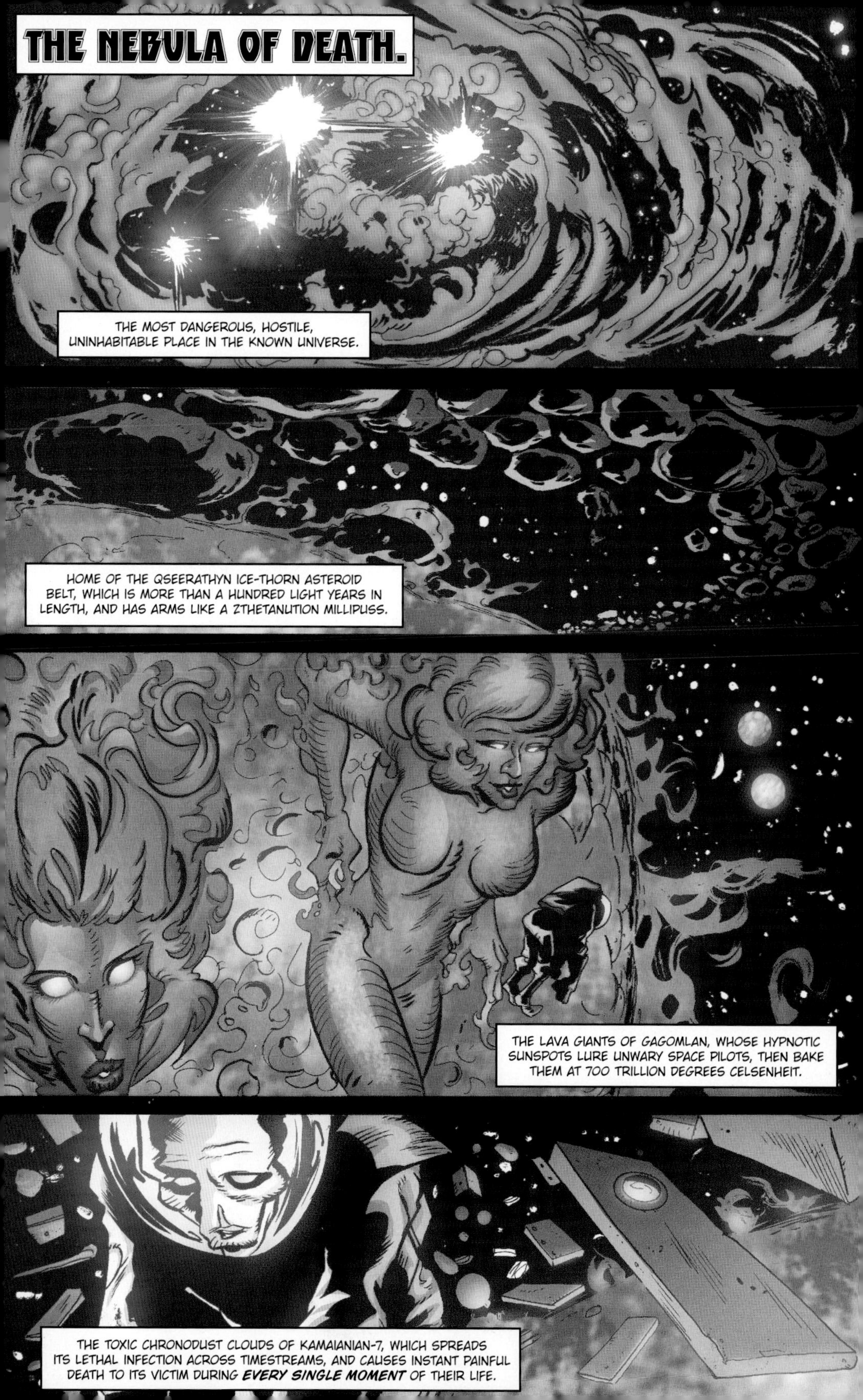
THE NEBULA OF DEATH.
THE MOST DANGEROUS, HOSTILE, UNINHABITABLE PLACE IN THE KNOWN UNIVERSE.
HOME OF THE QSEERATHYN ICE-THORN ASTEROID BELT, WHICH IS MORE THAN A HUNDRED LIGHT YEARS IN LENGTH, AND HAS ARMS LIKE A ZTHETANUTION MILLIPUSS.
THE LAVA GIANTS OF GAGOMLAN, WHOSE HYPNOTIC SUNSPOTS LURE UNWARY SPACE PILOTS, THEN BAKE THEM AT 700 TRILLION DEGREES CELSENHEIT.
THE TOXIC CHRONODUST CLOUDS OF KAMAIANIAN-7, WHICH SPREADS ITS LETHAL INFECTION ACROSS TIMESTREAMS, AND CAUSES INSTANT PAINFUL DEATH TO ITS VICTIM DURING ***EVERY SINGLE MOMENT*** OF THEIR LIFE.

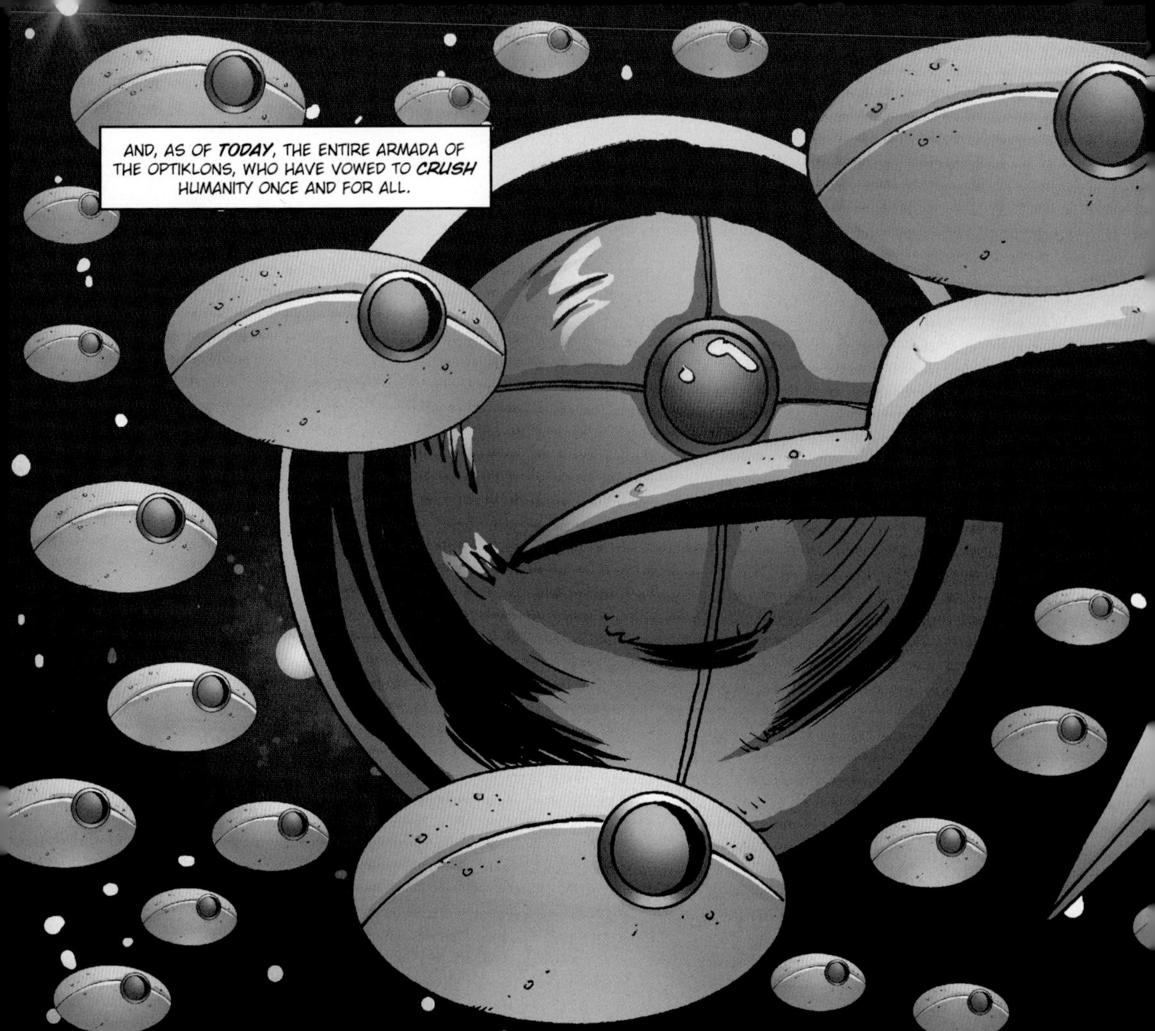
AND, AS OF *TODAY*, THE ENTIRE ARMADA OF THE OPTIKLONS, WHO HAVE VOWED TO *CRUSH* HUMANITY ONCE AND FOR ALL.

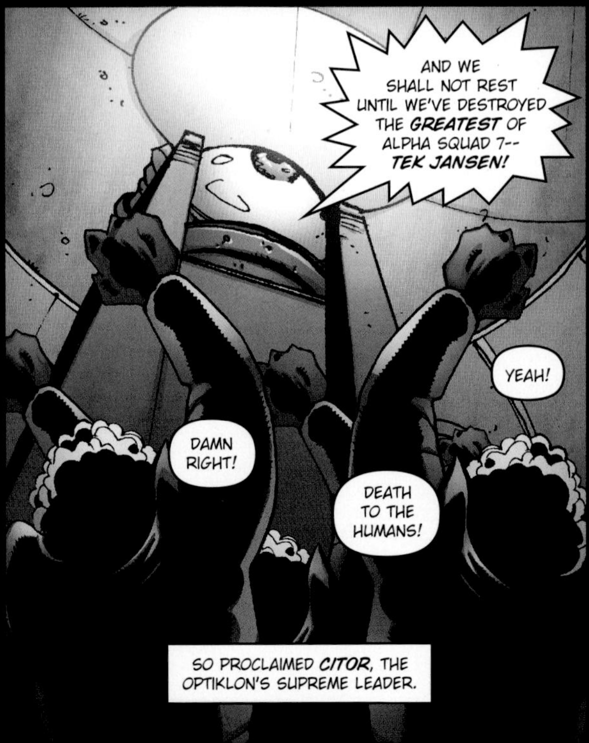
AND WE SHALL NOT REST UNTIL WE'VE DESTROYED THE *GREATEST* OF ALPHA SQUAD 7-- *TEK JANSEN!*
YEAH!
DAMN RIGHT!
DEATH TO THE HUMANS!
SO PROCLAIMED *CITOR*, THE OPTIKLON'S SUPREME LEADER.

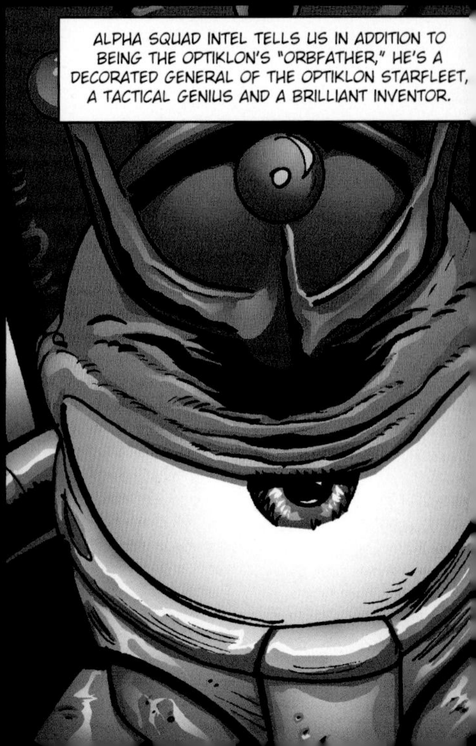
ALPHA SQUAD INTEL TELLS US IN ADDITION TO BEING THE OPTIKLON'S "ORBFATHER," HE'S A DECORATED GENERAL OF THE OPTIKLON STARFLEET, A TACTICAL GENIUS AND A BRILLIANT INVENTOR.

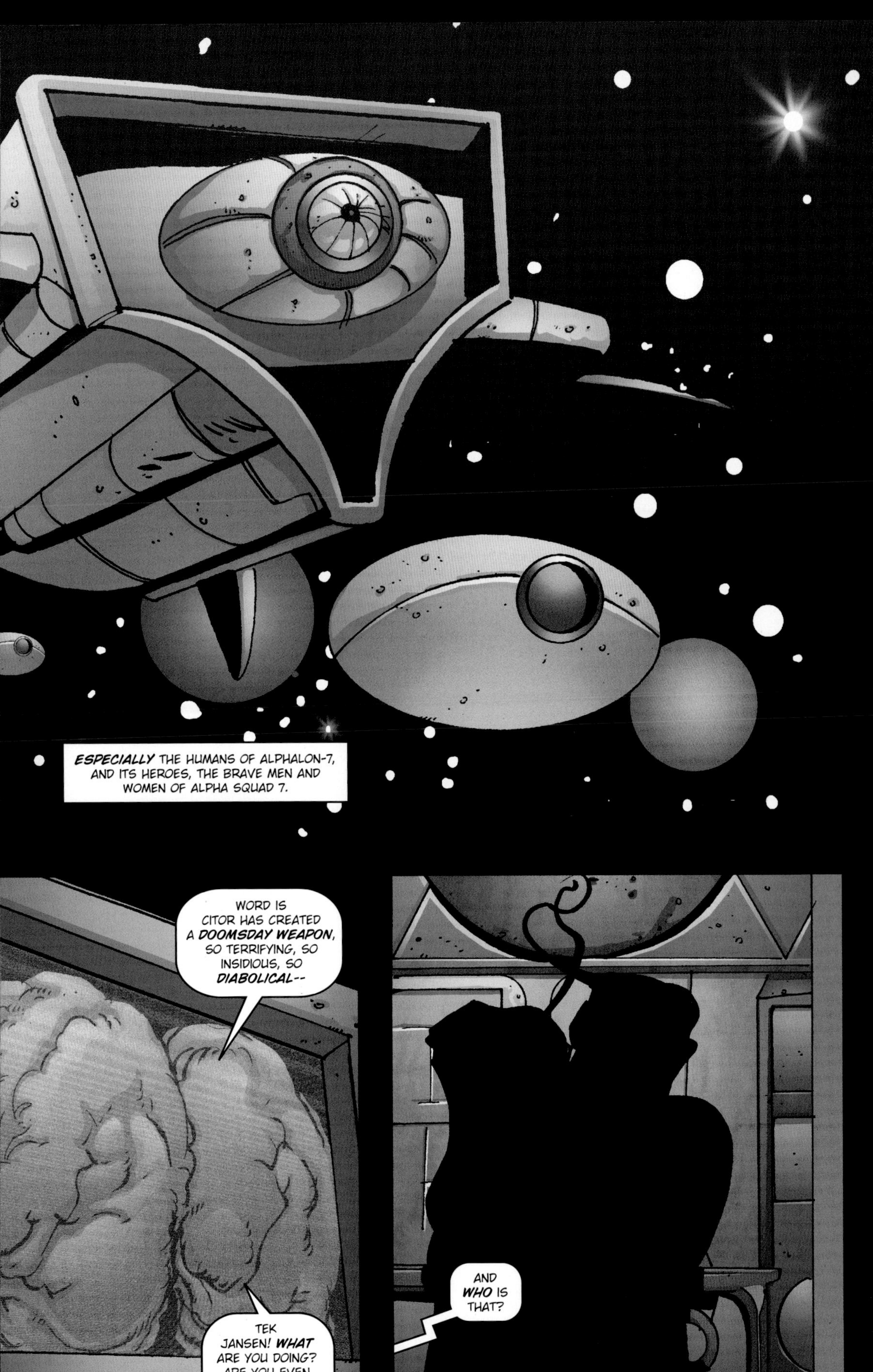
ESPECIALLY THE HUMANS OF ALPHALON-7, AND ITS HEROES, THE BRAVE MEN AND WOMEN OF ALPHA SQUAD 7.
WORD IS CITOR HAS CREATED A DOOMSDAY WEAPON, SO TERRIFYING, SO INSIDIOUS, SO DIABOLICAL--
TEK JANSEN! WHAT ARE YOU DOING? ARE YOU EVEN LISTENING TO ME?
AND WHO IS THAT?

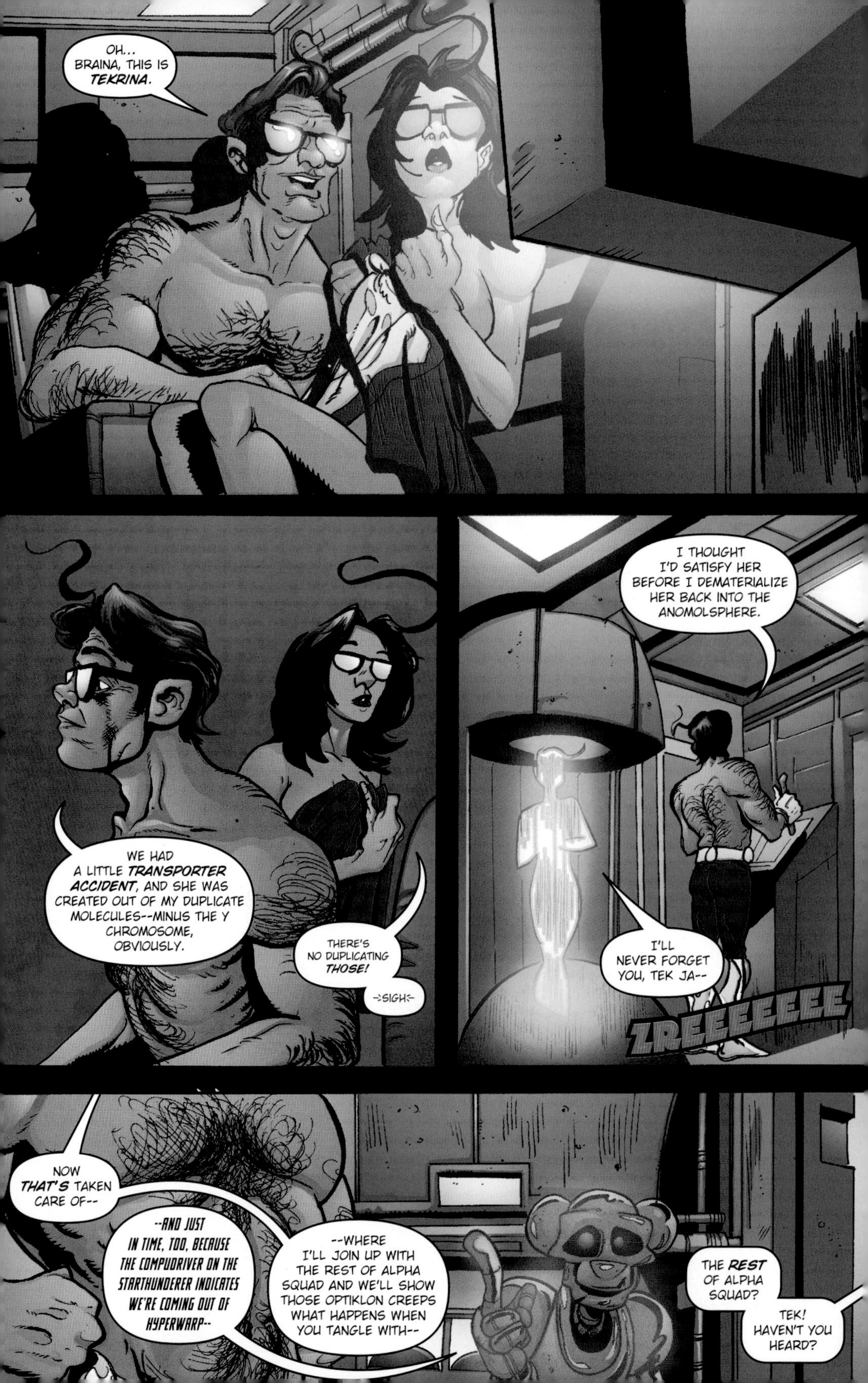
OH... BRAINA, THIS IS *TEKRINA*.
WE HAD A LITTLE ***TRANSPORTER ACCIDENT***, AND SHE WAS CREATED OUT OF MY DUPLICATE MOLECULES--MINUS THE Y CHROMOSOME, OBVIOUSLY.
THERE'S NO DUPLICATING ***THOSE!***
-SIGH-
I THOUGHT I'D SATISFY HER BEFORE I DEMATERIALIZE HER BACK INTO THE ANOMOLSPHERE.
I'LL NEVER FORGET YOU, TEK JA--
ZREEEEEEE
NOW ***THAT'S*** TAKEN CARE OF--
--AND JUST IN TIME, TOO, BECAUSE THE COMPUDRIVER ON THE STARTHUNDERER INDICATES WE'RE COMING OUT OF HYPERWARP--
--WHERE I'LL JOIN UP WITH THE REST OF ALPHA SQUAD AND WE'LL SHOW THOSE OPTIKLON CREEPS WHAT HAPPENS WHEN YOU TANGLE WITH--
THE ***REST*** OF ALPHA SQUAD?
TEK! HAVEN'T YOU HEARD?

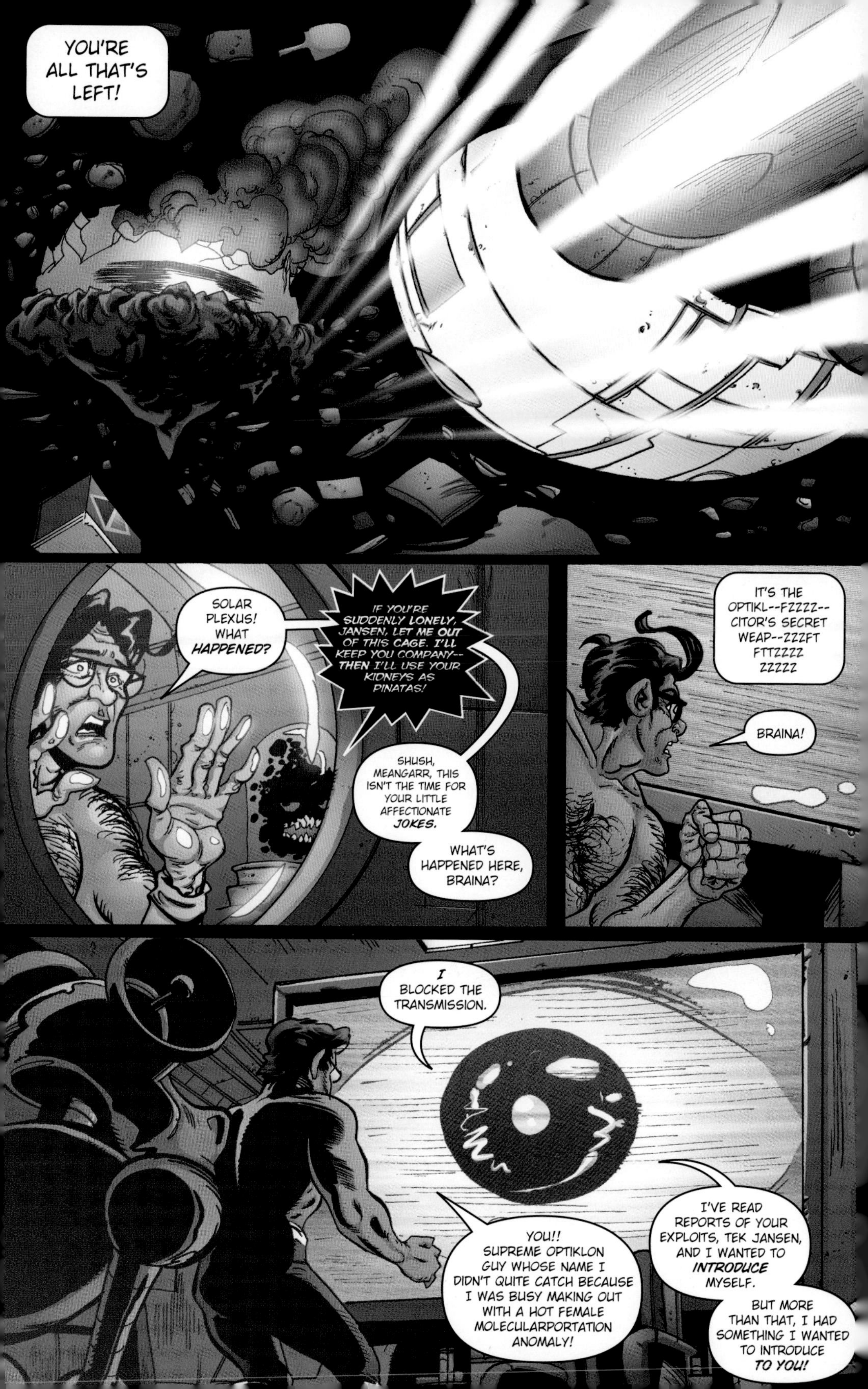
YOU'RE ALL THAT'S LEFT!
SOLAR PLEXUS! WHAT HAPPENED?
IF YOU'RE SUDDENLY LONELY, JANSEN, LET ME OUT OF THIS CAGE. I'LL KEEP YOU COMPANY-- THEN I'LL USE YOUR KIDNEYS AS PINATAS!
SHUSH, MEANGARR, THIS ISN'T THE TIME FOR YOUR LITTLE AFFECTIONATE JOKES.
WHAT'S HAPPENED HERE, BRAINA?
IT'S THE OPTIKL--FZZZZ--CITOR'S SECRET WEAP--ZZZFT FTTZZZZ ZZZZZ
BRAINA!
I BLOCKED THE TRANSMISSION.
YOU!! SUPREME OPTIKLON GUY WHOSE NAME I DIDN'T QUITE CATCH BECAUSE I WAS BUSY MAKING OUT WITH A HOT FEMALE MOLECULARPORTATION ANOMALY!
I'VE READ REPORTS OF YOUR EXPLOITS, TEK JANSEN, AND I WANTED TO INTRODUCE MYSELF.
BUT MORE THAN THAT, I HAD SOMETHING I WANTED TO INTRODUCE TO YOU!

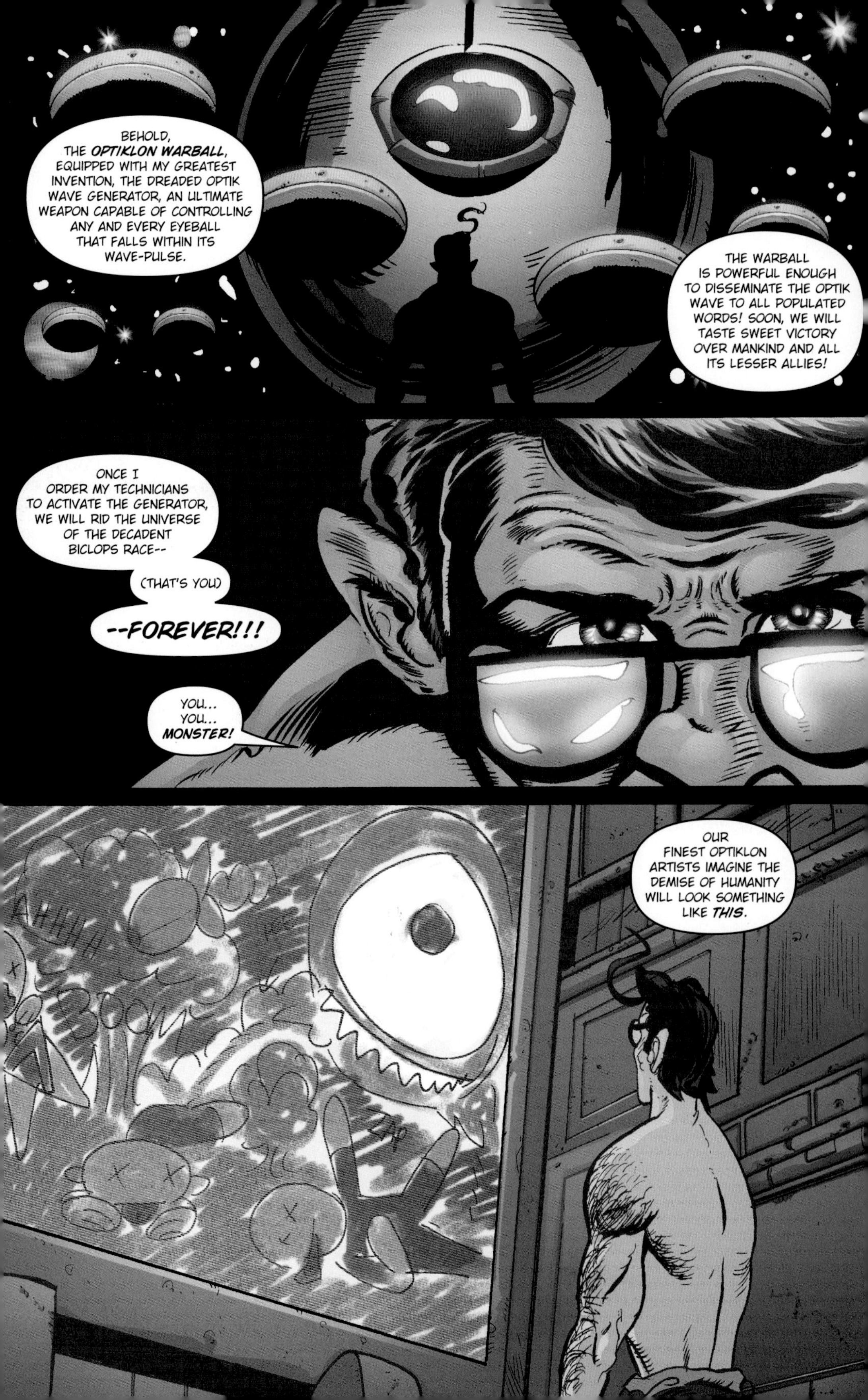
BEHOLD, THE **OPTIKLON WARBALL**, EQUIPPED WITH MY GREATEST INVENTION, THE DREADED OPTIK WAVE GENERATOR, AN ULTIMATE WEAPON CAPABLE OF CONTROLLING ANY AND EVERY EYEBALL THAT FALLS WITHIN ITS WAVE-PULSE.
THE WARBALL IS POWERFUL ENOUGH TO DISSEMINATE THE OPTIK WAVE TO ALL POPULATED WORDS! SOON, WE WILL TASTE SWEET VICTORY OVER MANKIND AND ALL ITS LESSER ALLIES!
ONCE I ORDER MY TECHNICIANS TO ACTIVATE THE GENERATOR, WE WILL RID THE UNIVERSE OF THE DECADENT BICLOPS RACE--
(THAT'S YOU)
--FOREVER!!!
YOU... YOU... **MONSTER!**
BOOM
OUR FINEST OPTIKLON ARTISTS IMAGINE THE DEMISE OF HUMANITY WILL LOOK SOMETHING LIKE **THIS**.

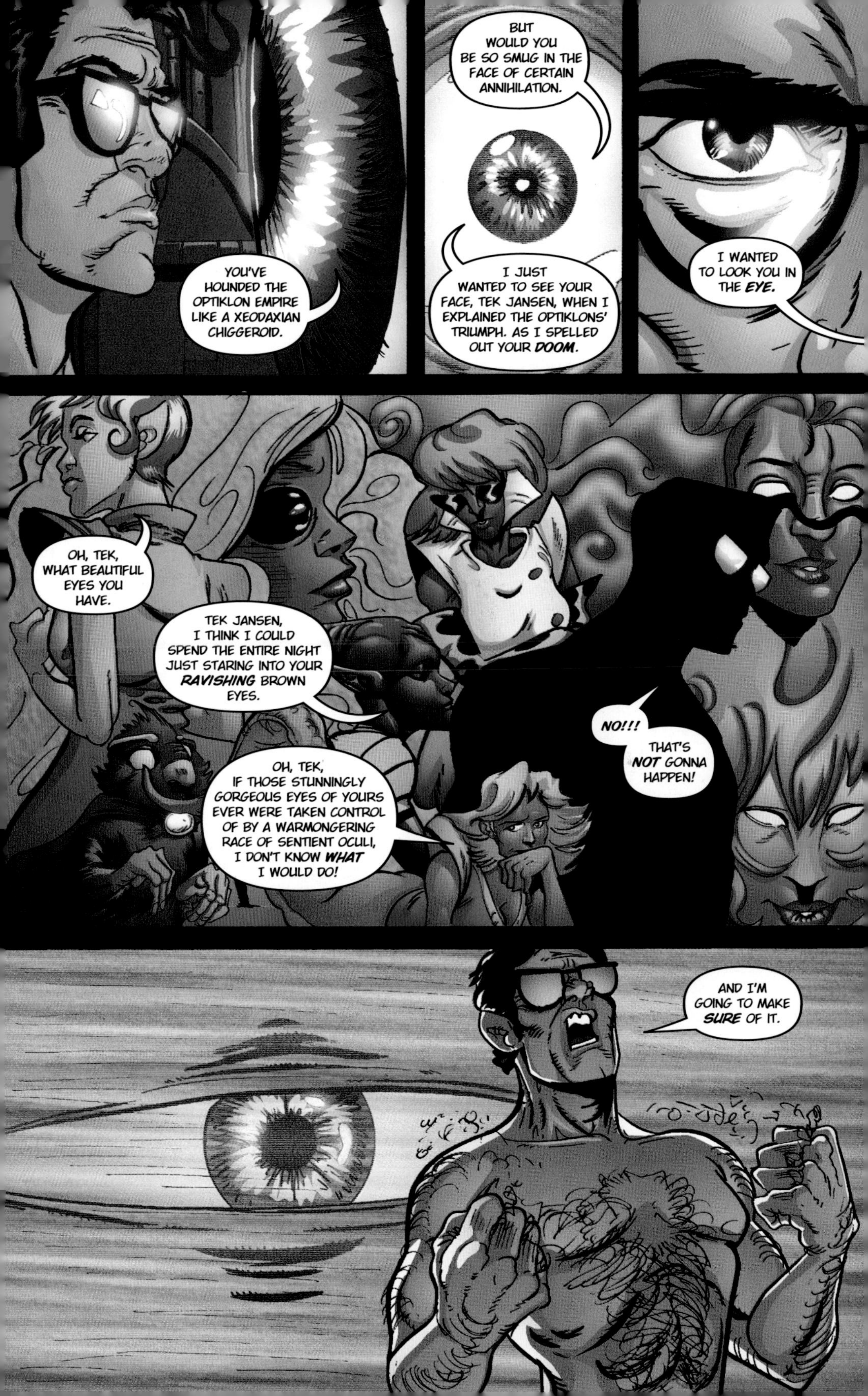
YOU'VE HOUNDED THE OPTIKLON EMPIRE LIKE A XEODAXIAN CHIGGEROID.
BUT WOULD YOU BE SO SMUG IN THE FACE OF CERTAIN ANNIHILATION.
I JUST WANTED TO SEE YOUR FACE, TEK JANSEN, WHEN I EXPLAINED THE OPTIKLONS' TRIUMPH. AS I SPELLED OUT YOUR ***DOOM***.
I WANTED TO LOOK YOU IN THE ***EYE.***
OH, TEK, WHAT BEAUTIFUL EYES YOU HAVE.
TEK JANSEN, I THINK I COULD SPEND THE ENTIRE NIGHT JUST STARING INTO YOUR ***RAVISHING*** BROWN EYES.
OH, TEK, IF THOSE STUNNINGLY GORGEOUS EYES OF YOURS EVER WERE TAKEN CONTROL OF BY A WARMONGERING RACE OF SENTIENT OCULI, I DON'T KNOW ***WHAT*** I WOULD DO!
NO!!!
THAT'S ***NOT*** GONNA HAPPEN!
AND I'M GOING TO MAKE ***SURE*** OF IT.

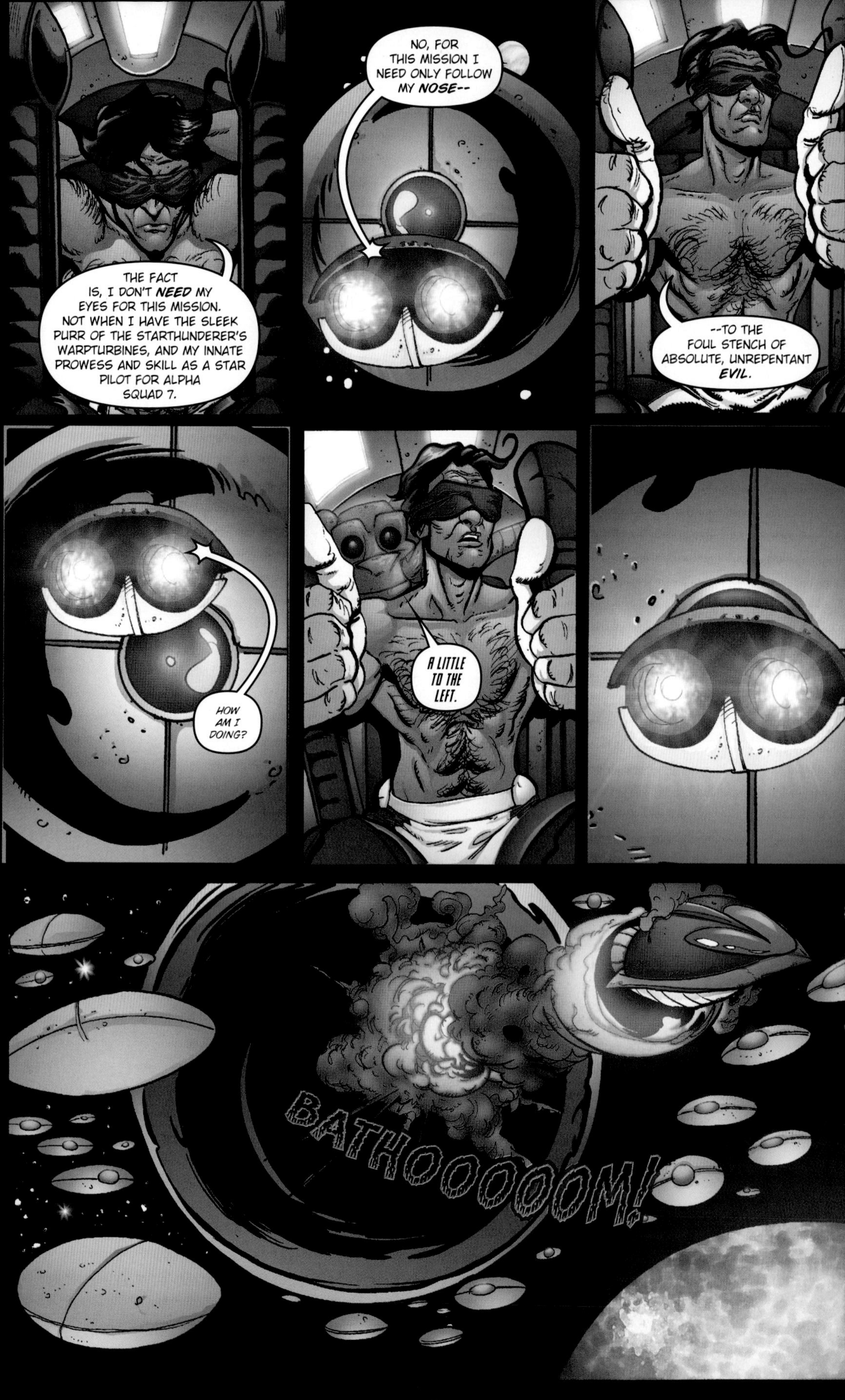
THE FACT IS, I DON'T **NEED** MY EYES FOR THIS MISSION. NOT WHEN I HAVE THE SLEEK PURR OF THE STARTHUNDERER'S WARPTURBINES, AND MY INNATE PROWESS AND SKILL AS A STAR PILOT FOR ALPHA SQUAD 7.
NO, FOR THIS MISSION I NEED ONLY FOLLOW MY **NOSE**--
--TO THE FOUL STENCH OF ABSOLUTE, UNREPENTANT **EVIL**.
HOW AM I DOING?
A LITTLE TO THE LEFT.
BATHOOOOOOM!

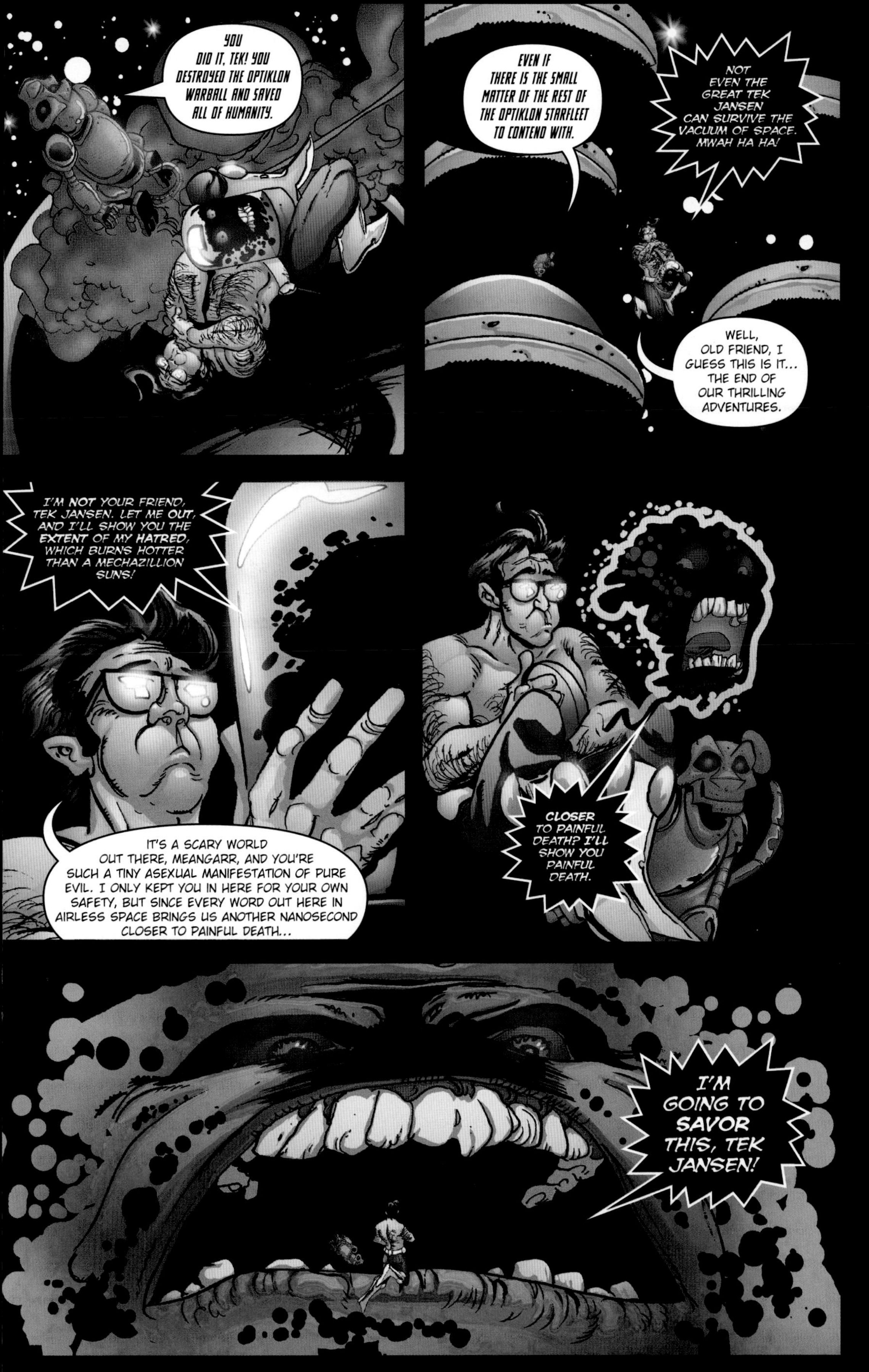
YOU DID IT, TEK! YOU DESTROYED THE OPTIKLON WARBALL AND SAVED ALL OF HUMANITY.
EVEN IF THERE IS THE SMALL MATTER OF THE REST OF THE OPTIKLON STARFLEET TO CONTEND WITH.
NOT EVEN THE GREAT TEK JANSEN CAN SURVIVE THE VACUUM OF SPACE. MWAH HA HA!
WELL, OLD FRIEND, I GUESS THIS IS IT... THE END OF OUR THRILLING ADVENTURES.
I'M **NOT** YOUR FRIEND, TEK JANSEN. LET ME **OUT**, AND I'LL SHOW YOU THE **EXTENT** OF MY **HATRED**, WHICH BURNS HOTTER THAN A MECHAZILLION SUNS!
IT'S A SCARY WORLD OUT THERE, MEANGARR, AND YOU'RE SUCH A TINY ASEXUAL MANIFESTATION OF PURE EVIL. I ONLY KEPT YOU IN HERE FOR YOUR OWN SAFETY, BUT SINCE EVERY WORD OUT HERE IN AIRLESS SPACE BRINGS US ANOTHER NANOSECOND CLOSER TO PAINFUL DEATH...
CLOSER TO PAINFUL DEATH? **I'LL** SHOW YOU PAINFUL DEATH.
I'M GOING TO **SAVOR** THIS, TEK JANSEN!

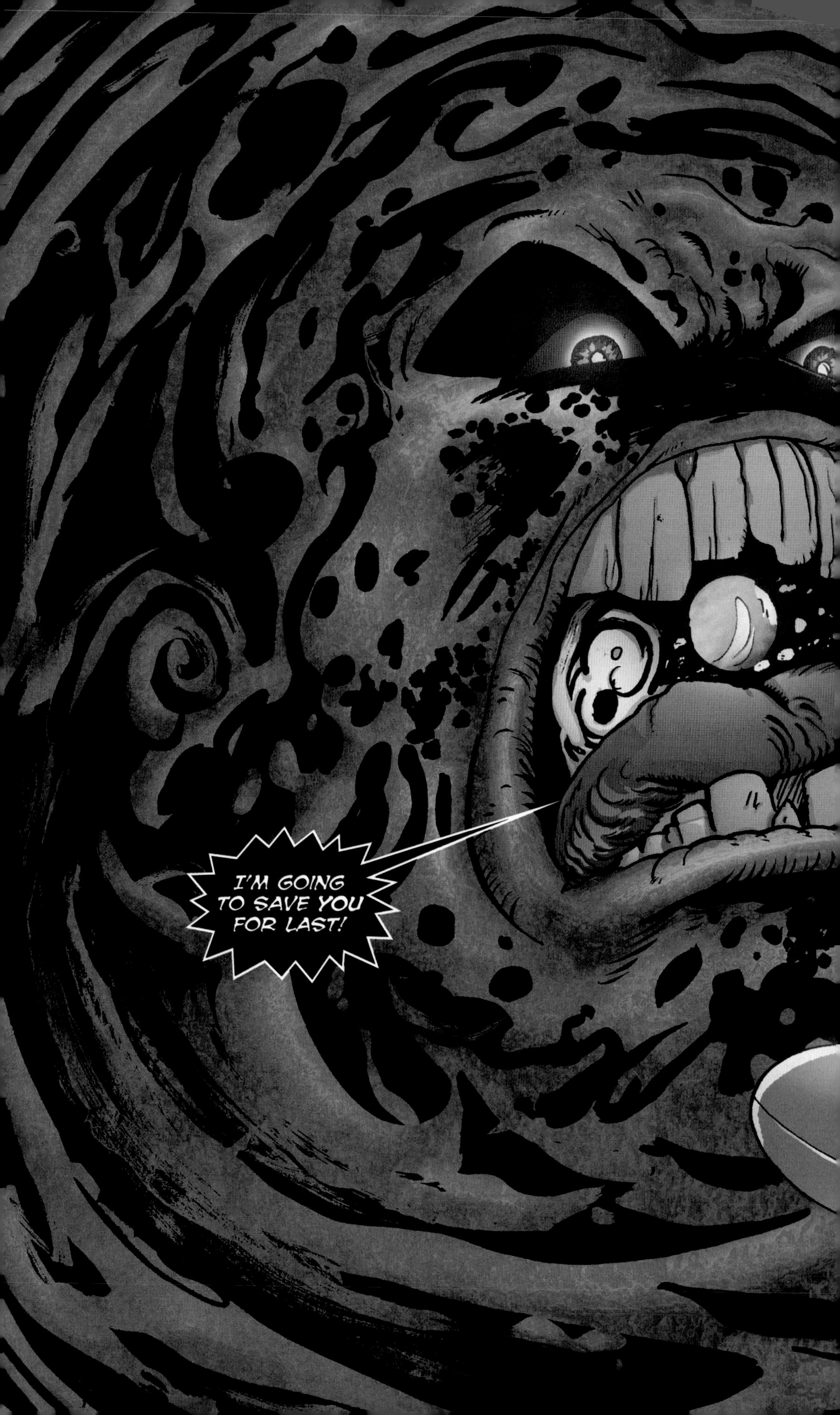
I'M GOING TO SAVE YOU FOR LAST!

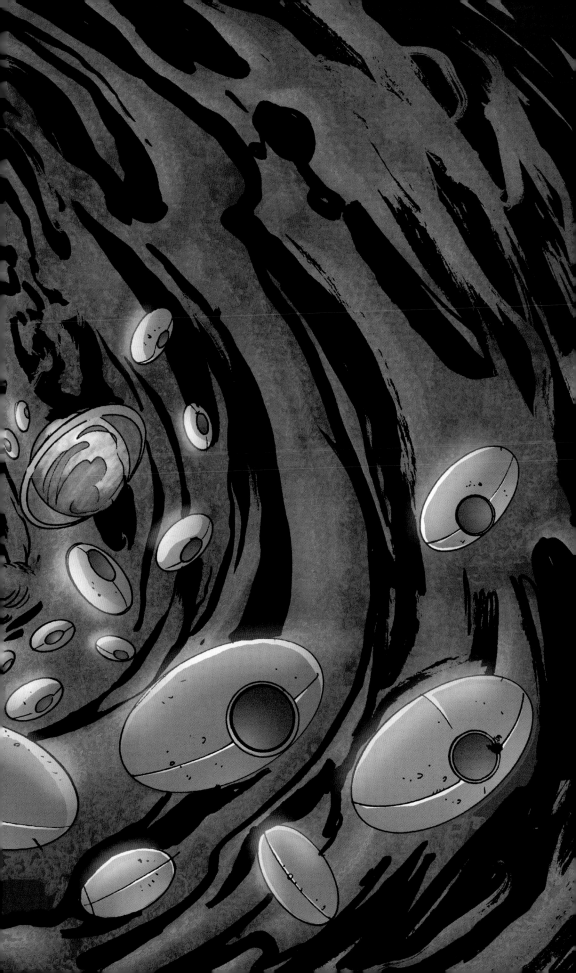

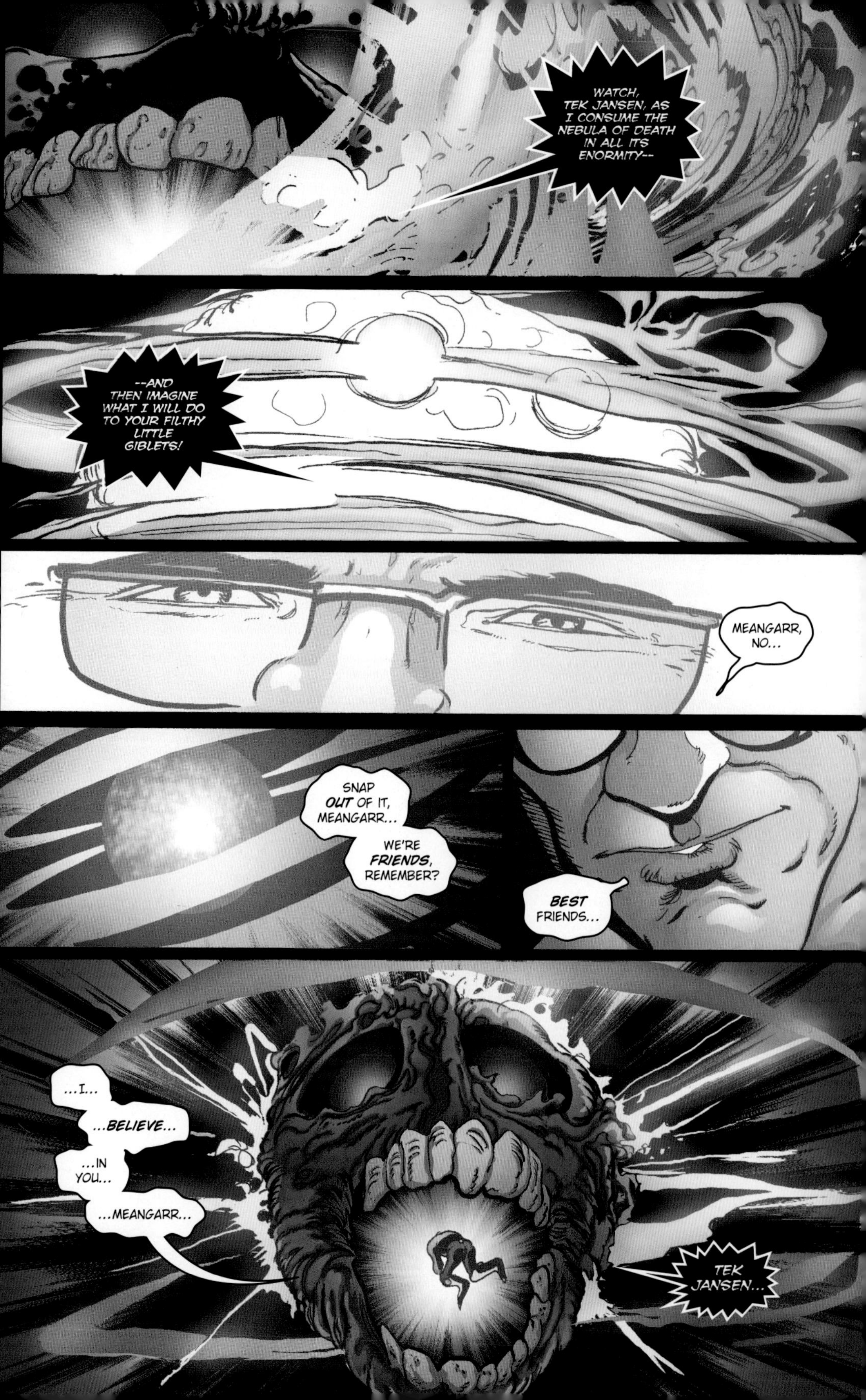
WATCH, TEK JANSEN, AS I CONSUME THE NEBULA OF DEATH IN ALL ITS ENORMITY--
--AND THEN IMAGINE WHAT I WILL DO TO YOUR FILTHY LITTLE GIBLETS!
MEANGARR, NO...
SNAP OUT OF IT, MEANGARR...
WE'RE FRIENDS, REMEMBER?
BEST FRIENDS...
...I...
...BELIEVE...
...IN YOU...
...MEANGARR...
TEK JANSEN...

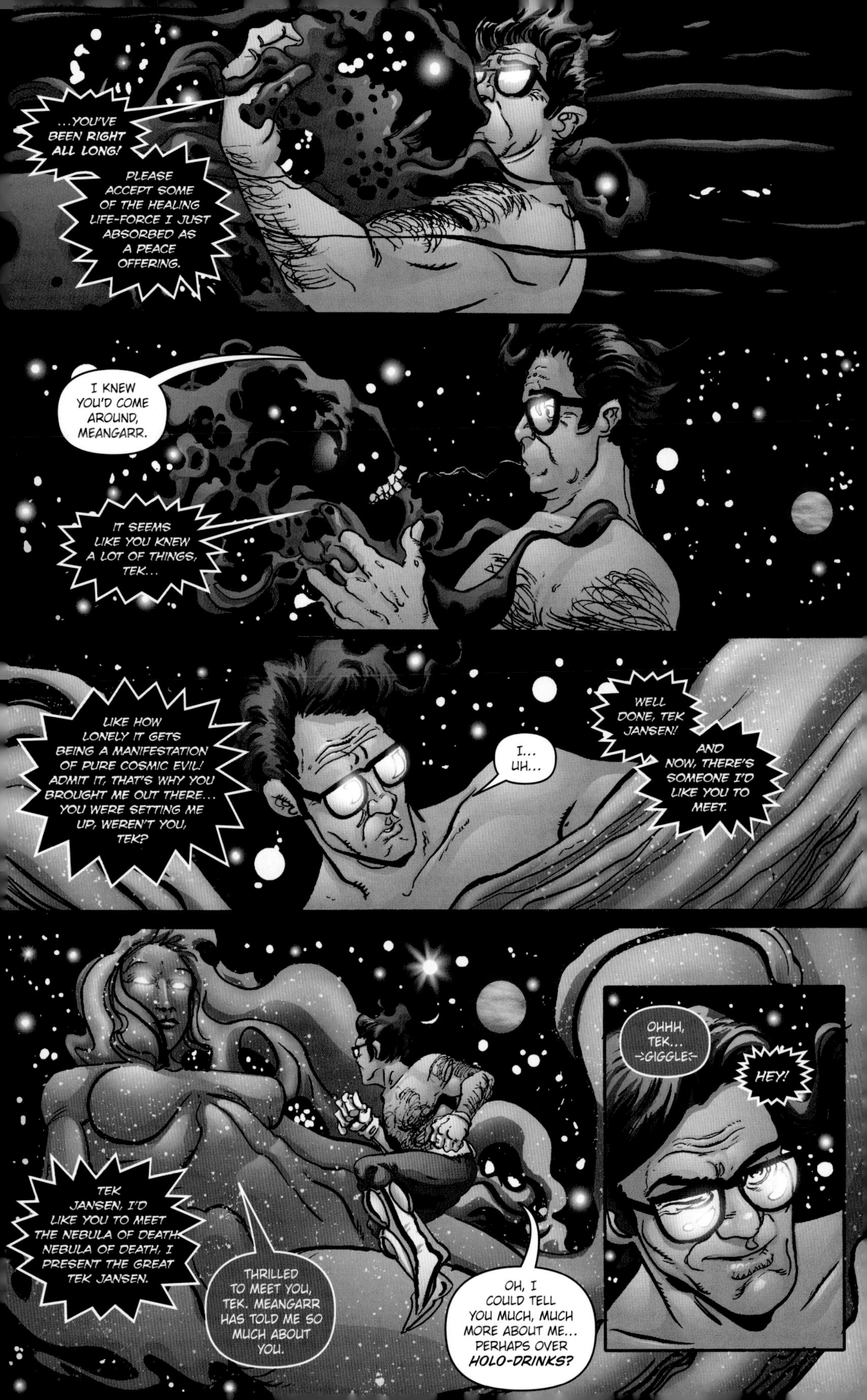
...YOU'VE BEEN RIGHT ALL LONG!
PLEASE ACCEPT SOME OF THE HEALING LIFE-FORCE I JUST ABSORBED AS A PEACE OFFERING.
I KNEW YOU'D COME AROUND, MEANGARR.
IT SEEMS LIKE YOU KNEW A LOT OF THINGS, TEK...
LIKE HOW LONELY IT GETS BEING A MANIFESTATION OF PURE COSMIC EVIL! ADMIT IT, THAT'S WHY YOU BROUGHT ME OUT THERE... YOU WERE SETTING ME UP, WEREN'T YOU, TEK?
I... UH...
WELL DONE, TEK JANSEN!
AND NOW, THERE'S SOMEONE I'D LIKE YOU TO MEET.
TEK JANSEN, I'D LIKE YOU TO MEET THE NEBULA OF DEATH. NEBULA OF DEATH, I PRESENT THE GREAT TEK JANSEN.
THRILLED TO MEET YOU, TEK. MEANGARR HAS TOLD ME SO MUCH ABOUT YOU.
OH, I COULD TELL YOU MUCH, MUCH MORE ABOUT ME... PERHAPS OVER HOLO-DRINKS?
OHHH, TEK... -:GIGGLE:-
HEY!

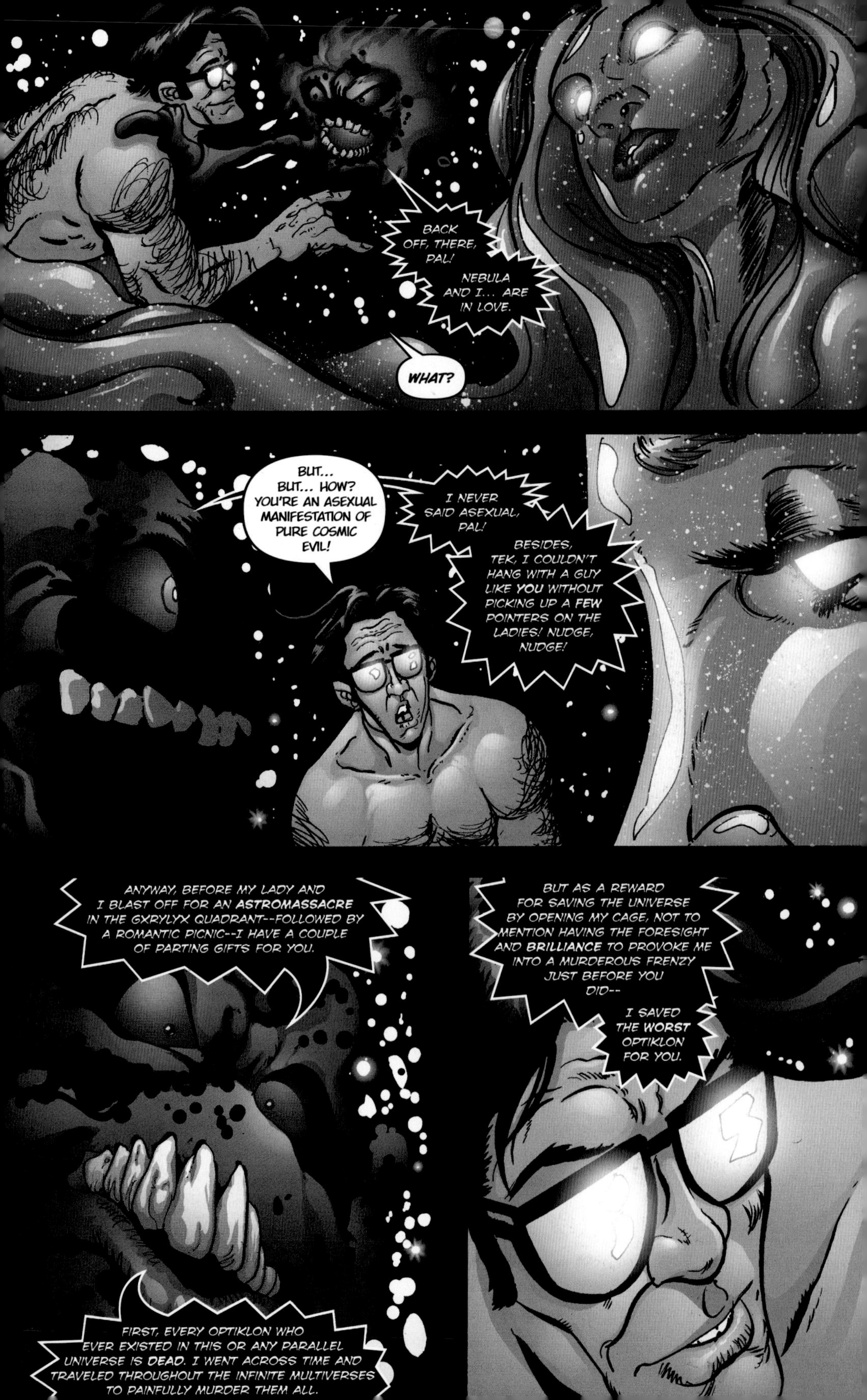
BACK OFF, THERE, PAL!
NEBULA AND I... ARE IN LOVE.
WHAT?
BUT... BUT... HOW? YOU'RE AN ASEXUAL MANIFESTATION OF PURE COSMIC EVIL!
I NEVER SAID ASEXUAL, PAL!
BESIDES, TEK, I COULDN'T HANG WITH A GUY LIKE YOU WITHOUT PICKING UP A FEW POINTERS ON THE LADIES! NUDGE, NUDGE!
ANYWAY, BEFORE MY LADY AND I BLAST OFF FOR AN ASTROMASSACRE IN THE GXRYLYX QUADRANT--FOLLOWED BY A ROMANTIC PICNIC--I HAVE A COUPLE OF PARTING GIFTS FOR YOU.
FIRST, EVERY OPTIKLON WHO EVER EXISTED IN THIS OR ANY PARALLEL UNIVERSE IS DEAD. I WENT ACROSS TIME AND TRAVELED THROUGHOUT THE INFINITE MULTIVERSES TO PAINFULLY MURDER THEM ALL.
BUT AS A REWARD FOR SAVING THE UNIVERSE BY OPENING MY CAGE, NOT TO MENTION HAVING THE FORESIGHT AND BRILLIANCE TO PROVOKE ME INTO A MURDEROUS FRENZY JUST BEFORE YOU DID--
I SAVED THE WORST OPTIKLON FOR YOU.

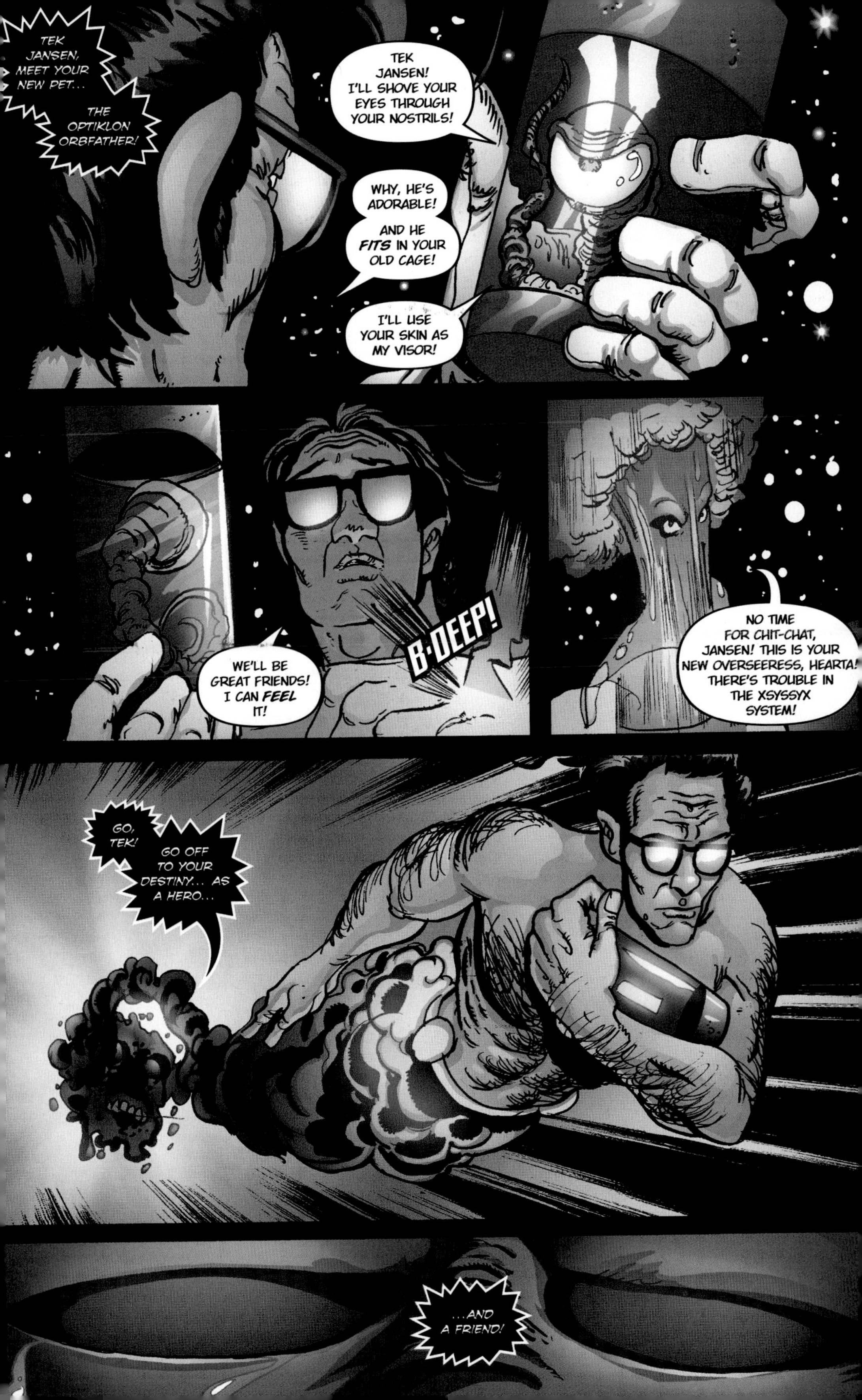
TEK JANSEN, MEET YOUR NEW PET...
THE OPTIKLON ORBFATHER!
TEK JANSEN! I'LL SHOVE YOUR EYES THROUGH YOUR NOSTRILS!
WHY, HE'S ADORABLE!
AND HE FITS IN YOUR OLD CAGE!
I'LL USE YOUR SKIN AS MY VISOR!
WE'LL BE GREAT FRIENDS! I CAN FEEL IT!
B-DEEP!
NO TIME FOR CHIT-CHAT, JANSEN! THIS IS YOUR NEW OVERSEERESS, HEARTA! THERE'S TROUBLE IN THE XSYSSYX SYSTEM!
GO, TEK!
GO OFF TO YOUR DESTINY... AS A HERO...
...AND A FRIEND!

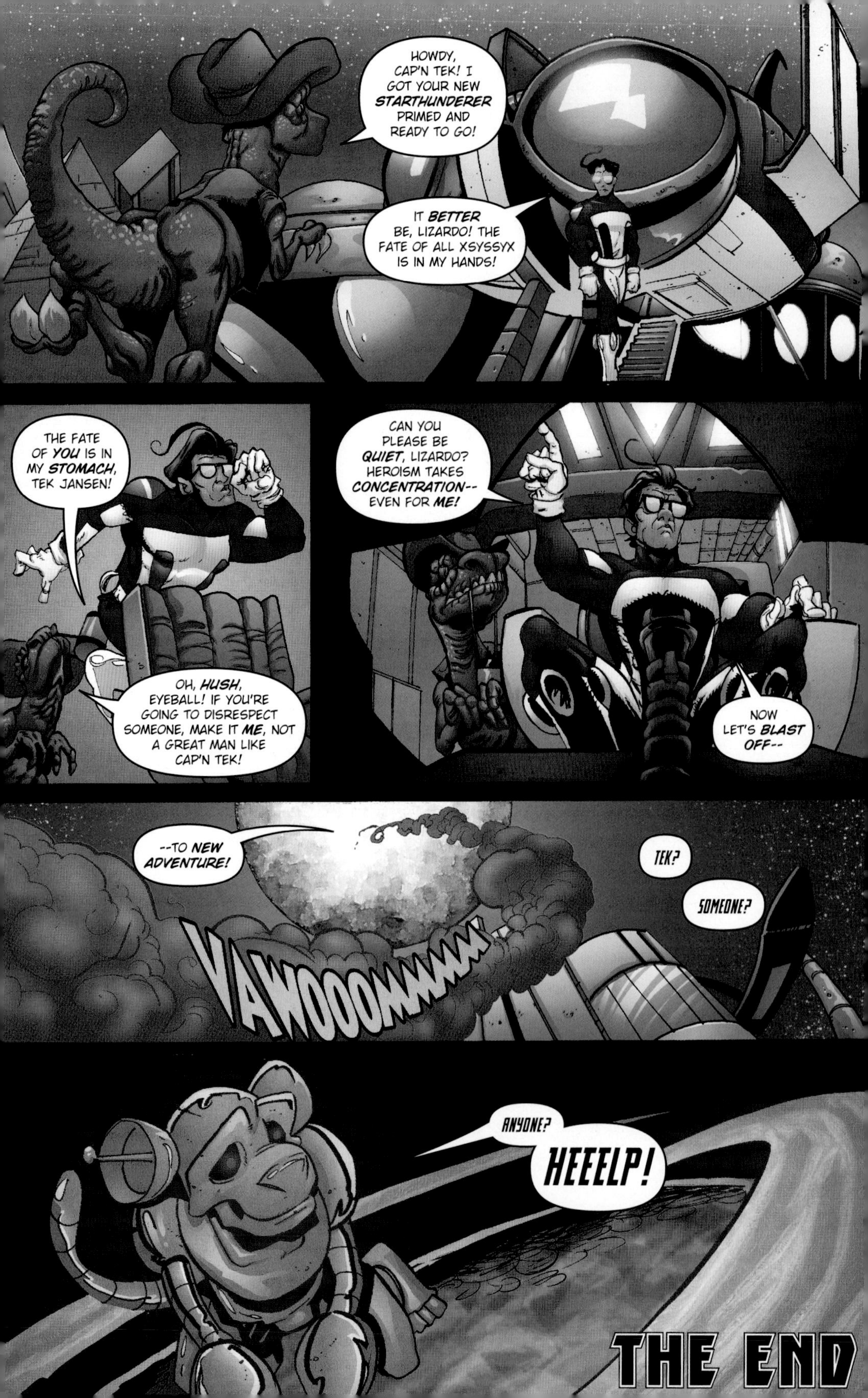
HOWDY, CAP'N TEK! I GOT YOUR NEW STARTHUNDERER PRIMED AND READY TO GO!
IT BETTER BE, LIZARDO! THE FATE OF ALL XSYSSYX IS IN MY HANDS!
THE FATE OF YOU IS IN MY STOMACH, TEK JANSEN!
OH, HUSH, EYEBALL! IF YOU'RE GOING TO DISRESPECT SOMEONE, MAKE IT ME, NOT A GREAT MAN LIKE CAP'N TEK!
CAN YOU PLEASE BE QUIET, LIZARDO? HEROISM TAKES CONCENTRATION-- EVEN FOR ME!
NOW LET'S BLAST OFF--
--TO NEW ADVENTURE!
VAWOOOMMMM
TEK?
SOMEONE?
ANYONE?
HEEELP!
THE END

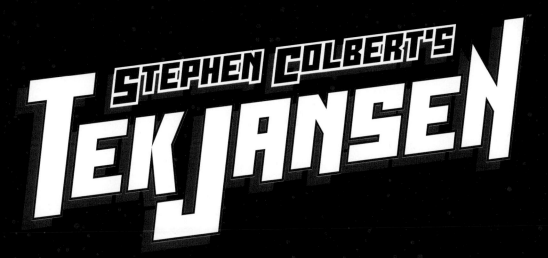

STEPHEN COLBERT'S TEK JANSEN

THE TEK JANSEN CASE FILES

WRITTEN BY **JIM MASSEY**

ILLUSTRATED BY **ROBBI RODRIGUEZ**

COLORED BY **DAVE McCAIG** & **NATHAN FAIRBAIRN**

LETTERED BY **DOUGLAS E. SHERWOOD**

EDITED BY **JAMES LUCAS JONES** & **RANDAL C. JARRELL**

DESIGNED BY **KEITH WOOD**

FLEET COMMANDED BY **RICHARD DAHM**

GALACTIC OVERLORDING BY **STEPHEN COLBERT**

APPROVED BY THE COLBERT NATION AUTHORITY

A SQUAD

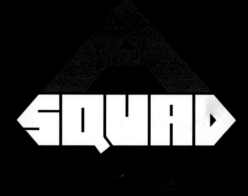

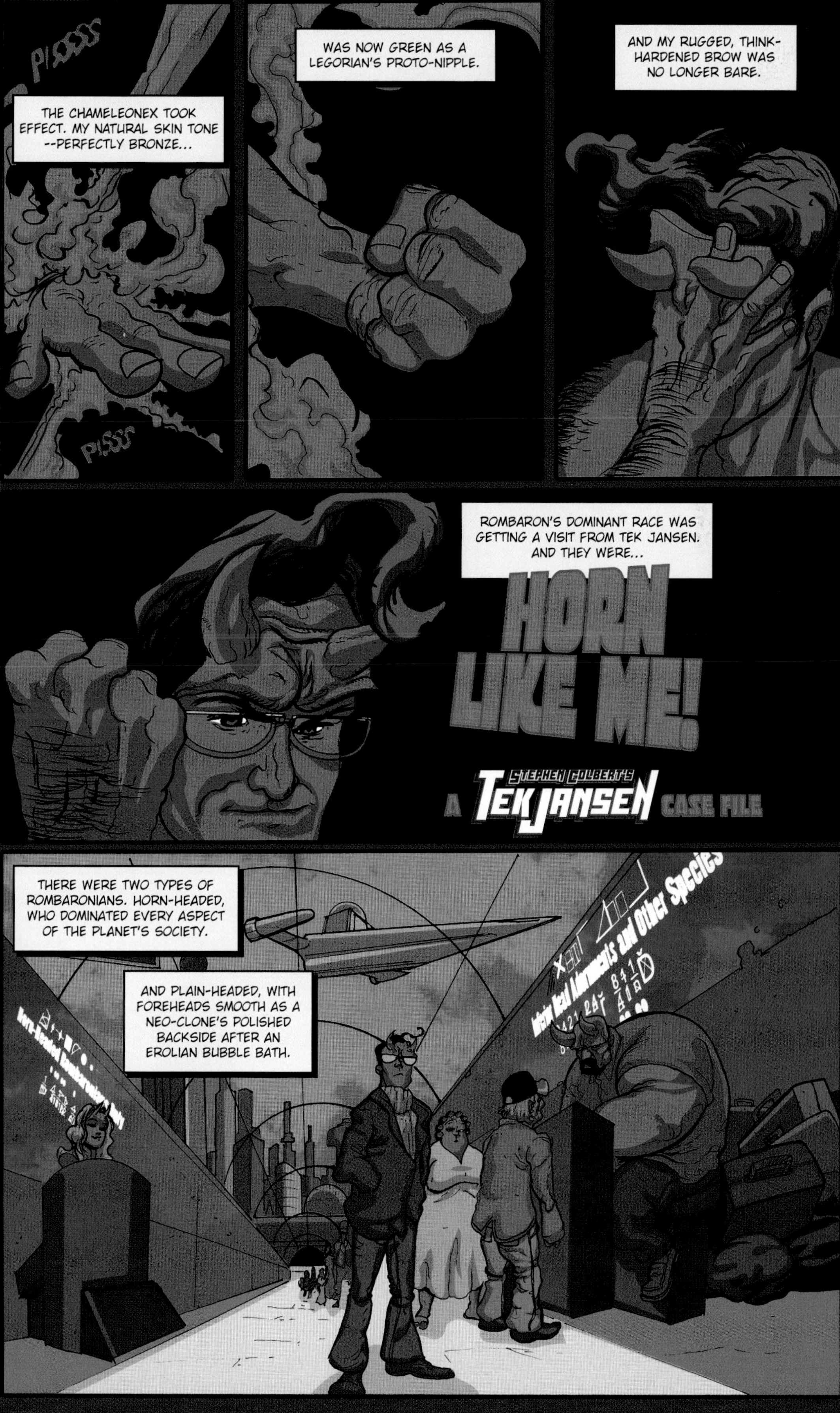
PISSSS
THE CHAMELEONEX TOOK EFFECT. MY NATURAL SKIN TONE --PERFECTLY BRONZE...
PISSSS
WAS NOW GREEN AS A LEGORIAN'S PROTO-NIPPLE.
AND MY RUGGED, THINK-HARDENED BROW WAS NO LONGER BARE.
ROMBARON'S DOMINANT RACE WAS GETTING A VISIT FROM TEK JANSEN. AND THEY WERE...
HORN LIKE ME!
A STEPHEN COLBERT'S TEK JANSEN CASE FILE
THERE WERE TWO TYPES OF ROMBARONIANS. HORN-HEADED, WHO DOMINATED EVERY ASPECT OF THE PLANET'S SOCIETY.
AND PLAIN-HEADED, WITH FOREHEADS SMOOTH AS A NEO-CLONE'S POLISHED BACKSIDE AFTER AN EROLIAN BUBBLE BATH.

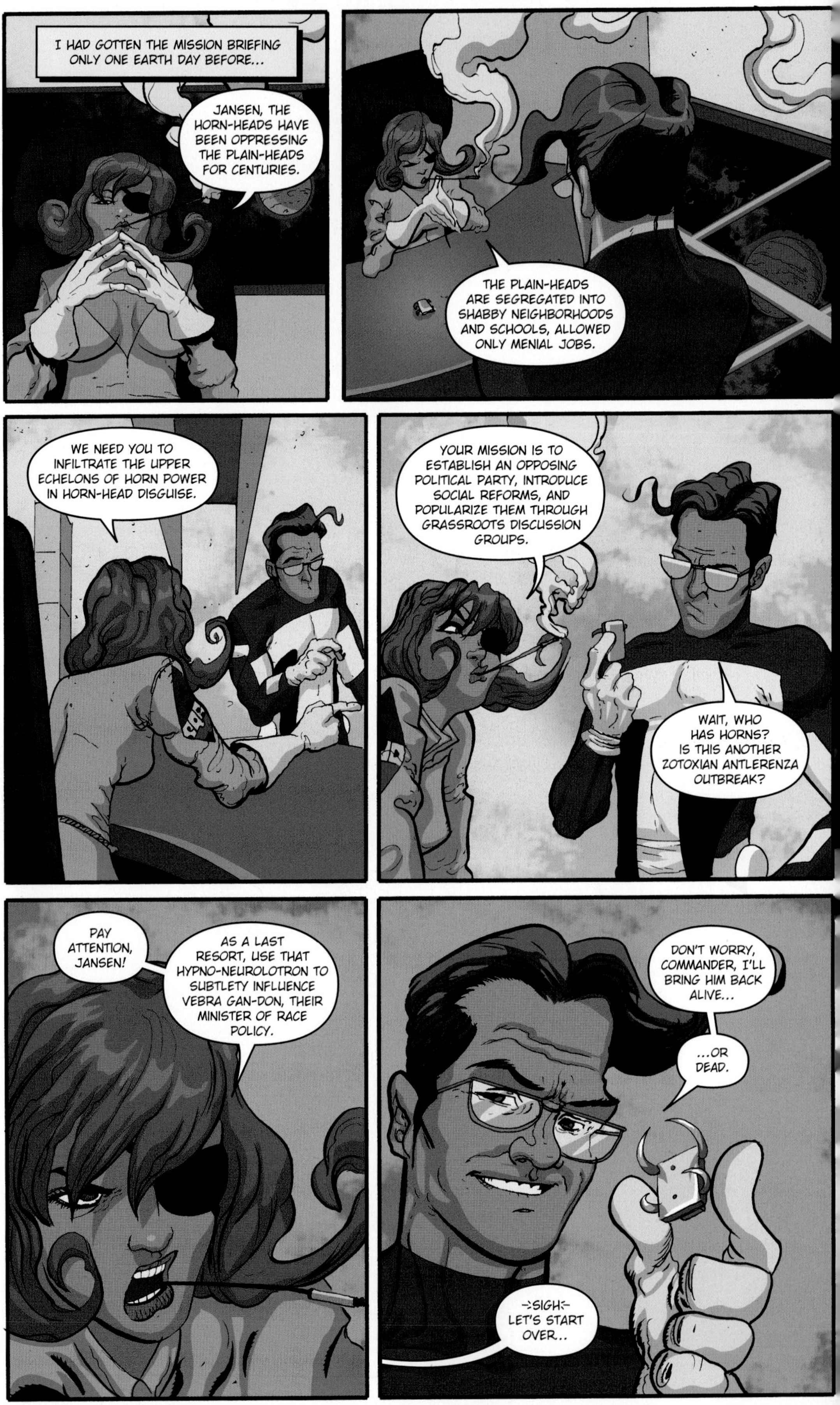
I HAD GOTTEN THE MISSION BRIEFING ONLY ONE EARTH DAY BEFORE...
JANSEN, THE HORN-HEADS HAVE BEEN OPPRESSING THE PLAIN-HEADS FOR CENTURIES.
THE PLAIN-HEADS ARE SEGREGATED INTO SHABBY NEIGHBORHOODS AND SCHOOLS, ALLOWED ONLY MENIAL JOBS.
WE NEED YOU TO INFILTRATE THE UPPER ECHELONS OF HORN POWER IN HORN-HEAD DISGUISE.
YOUR MISSION IS TO ESTABLISH AN OPPOSING POLITICAL PARTY, INTRODUCE SOCIAL REFORMS, AND POPULARIZE THEM THROUGH GRASSROOTS DISCUSSION GROUPS.
WAIT, WHO HAS HORNS? IS THIS ANOTHER ZOTOXIAN ANTLERENZA OUTBREAK?
PAY ATTENTION, JANSEN!
AS A LAST RESORT, USE THAT HYPNO-NEUROLOTRON TO SUBTLETY INFLUENCE VEBRA GAN-DON, THEIR MINISTER OF RACE POLICY.
DON'T WORRY, COMMANDER, I'LL BRING HIM BACK ALIVE...
...OR DEAD.
-SIGH- LET'S START OVER..

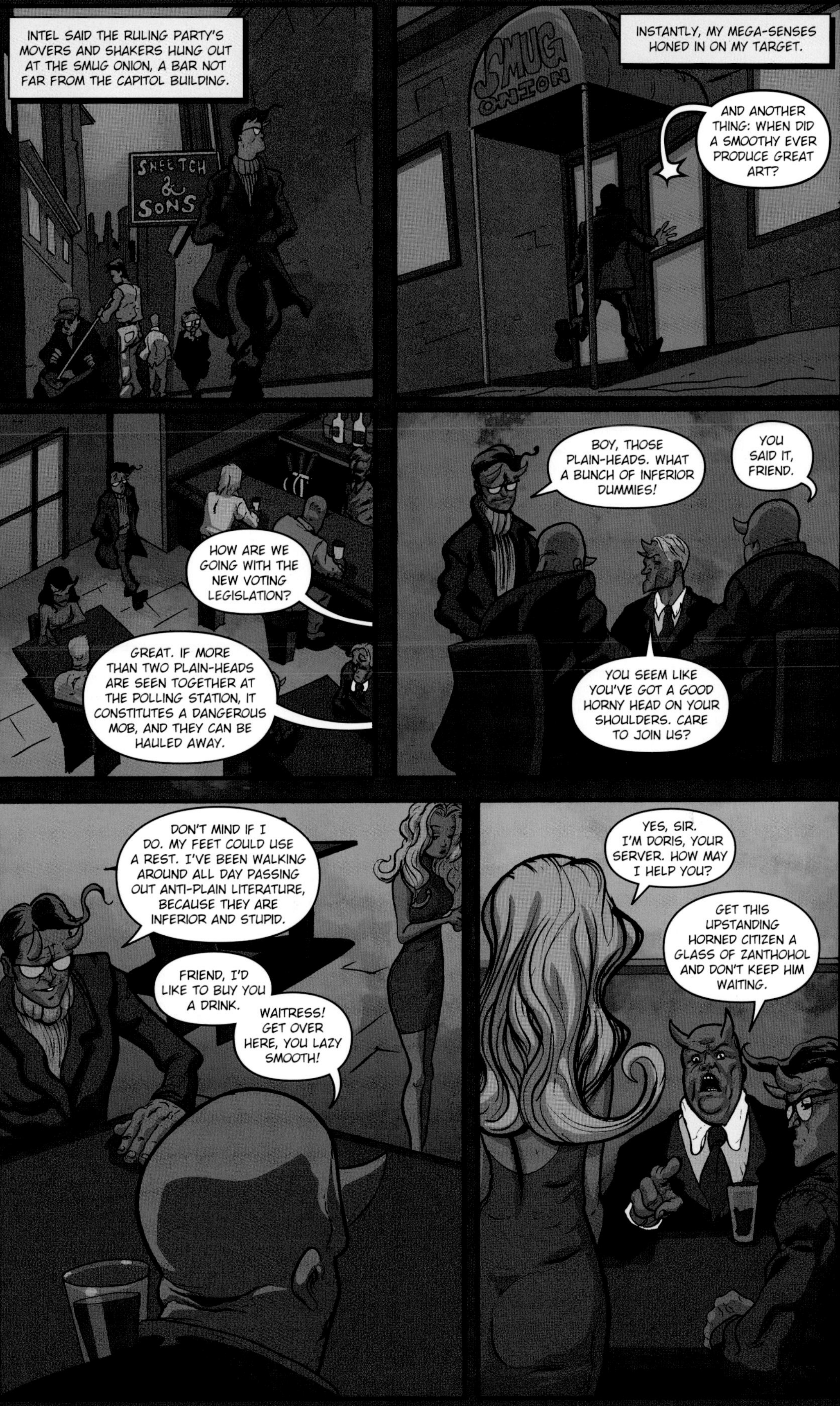

INTEL SAID THE RULING PARTY'S MOVERS AND SHAKERS HUNG OUT AT THE SMUG ONION, A BAR NOT FAR FROM THE CAPITOL BUILDING.
SNEETCH & SONS
INSTANTLY, MY MEGA-SENSES HONED IN ON MY TARGET.
SMUG ONION
AND ANOTHER THING: WHEN DID A SMOOTHY EVER PRODUCE GREAT ART?
HOW ARE WE GOING WITH THE NEW VOTING LEGISLATION?
GREAT. IF MORE THAN TWO PLAIN-HEADS ARE SEEN TOGETHER AT THE POLLING STATION, IT CONSTITUTES A DANGEROUS MOB, AND THEY CAN BE HAULED AWAY.
BOY, THOSE PLAIN-HEADS. WHAT A BUNCH OF INFERIOR DUMMIES!
YOU SAID IT, FRIEND.
YOU SEEM LIKE YOU'VE GOT A GOOD HORNY HEAD ON YOUR SHOULDERS. CARE TO JOIN US?
DON'T MIND IF I DO. MY FEET COULD USE A REST. I'VE BEEN WALKING AROUND ALL DAY PASSING OUT ANTI-PLAIN LITERATURE, BECAUSE THEY ARE INFERIOR AND STUPID.
FRIEND, I'D LIKE TO BUY YOU A DRINK.
WAITRESS! GET OVER HERE, YOU LAZY SMOOTH!
YES, SIR. I'M DORIS, YOUR SERVER. HOW MAY I HELP YOU?
GET THIS UPSTANDING HORNED CITIZEN A GLASS OF ZANTHOHOL AND DON'T KEEP HIM WAITING.

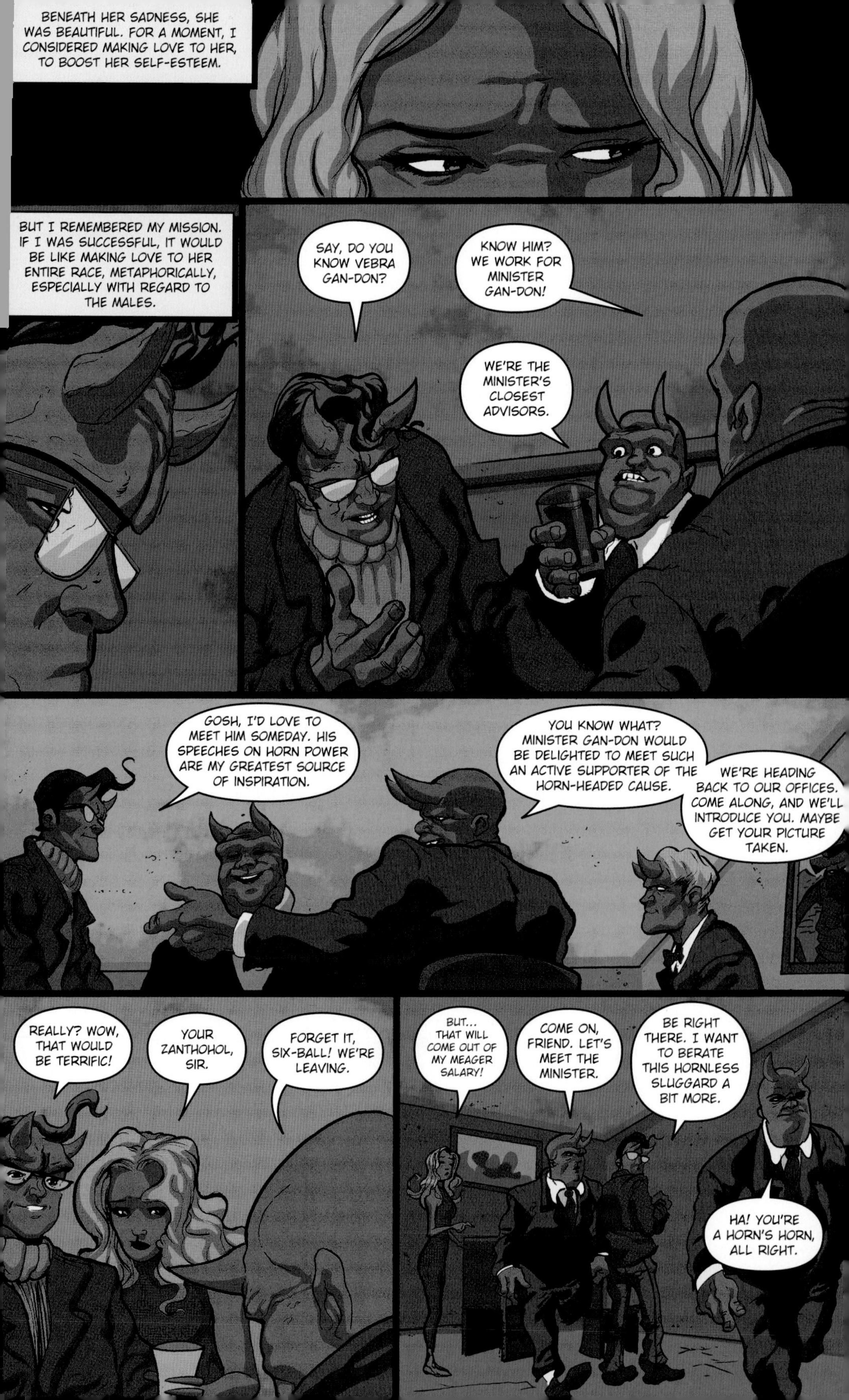
BENEATH HER SADNESS, SHE WAS BEAUTIFUL. FOR A MOMENT, I CONSIDERED MAKING LOVE TO HER, TO BOOST HER SELF-ESTEEM.
BUT I REMEMBERED MY MISSION. IF I WAS SUCCESSFUL, IT WOULD BE LIKE MAKING LOVE TO HER ENTIRE RACE, METAPHORICALLY, ESPECIALLY WITH REGARD TO THE MALES.
SAY, DO YOU KNOW VEBRA GAN-DON?
KNOW HIM? WE WORK FOR MINISTER GAN-DON!
WE'RE THE MINISTER'S CLOSEST ADVISORS.
GOSH, I'D LOVE TO MEET HIM SOMEDAY. HIS SPEECHES ON HORN POWER ARE MY GREATEST SOURCE OF INSPIRATION.
YOU KNOW WHAT? MINISTER GAN-DON WOULD BE DELIGHTED TO MEET SUCH AN ACTIVE SUPPORTER OF THE HORN-HEADED CAUSE.
WE'RE HEADING BACK TO OUR OFFICES. COME ALONG, AND WE'LL INTRODUCE YOU. MAYBE GET YOUR PICTURE TAKEN.
REALLY? WOW, THAT WOULD BE TERRIFIC!
YOUR ZANTHOHOL, SIR.
FORGET IT, SIX-BALL! WE'RE LEAVING.
BUT... THAT WILL COME OUT OF MY MEAGER SALARY!
COME ON, FRIEND. LET'S MEET THE MINISTER.
BE RIGHT THERE. I WANT TO BERATE THIS HORNLESS SLUGGARD A BIT MORE.
HA! YOU'RE A HORN'S HORN, ALL RIGHT.

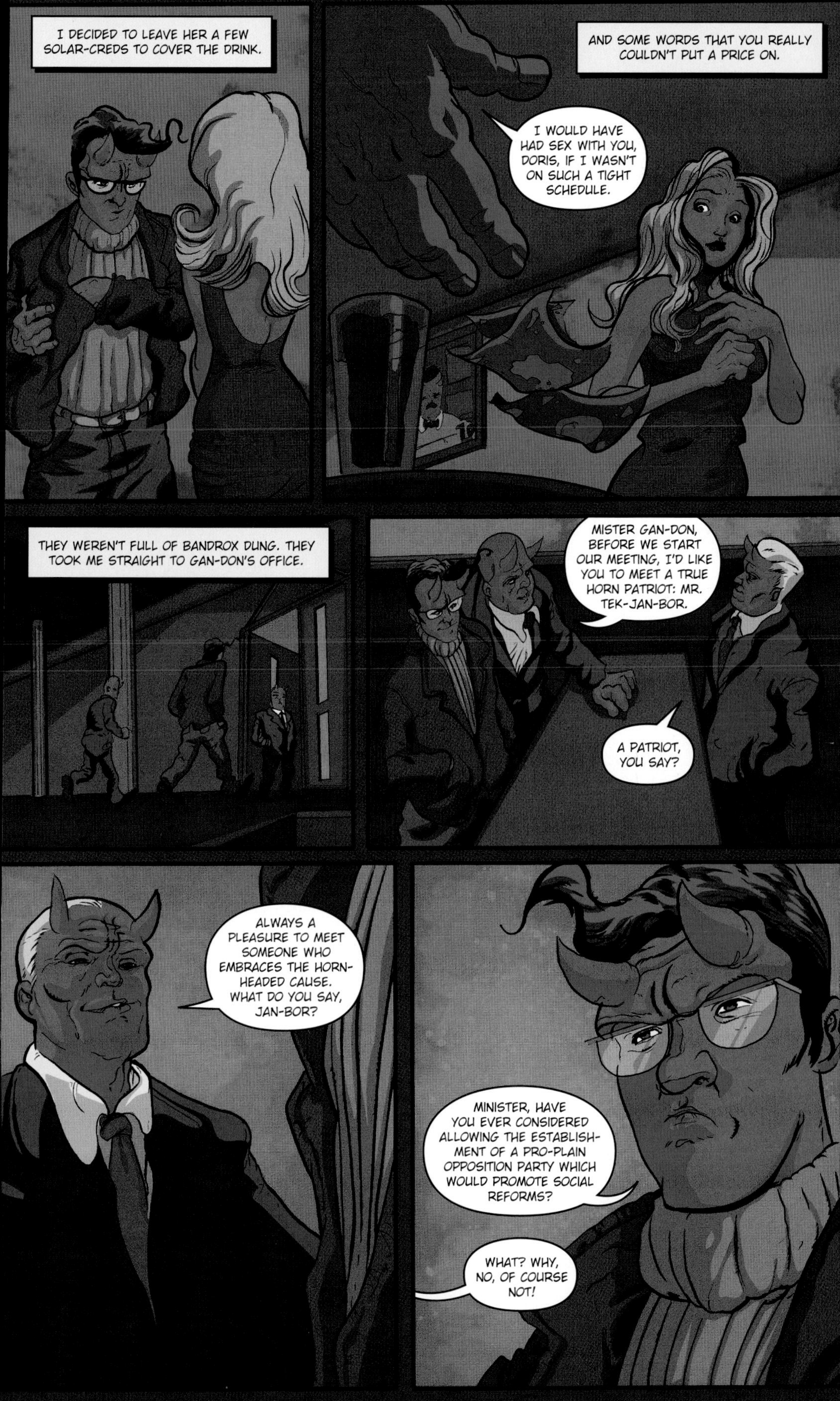
I DECIDED TO LEAVE HER A FEW SOLAR-CREDS TO COVER THE DRINK.
AND SOME WORDS THAT YOU REALLY COULDN'T PUT A PRICE ON.
I WOULD HAVE HAD SEX WITH YOU, DORIS, IF I WASN'T ON SUCH A TIGHT SCHEDULE.
THEY WEREN'T FULL OF BANDROX DUNG. THEY TOOK ME STRAIGHT TO GAN-DON'S OFFICE.
MISTER GAN-DON, BEFORE WE START OUR MEETING, I'D LIKE YOU TO MEET A TRUE HORN PATRIOT: MR. TEK-JAN-BOR.
A PATRIOT, YOU SAY?
ALWAYS A PLEASURE TO MEET SOMEONE WHO EMBRACES THE HORN-HEADED CAUSE. WHAT DO YOU SAY, JAN-BOR?
MINISTER, HAVE YOU EVER CONSIDERED ALLOWING THE ESTABLISHMENT OF A PRO-PLAIN OPPOSITION PARTY WHICH WOULD PROMOTE SOCIAL REFORMS?
WHAT? WHY, NO, OF COURSE NOT!

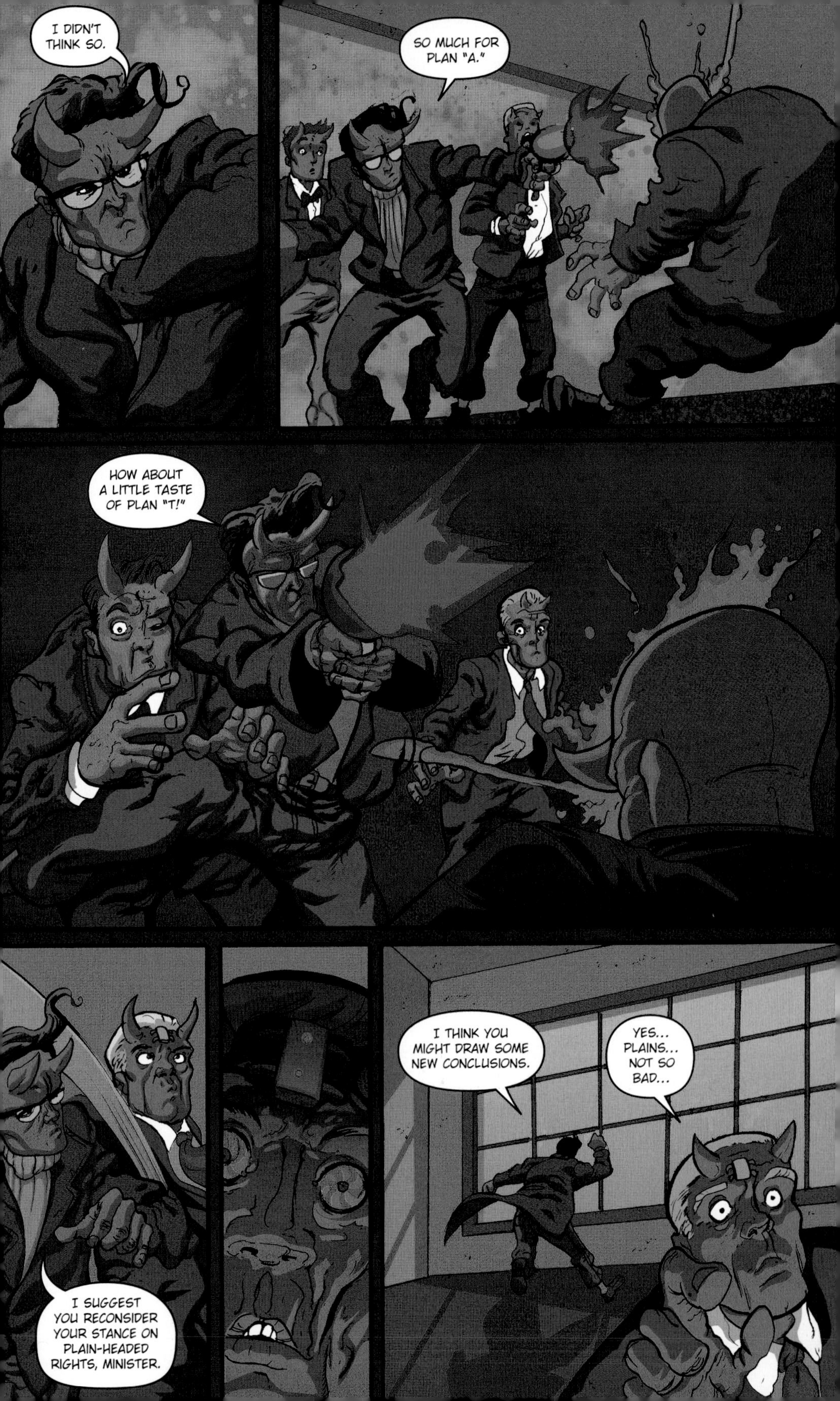
I DIDN'T THINK SO.
SO MUCH FOR PLAN "A."
HOW ABOUT A LITTLE TASTE OF PLAN "T!"
I SUGGEST YOU RECONSIDER YOUR STANCE ON PLAIN-HEADED RIGHTS, MINISTER.
I THINK YOU MIGHT DRAW SOME NEW CONCLUSIONS.
YES... PLAINS... NOT SO BAD...

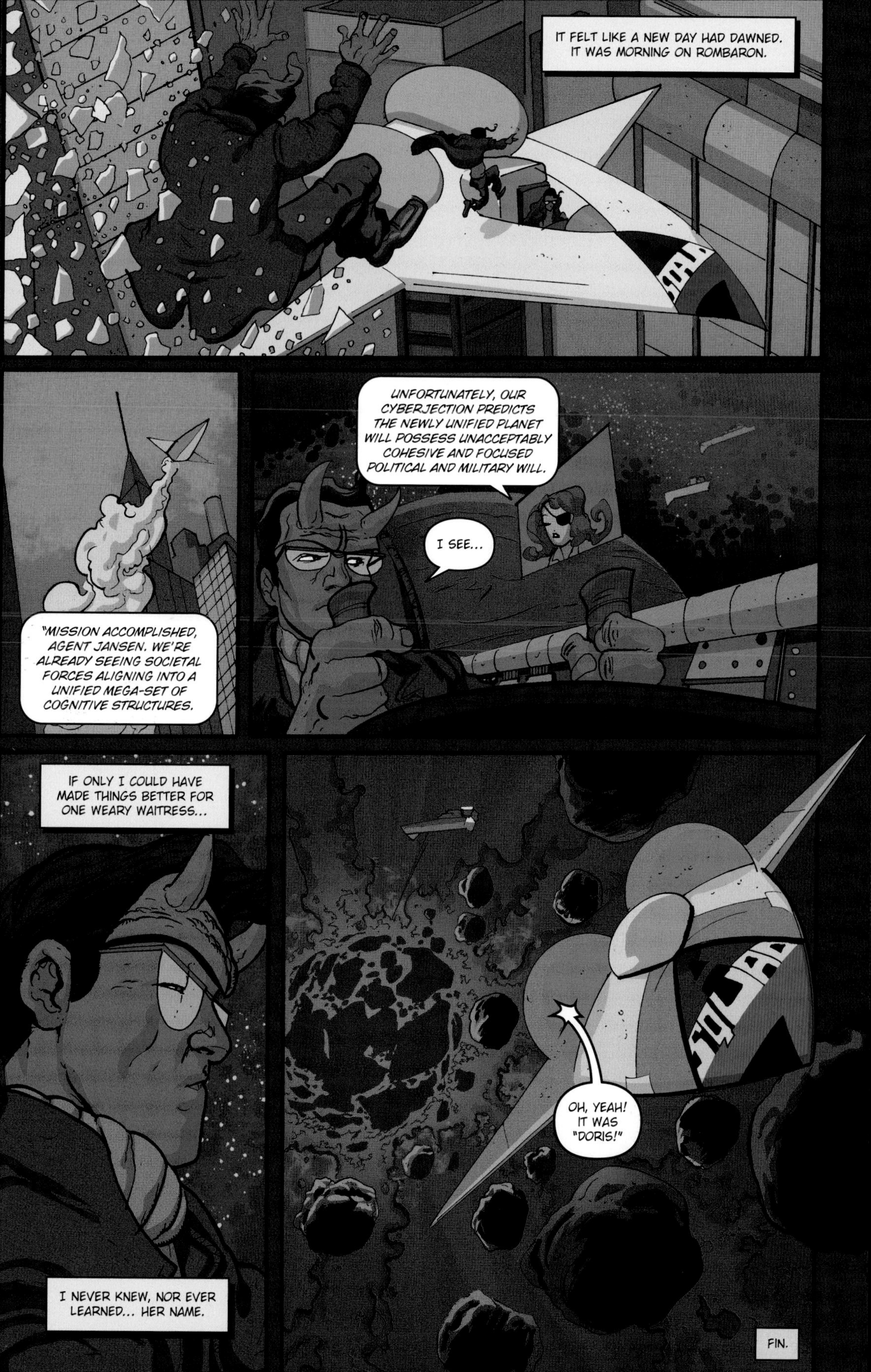
IT FELT LIKE A NEW DAY HAD DAWNED. IT WAS MORNING ON ROMBARON.
"MISSION ACCOMPLISHED, AGENT JANSEN. WE'RE ALREADY SEEING SOCIETAL FORCES ALIGNING INTO A UNIFIED MEGA-SET OF COGNITIVE STRUCTURES.
UNFORTUNATELY, OUR CYBERJECTION PREDICTS THE NEWLY UNIFIED PLANET WILL POSSESS UNACCEPTABLY COHESIVE AND FOCUSED POLITICAL AND MILITARY WILL.
I SEE...
IF ONLY I COULD HAVE MADE THINGS BETTER FOR ONE WEARY WAITRESS...
I NEVER KNEW, NOR EVER LEARNED... HER NAME.
OH, YEAH! IT WAS "DORIS!"
FIN.

SQUAD

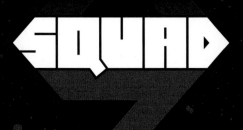

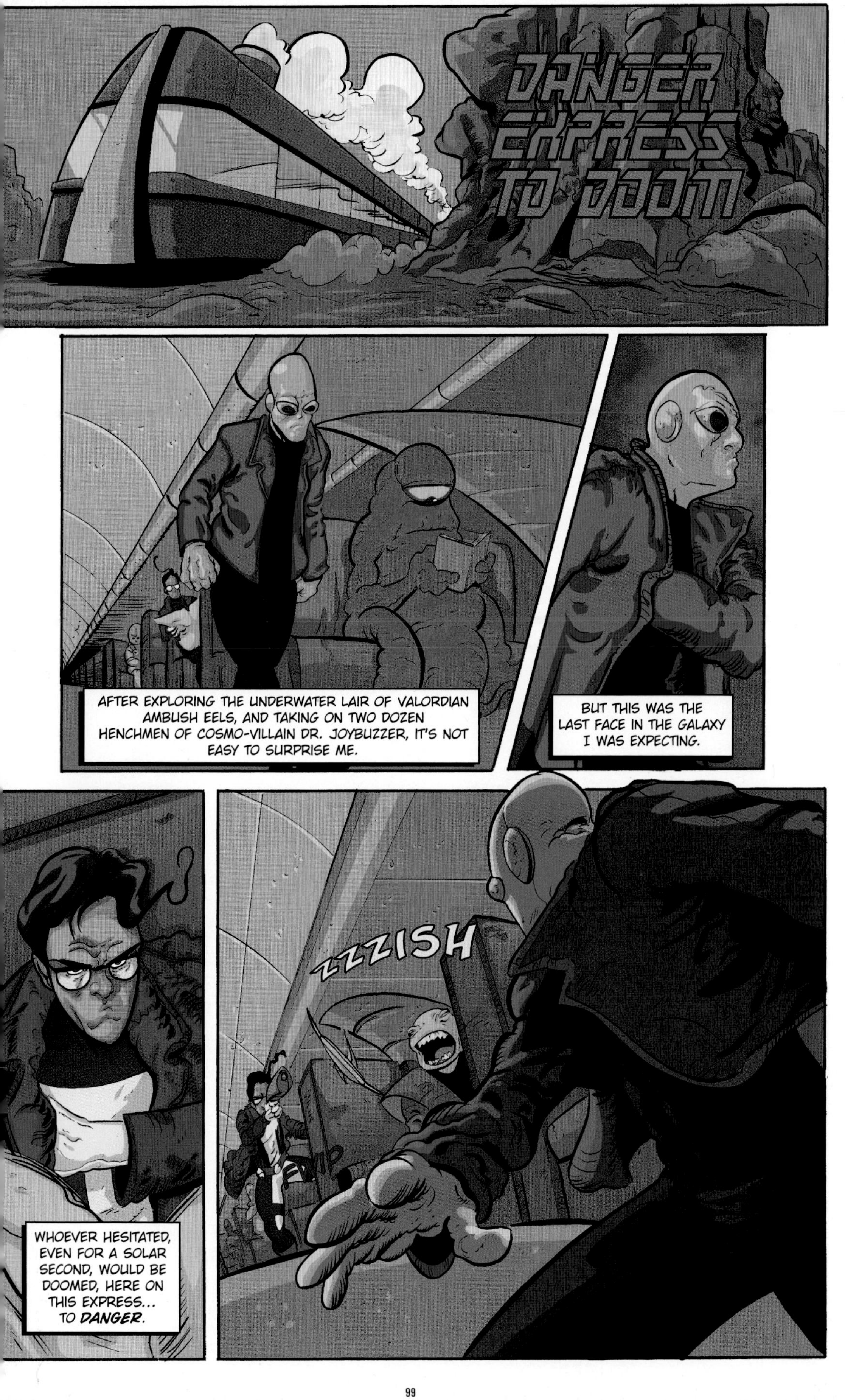
DANGER EXPRESS TO DOOM
AFTER EXPLORING THE UNDERWATER LAIR OF VALORDIAN AMBUSH EELS, AND TAKING ON TWO DOZEN HENCHMEN OF COSMO-VILLAIN DR. JOYBUZZER, IT'S NOT EASY TO SURPRISE ME.
BUT THIS WAS THE LAST FACE IN THE GALAXY I WAS EXPECTING.
WHOEVER HESITATED, EVEN FOR A SOLAR SECOND, WOULD BE DOOMED, HERE ON THIS EXPRESS... TO ***DANGER***.
ZZZISH

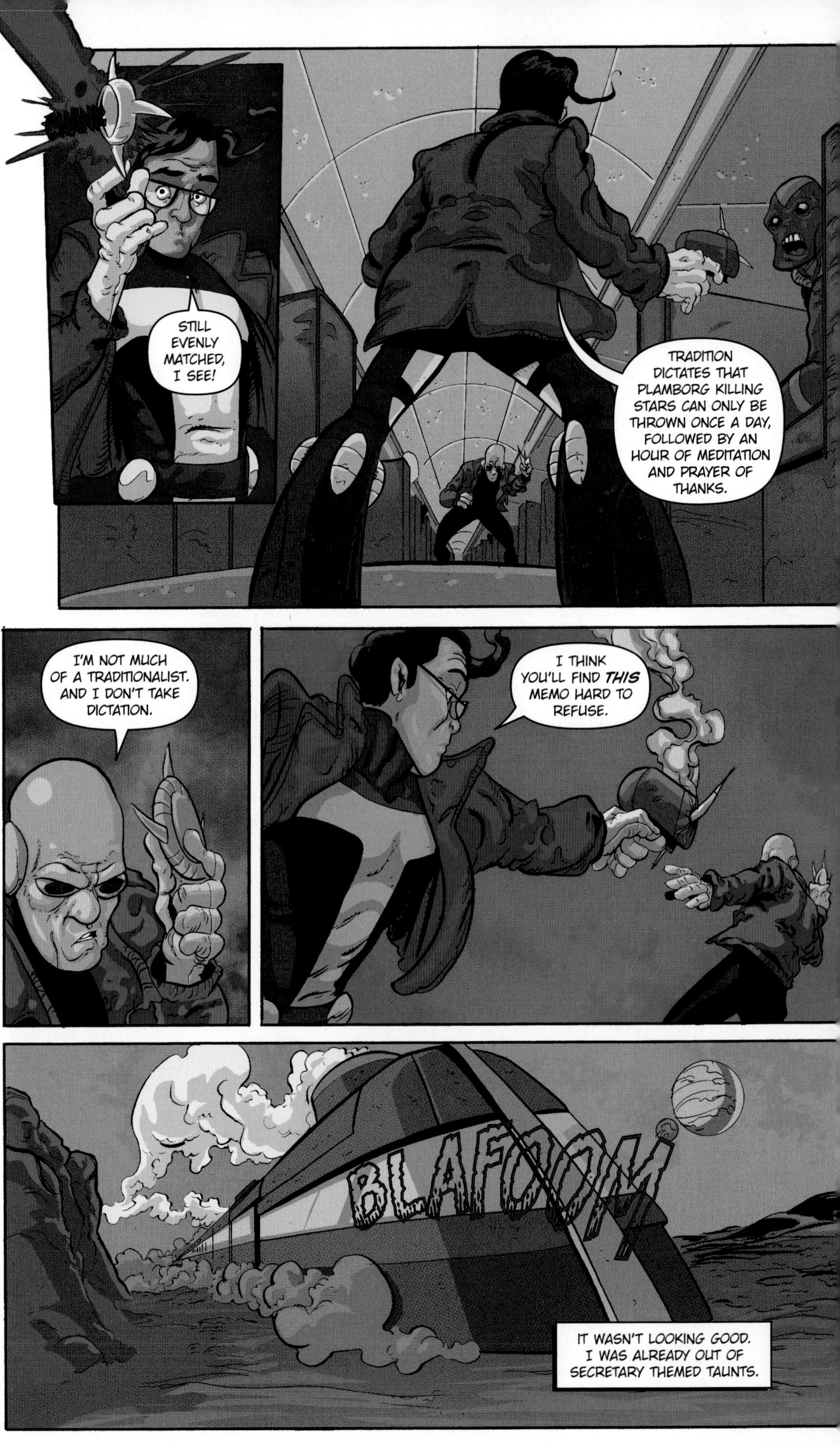
STILL EVENLY MATCHED, I SEE!
TRADITION DICTATES THAT PLAMBORG KILLING STARS CAN ONLY BE THROWN ONCE A DAY, FOLLOWED BY AN HOUR OF MEDITATION AND PRAYER OF THANKS.
I'M NOT MUCH OF A TRADITIONALIST. AND I DON'T TAKE DICTATION.
I THINK YOU'LL FIND *THIS* MEMO HARD TO REFUSE.
BLAFOOM
IT WASN'T LOOKING GOOD. I WAS ALREADY OUT OF SECRETARY THEMED TAUNTS.

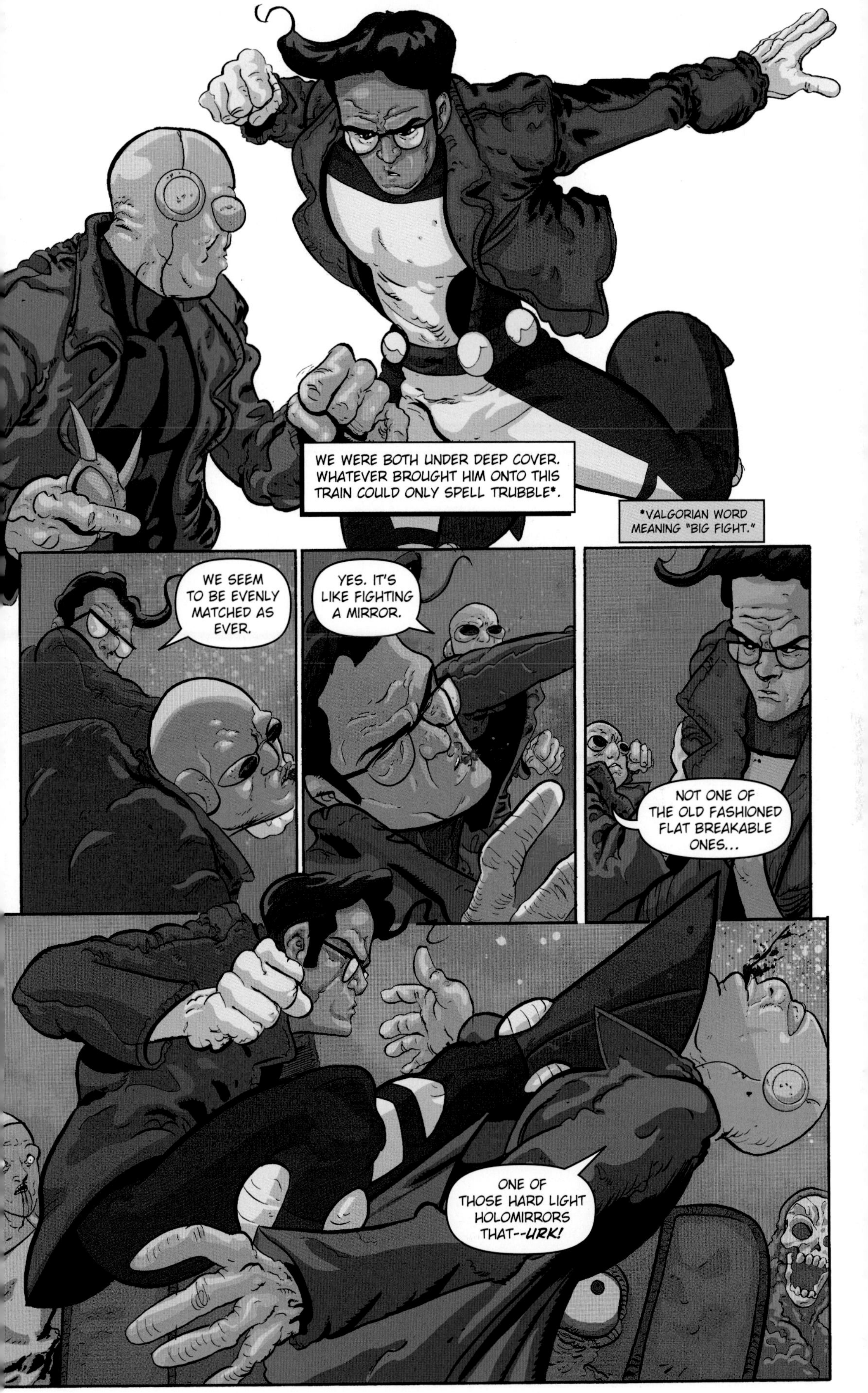

WE WERE BOTH UNDER DEEP COVER. WHATEVER BROUGHT HIM ONTO THIS TRAIN COULD ONLY SPELL TRUBBLE*.
*VALGORIAN WORD MEANING "BIG FIGHT."
WE SEEM TO BE EVENLY MATCHED AS EVER.
YES. IT'S LIKE FIGHTING A MIRROR.
NOT ONE OF THE OLD FASHIONED FLAT BREAKABLE ONES...
ONE OF THOSE HARD LIGHT HOLOMIRRORS THAT--URK!

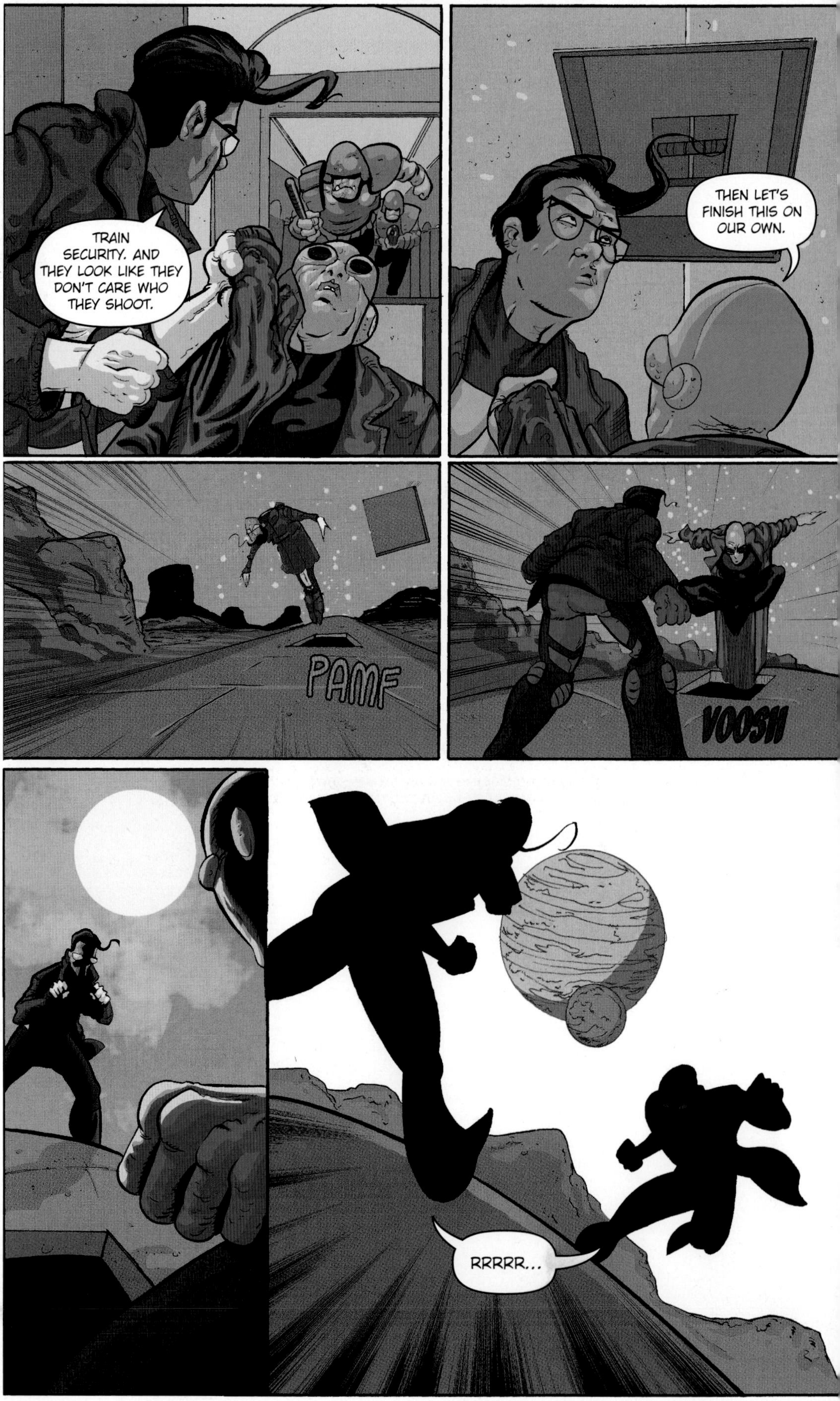
TRAIN SECURITY. AND THEY LOOK LIKE THEY DON'T CARE WHO THEY SHOOT.
THEN LET'S FINISH THIS ON OUR OWN.
PAMF
VOOSH
RRRRR...

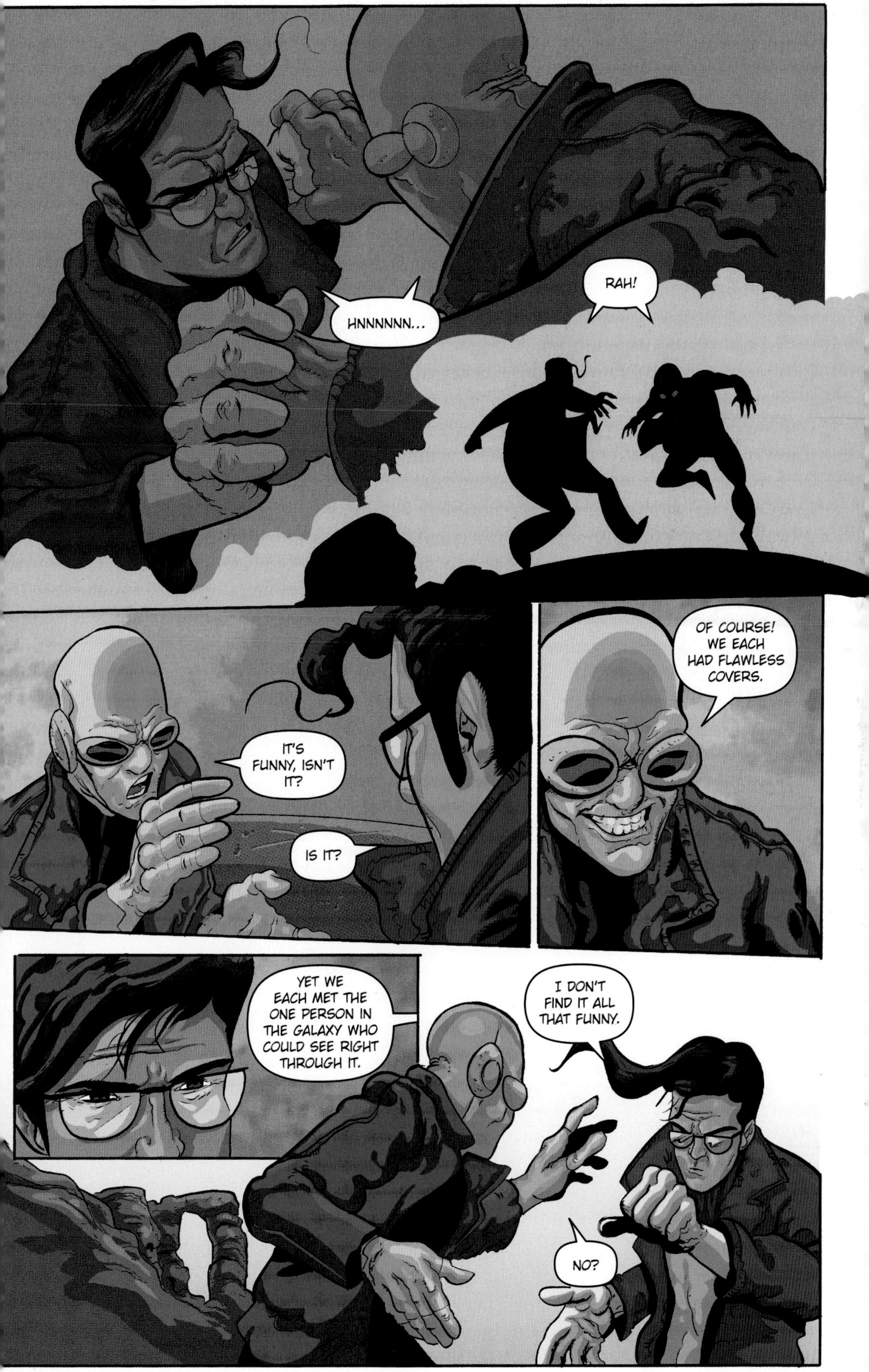
HNNNNNN...
RAH!
IT'S FUNNY, ISN'T IT?
IS IT?
OF COURSE! WE EACH HAD FLAWLESS COVERS.
YET WE EACH MET THE ONE PERSON IN THE GALAXY WHO COULD SEE RIGHT THROUGH IT.
I DON'T FIND IT ALL THAT FUNNY.
NO?

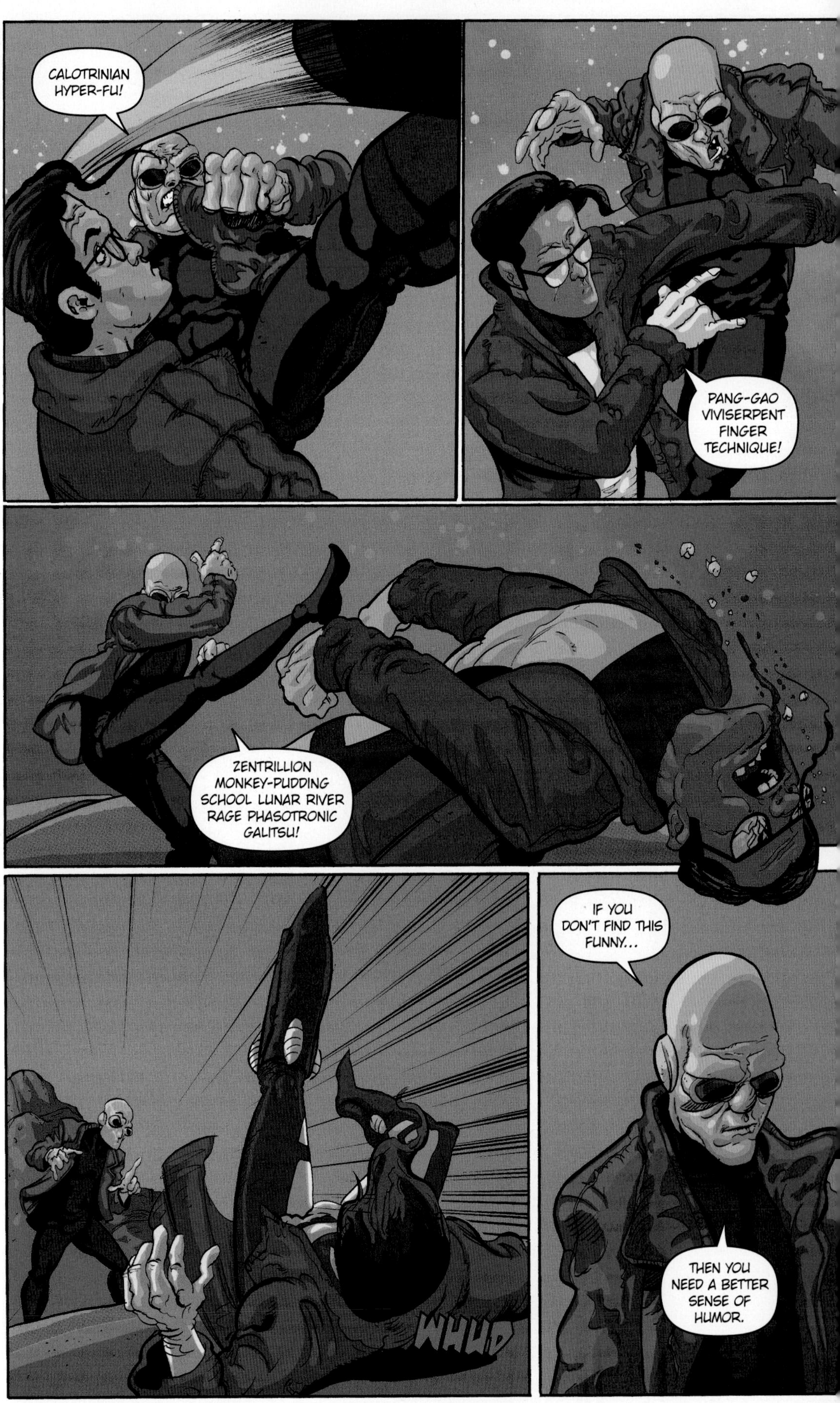
CALOTRINIAN HYPER-FU!
PANG-GAO VIVISERPENT FINGER TECHNIQUE!
ZENTRILLION MONKEY-PUDDING SCHOOL LUNAR RIVER RAGE PHASOTRONIC GALITSU!
WHUD
IF YOU DON'T FIND THIS FUNNY...
THEN YOU NEED A BETTER SENSE OF HUMOR.

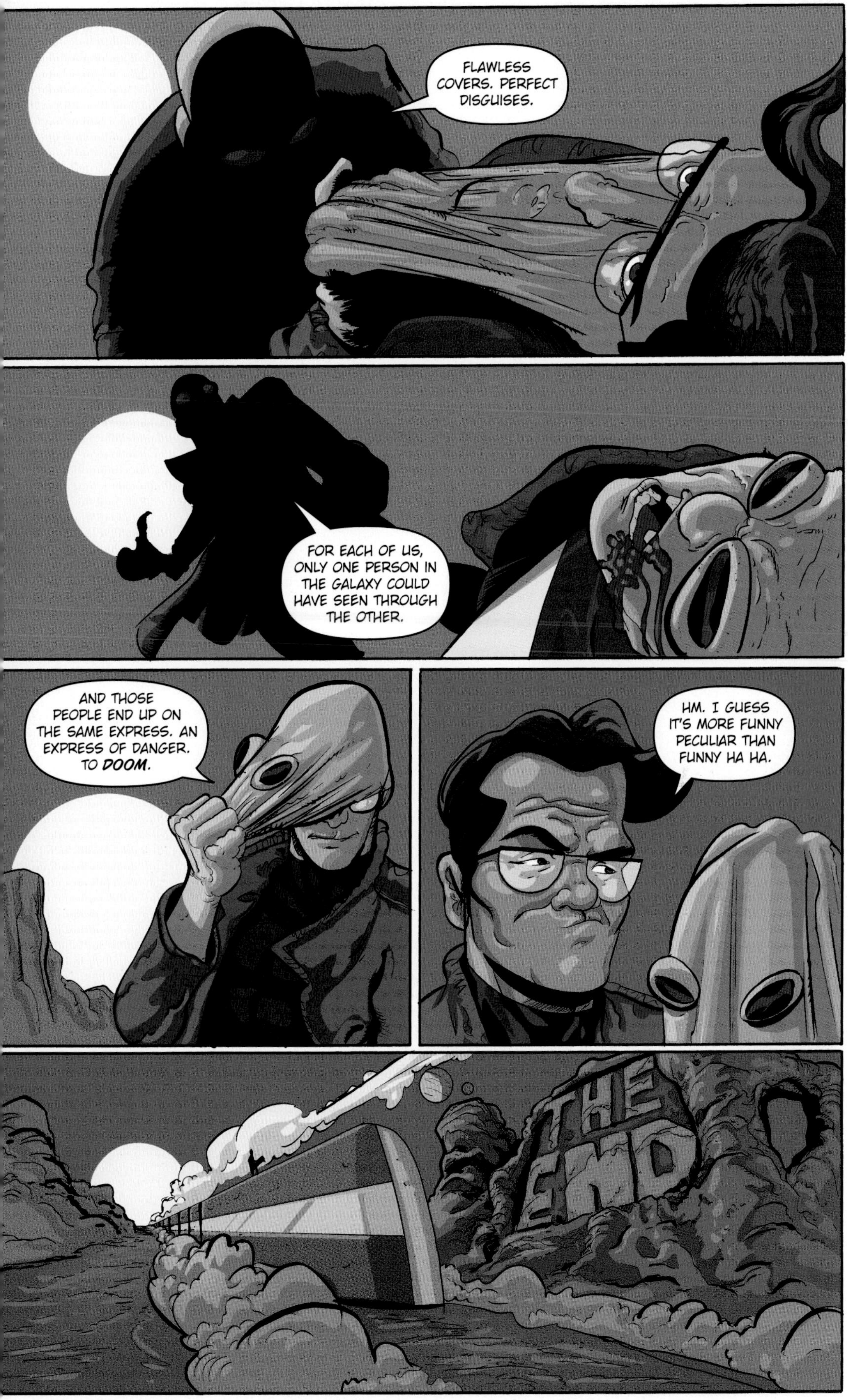
FLAWLESS COVERS. PERFECT DISGUISES.
FOR EACH OF US, ONLY ONE PERSON IN THE GALAXY COULD HAVE SEEN THROUGH THE OTHER.
AND THOSE PEOPLE END UP ON THE SAME EXPRESS. AN EXPRESS OF DANGER. TO ***DOOM***.
HM. I GUESS IT'S MORE FUNNY PECULIAR THAN FUNNY HA HA.
THE END

SQUAD

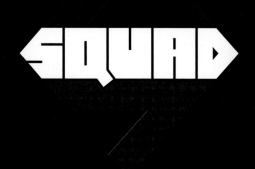

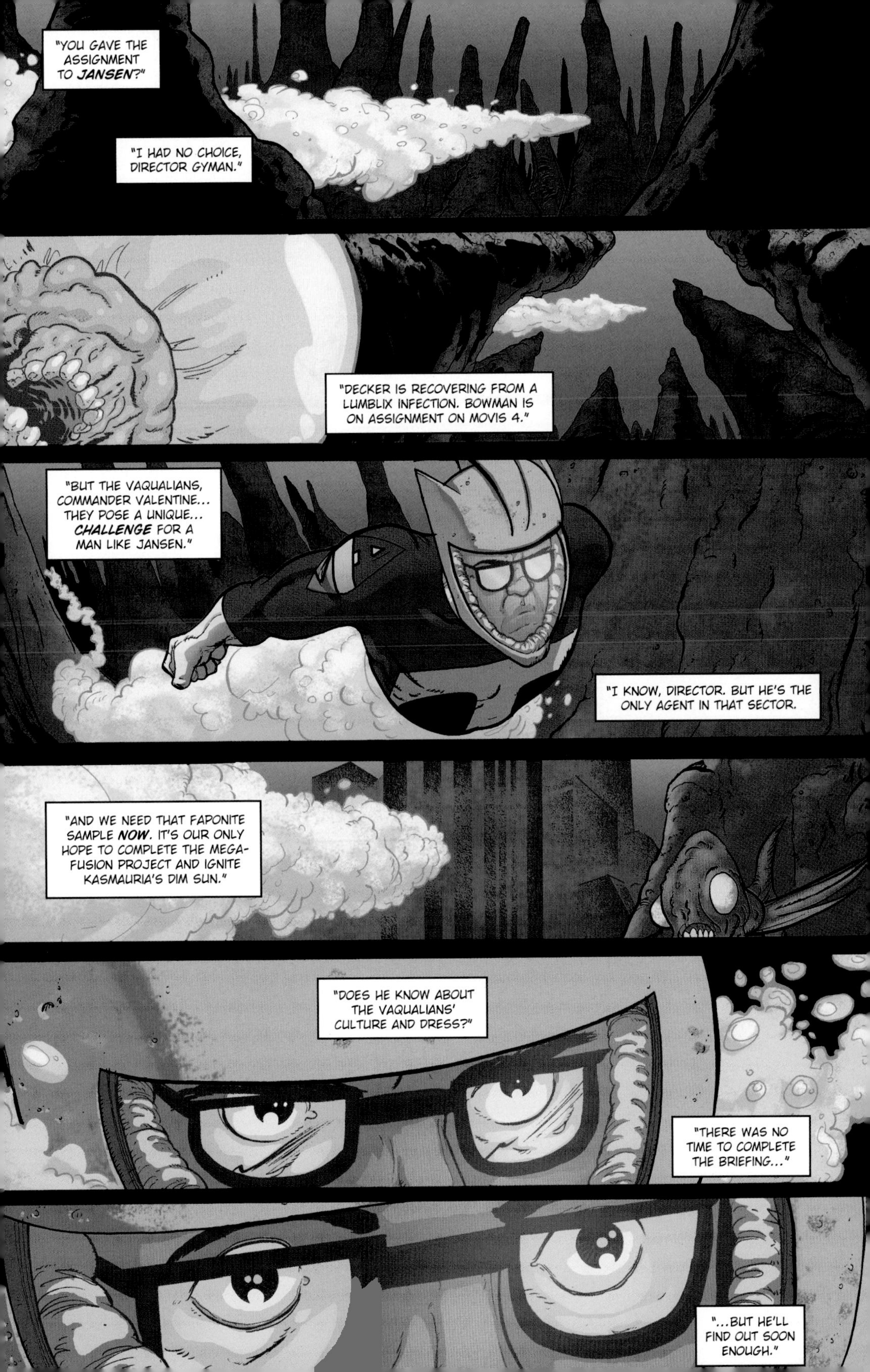
"YOU GAVE THE ASSIGNMENT TO JANSEN?"
"I HAD NO CHOICE, DIRECTOR GYMAN."
"DECKER IS RECOVERING FROM A LUMBLIX INFECTION. BOWMAN IS ON ASSIGNMENT ON MOVIS 4."
"BUT THE VAQUALIANS, COMMANDER VALENTINE... THEY POSE A UNIQUE... CHALLENGE FOR A MAN LIKE JANSEN."
"I KNOW, DIRECTOR. BUT HE'S THE ONLY AGENT IN THAT SECTOR.
"AND WE NEED THAT FAPONITE SAMPLE NOW. IT'S OUR ONLY HOPE TO COMPLETE THE MEGA-FUSION PROJECT AND IGNITE KASMAURIA'S DIM SUN."
"DOES HE KNOW ABOUT THE VAQUALIANS' CULTURE AND DRESS?"
"THERE WAS NO TIME TO COMPLETE THE BRIEFING..."
"...BUT HE'LL FIND OUT SOON ENOUGH."

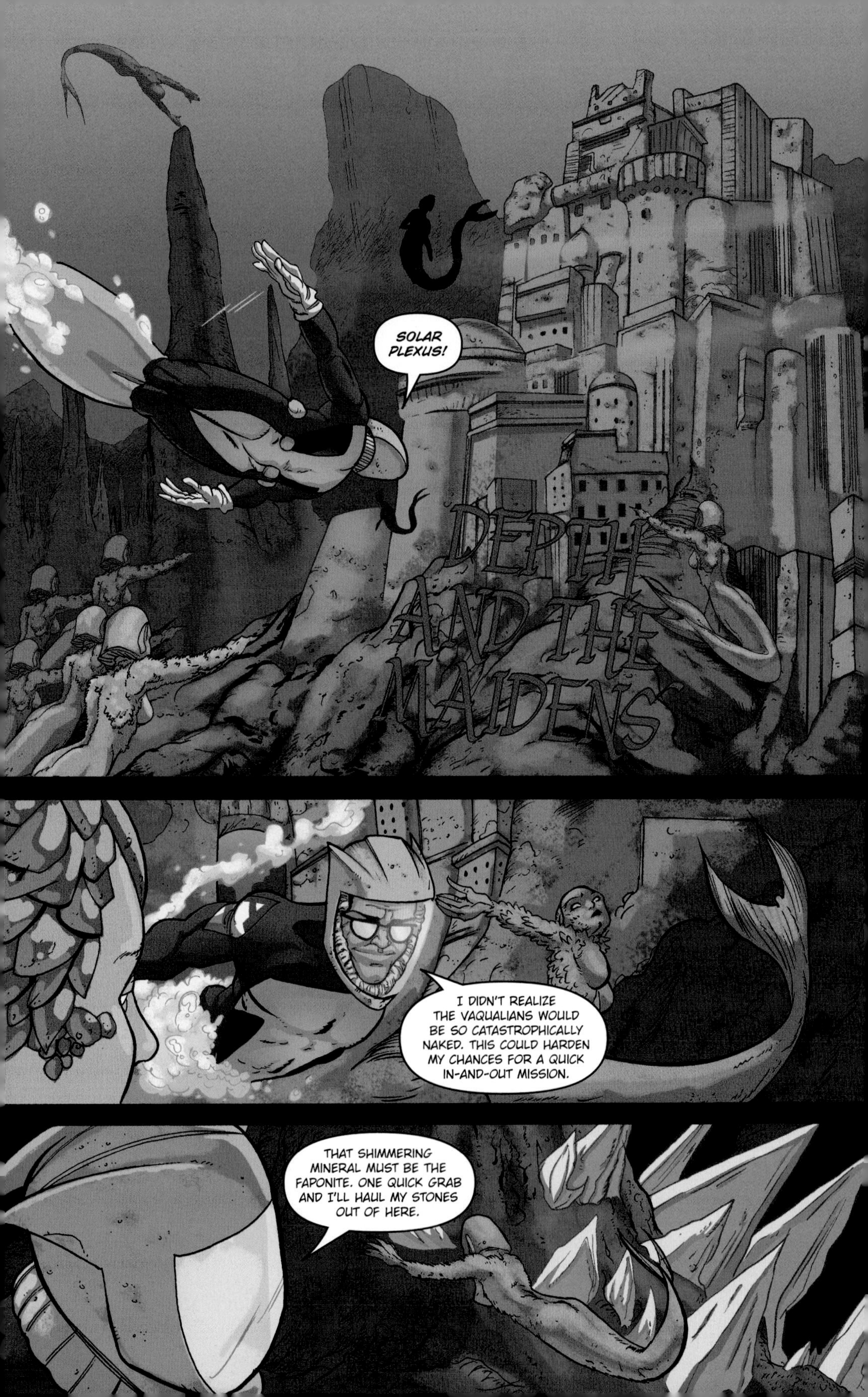
SOLAR PLEXUS!
DEPTH AND THE MAIDENS
I DIDN'T REALIZE THE VAQUALIANS WOULD BE SO CATASTROPHICALLY NAKED. THIS COULD HARDEN MY CHANCES FOR A QUICK IN-AND-OUT MISSION.
THAT SHIMMERING MINERAL MUST BE THE FAPONITE. ONE QUICK GRAB AND I'LL HAUL MY STONES OUT OF HERE.

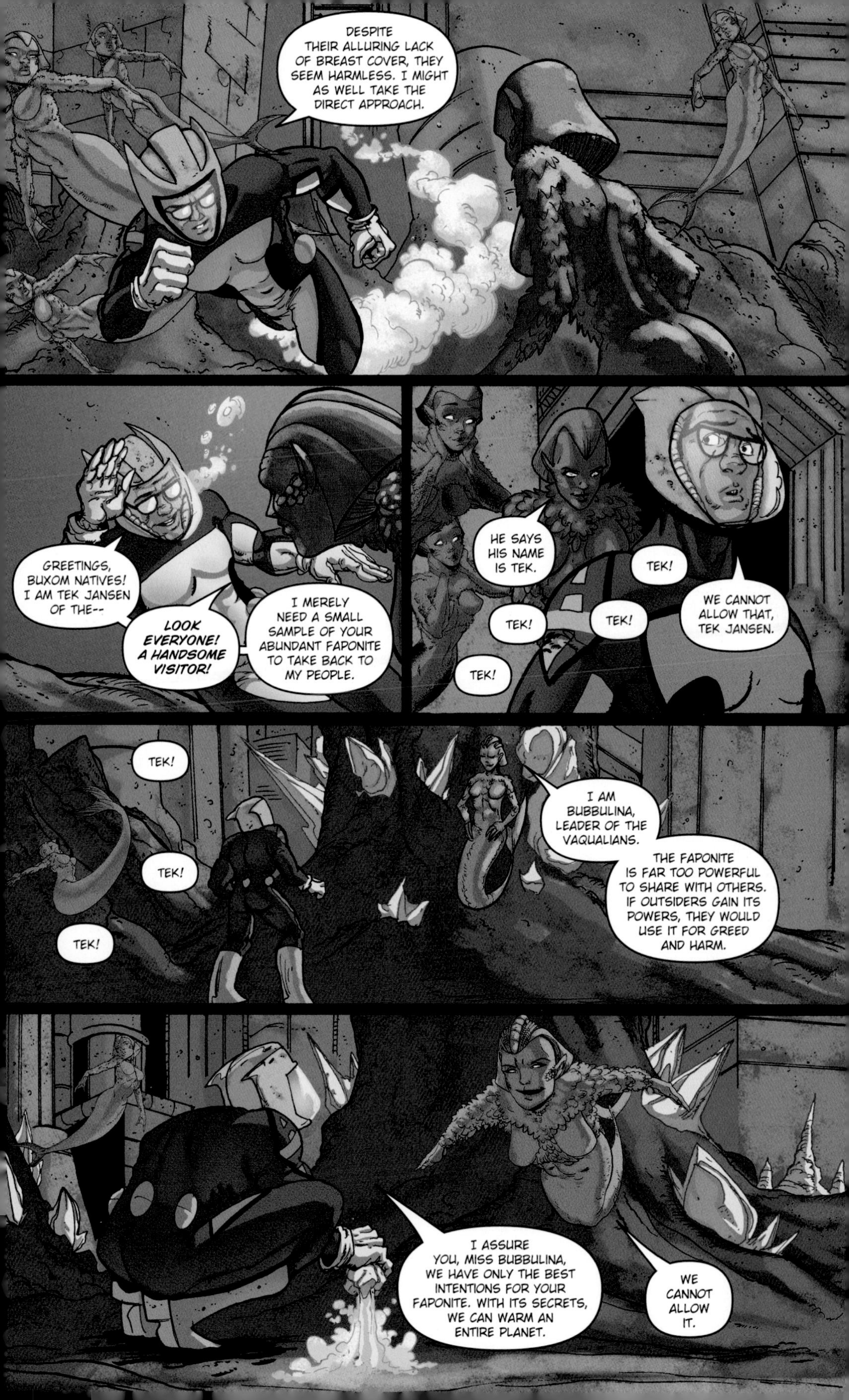

DESPITE THEIR ALLURING LACK OF BREAST COVER, THEY SEEM HARMLESS. I MIGHT AS WELL TAKE THE DIRECT APPROACH.
GREETINGS, BUXOM NATIVES! I AM TEK JANSEN OF THE--
LOOK EVERYONE! A HANDSOME VISITOR!
I MERELY NEED A SMALL SAMPLE OF YOUR ABUNDANT FAPONITE TO TAKE BACK TO MY PEOPLE.
HE SAYS HIS NAME IS TEK.
TEK!
TEK!
TEK!
TEK!
WE CANNOT ALLOW THAT, TEK JANSEN.
TEK!
TEK!
TEK!
I AM BUBBULINA, LEADER OF THE VAQUALIANS.
THE FAPONITE IS FAR TOO POWERFUL TO SHARE WITH OTHERS. IF OUTSIDERS GAIN ITS POWERS, THEY WOULD USE IT FOR GREED AND HARM.
I ASSURE YOU, MISS BUBBULINA, WE HAVE ONLY THE BEST INTENTIONS FOR YOUR FAPONITE. WITH ITS SECRETS, WE CAN WARM AN ENTIRE PLANET.
WE CANNOT ALLOW IT.

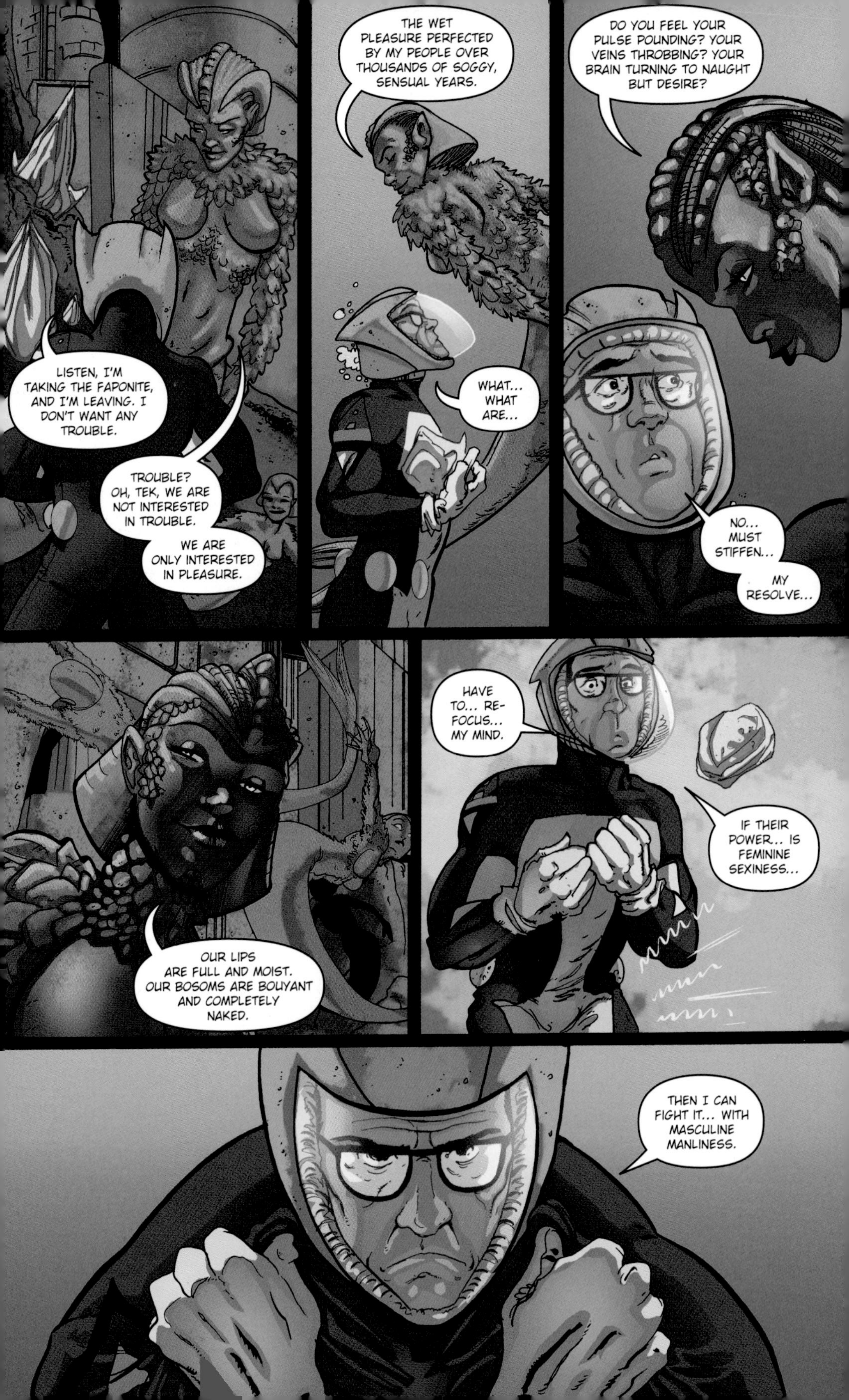
LISTEN, I'M TAKING THE FAPONITE, AND I'M LEAVING. I DON'T WANT ANY TROUBLE.
TROUBLE? OH, TEK, WE ARE NOT INTERESTED IN TROUBLE.
WE ARE ONLY INTERESTED IN PLEASURE.
THE WET PLEASURE PERFECTED BY MY PEOPLE OVER THOUSANDS OF SOGGY, SENSUAL YEARS.
WHAT... WHAT ARE...
DO YOU FEEL YOUR PULSE POUNDING? YOUR VEINS THROBBING? YOUR BRAIN TURNING TO NAUGHT BUT DESIRE?
NO... MUST STIFFEN...
MY RESOLVE...
OUR LIPS ARE FULL AND MOIST. OUR BOSOMS ARE BOUYANT AND COMPLETELY NAKED.
HAVE TO... RE-FOCUS... MY MIND.
IF THEIR POWER... IS FEMININE SEXINESS...
THEN I CAN FIGHT IT... WITH MASCULINE MANLINESS.

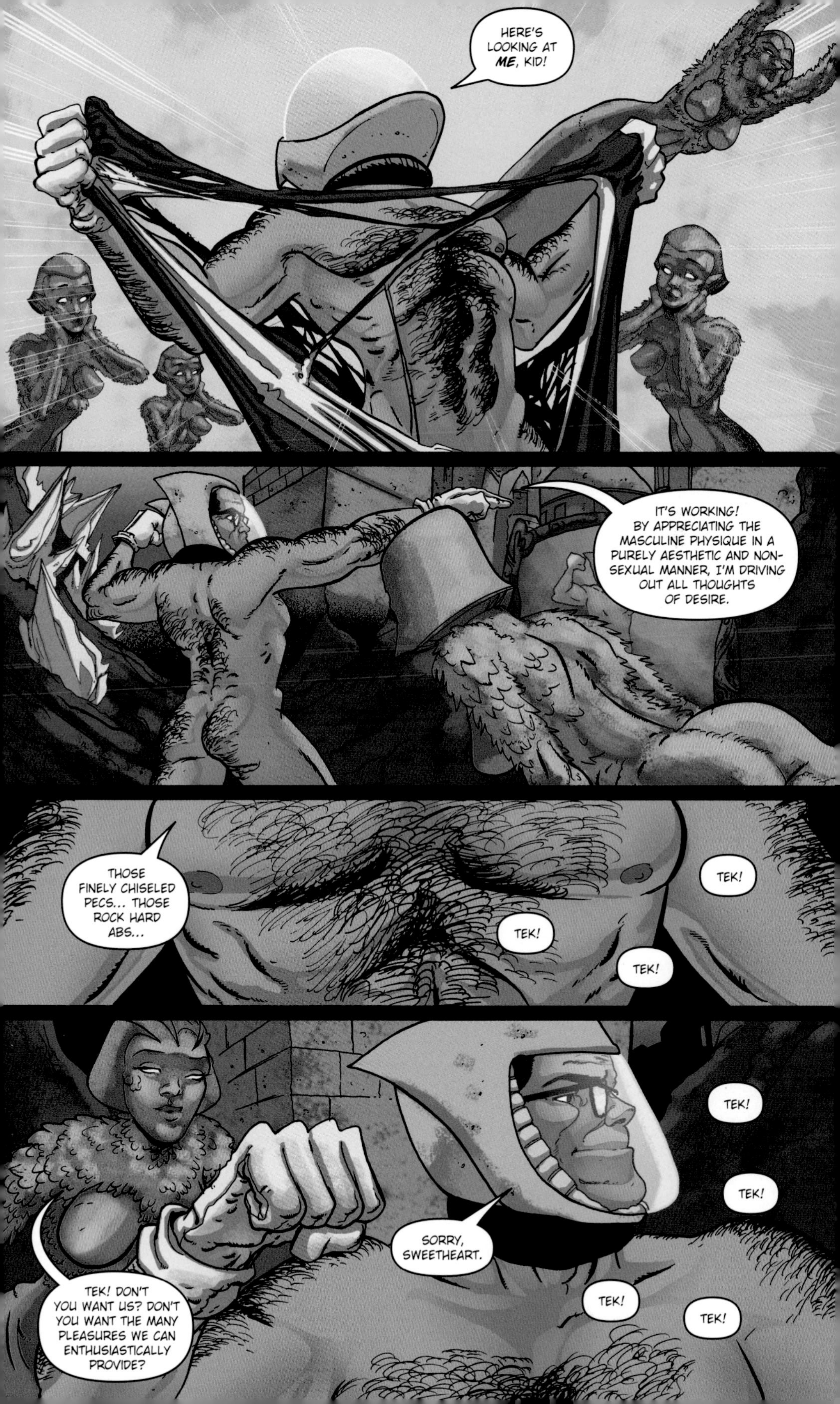
HERE'S LOOKING AT ME, KID!
IT'S WORKING! BY APPRECIATING THE MASCULINE PHYSIQUE IN A PURELY AESTHETIC AND NON-SEXUAL MANNER, I'M DRIVING OUT ALL THOUGHTS OF DESIRE.
THOSE FINELY CHISELED PECS... THOSE ROCK HARD ABS...
TEK!
TEK!
TEK!
TEK! DON'T YOU WANT US? DON'T YOU WANT THE MANY PLEASURES WE CAN ENTHUSIASTICALLY PROVIDE?
SORRY, SWEETHEART.
TEK!
TEK!
TEK!
TEK!

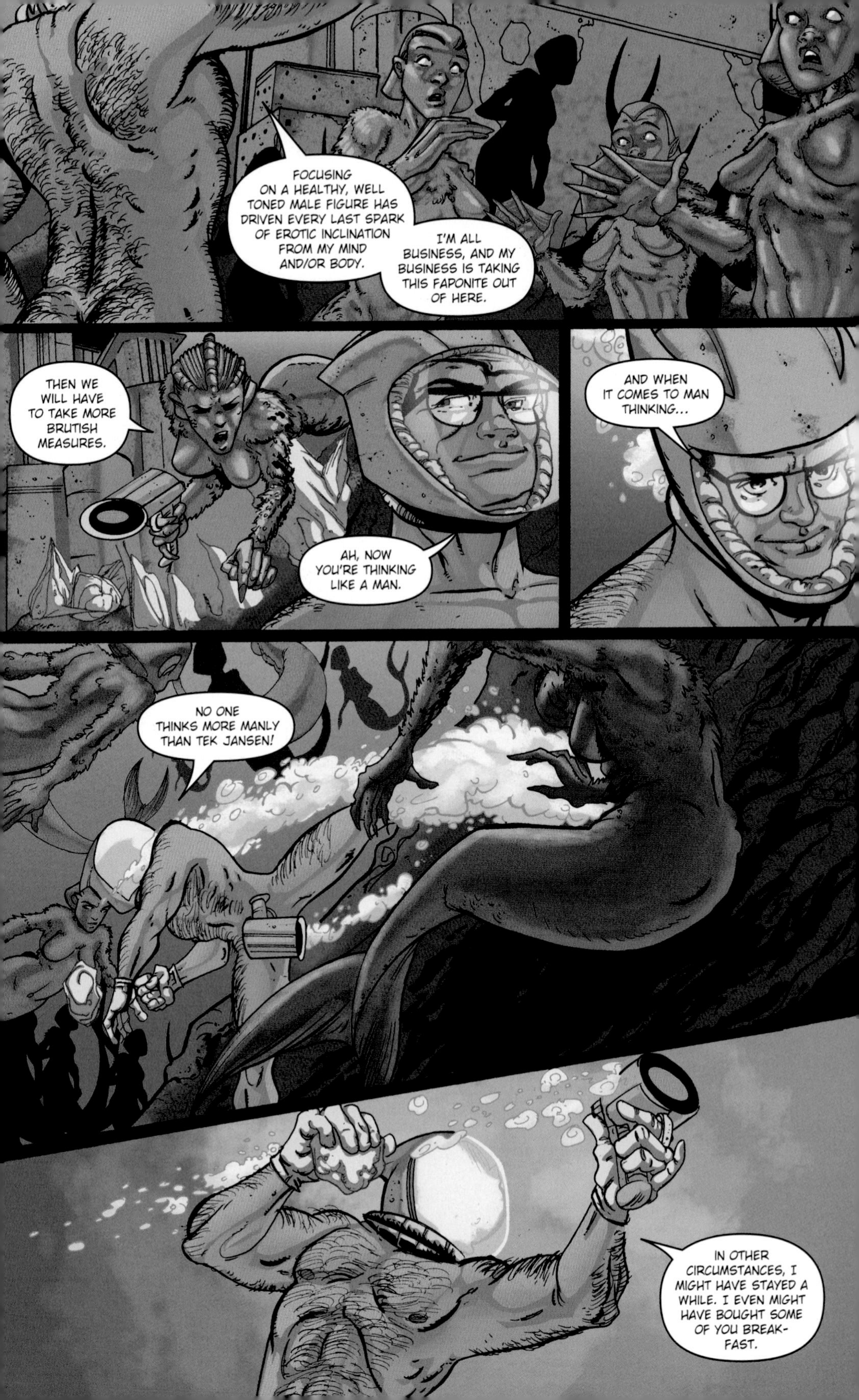
FOCUSING ON A HEALTHY, WELL TONED MALE FIGURE HAS DRIVEN EVERY LAST SPARK OF EROTIC INCLINATION FROM MY MIND AND/OR BODY.
I'M ALL BUSINESS, AND MY BUSINESS IS TAKING THIS FAPONITE OUT OF HERE.
THEN WE WILL HAVE TO TAKE MORE BRUTISH MEASURES.
AH, NOW YOU'RE THINKING LIKE A MAN.
AND WHEN IT COMES TO MAN THINKING...
NO ONE THINKS MORE MANLY THAN TEK JANSEN!
IN OTHER CIRCUMSTANCES, I MIGHT HAVE STAYED A WHILE. I EVEN MIGHT HAVE BOUGHT SOME OF YOU BREAK-FAST.

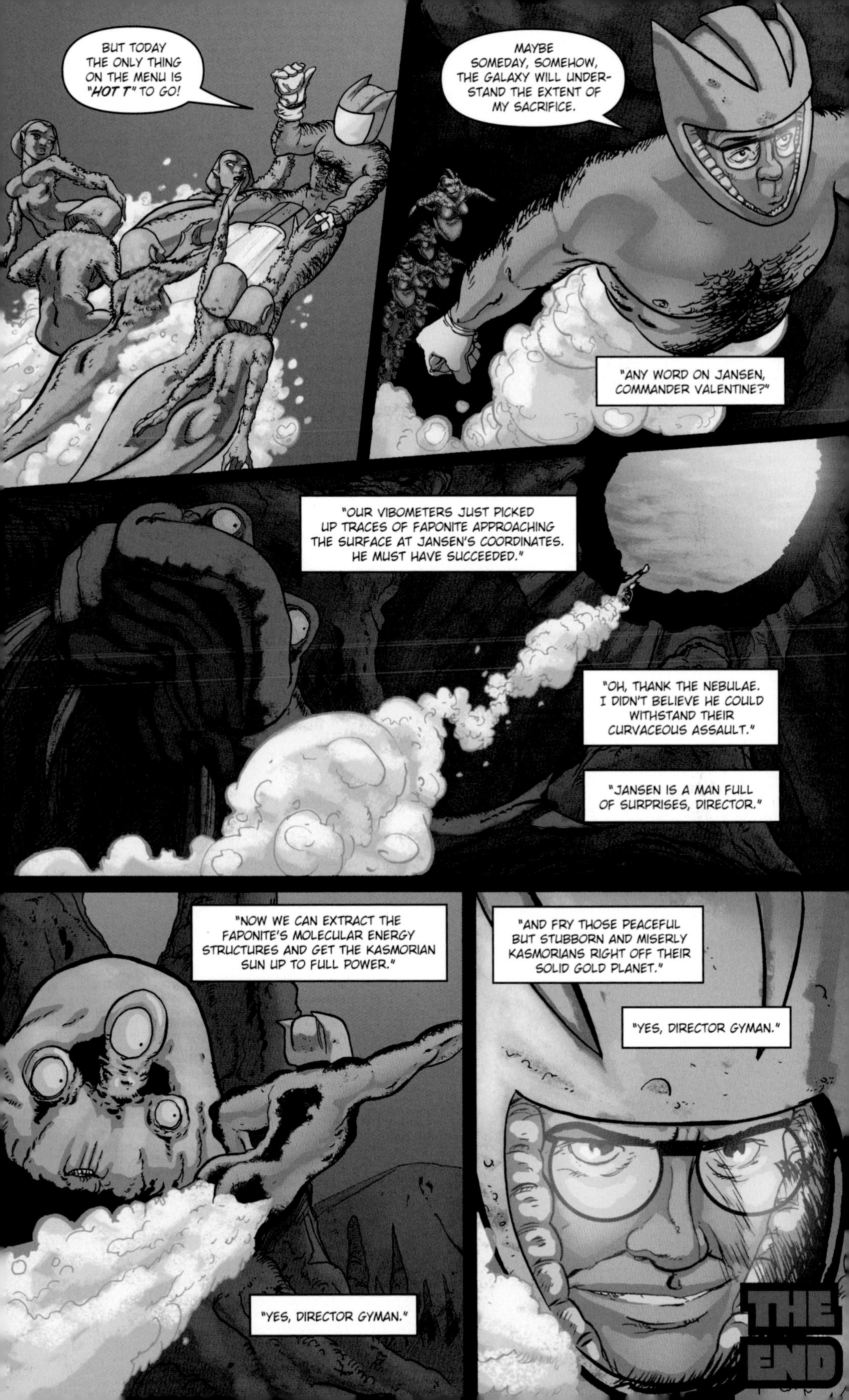
BUT TODAY THE ONLY THING ON THE MENU IS *"HOT T"* TO GO!
MAYBE SOMEDAY, SOMEHOW, THE GALAXY WILL UNDER-STAND THE EXTENT OF MY SACRIFICE.
"ANY WORD ON JANSEN, COMMANDER VALENTINE?"
"OUR VIBOMETERS JUST PICKED UP TRACES OF FAPONITE APPROACHING THE SURFACE AT JANSEN'S COORDINATES. HE MUST HAVE SUCCEEDED."
"OH, THANK THE NEBULAE. I DIDN'T BELIEVE HE COULD WITHSTAND THEIR CURVACEOUS ASSAULT."
"JANSEN IS A MAN FULL OF SURPRISES, DIRECTOR."
"NOW WE CAN EXTRACT THE FAPONITE'S MOLECULAR ENERGY STRUCTURES AND GET THE KASMORIAN SUN UP TO FULL POWER."
"YES, DIRECTOR GYMAN."
"AND FRY THOSE PEACEFUL BUT STUBBORN AND MISERLY KASMORIANS RIGHT OFF THEIR SOLID GOLD PLANET."
"YES, DIRECTOR GYMAN."
THE END

SQUAD

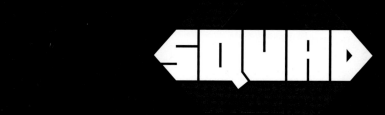

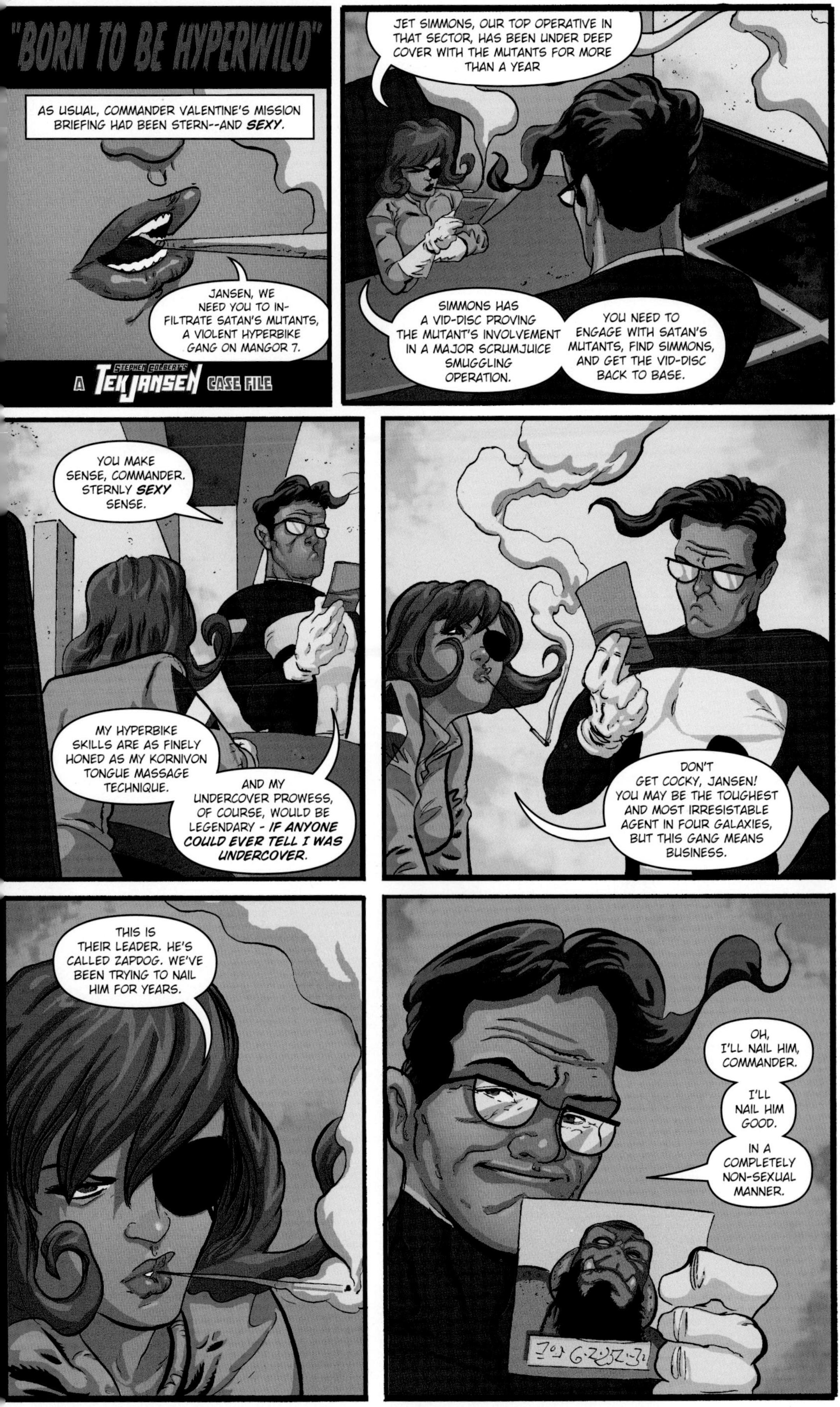
"BORN TO BE HYPERWILD"
AS USUAL, COMMANDER VALENTINE'S MISSION BRIEFING HAD BEEN STERN--AND SEXY.
JANSEN, WE NEED YOU TO IN-FILTRATE SATAN'S MUTANTS, A VIOLENT HYPERBIKE GANG ON MANGOR 7.
STEPHEN COLBERT'S A TEK JANSEN CASE FILE
JET SIMMONS, OUR TOP OPERATIVE IN THAT SECTOR, HAS BEEN UNDER DEEP COVER WITH THE MUTANTS FOR MORE THAN A YEAR
SIMMONS HAS A VID-DISC PROVING THE MUTANT'S INVOLVEMENT IN A MAJOR SCRUMJUICE SMUGGLING OPERATION.
YOU NEED TO ENGAGE WITH SATAN'S MUTANTS, FIND SIMMONS, AND GET THE VID-DISC BACK TO BASE.
YOU MAKE SENSE, COMMANDER. STERNLY SEXY SENSE.
MY HYPERBIKE SKILLS ARE AS FINELY HONED AS MY KORNIVON TONGUE MASSAGE TECHNIQUE.
AND MY UNDERCOVER PROWESS, OF COURSE, WOULD BE LEGENDARY - IF ANYONE COULD EVER TELL I WAS UNDERCOVER.
DON'T GET COCKY, JANSEN! YOU MAY BE THE TOUGHEST AND MOST IRRESISTABLE AGENT IN FOUR GALAXIES, BUT THIS GANG MEANS BUSINESS.
THIS IS THEIR LEADER. HE'S CALLED ZAPDOG. WE'VE BEEN TRYING TO NAIL HIM FOR YEARS.
OH, I'LL NAIL HIM, COMMANDER.
I'LL NAIL HIM GOOD.
IN A COMPLETELY NON-SEXUAL MANNER.

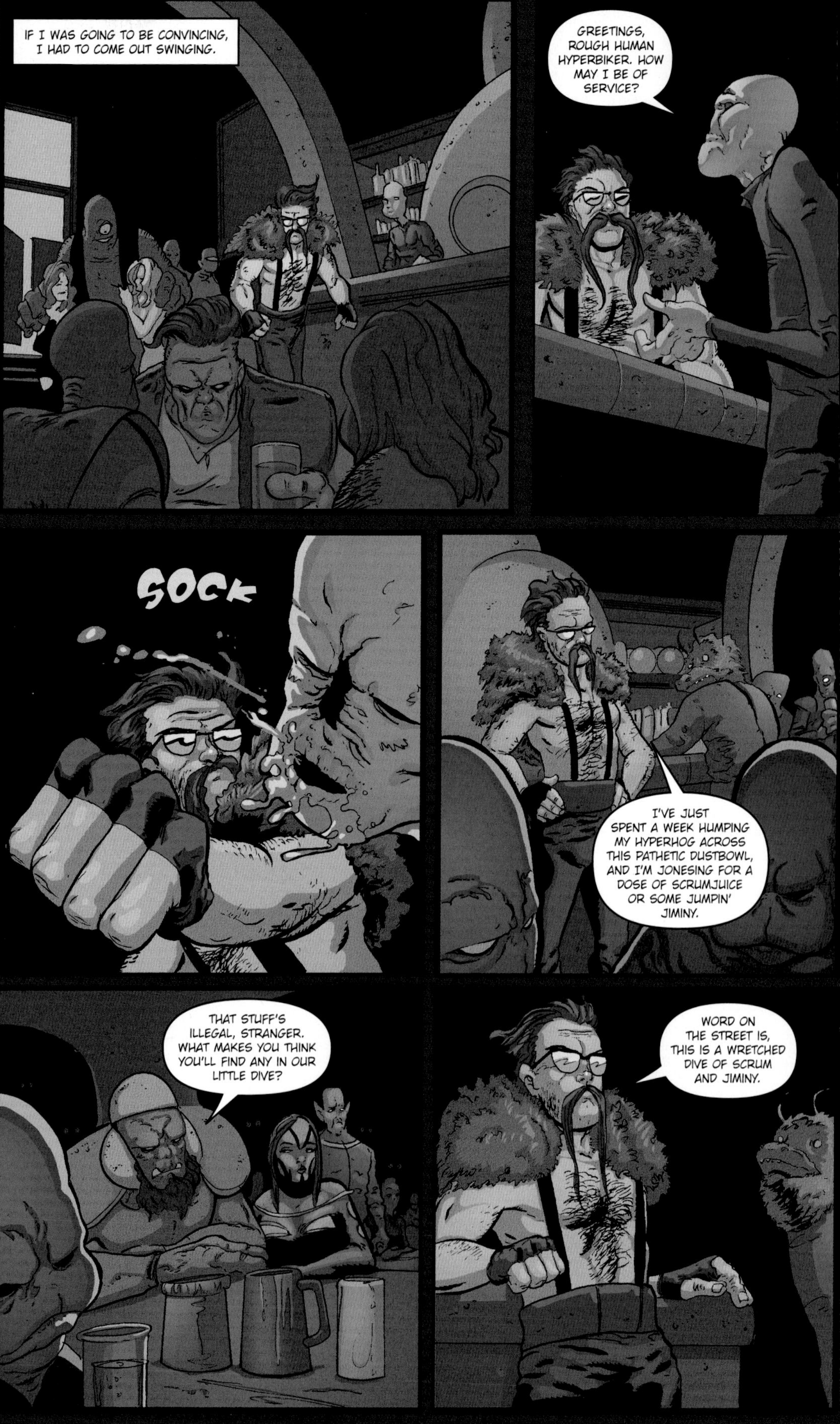
IF I WAS GOING TO BE CONVINCING, I HAD TO COME OUT SWINGING.
GREETINGS, ROUGH HUMAN HYPERBIKER. HOW MAY I BE OF SERVICE?
SOCK
I'VE JUST SPENT A WEEK HUMPING MY HYPERHOG ACROSS THIS PATHETIC DUSTBOWL, AND I'M JONESING FOR A DOSE OF SCRUMJUICE OR SOME JUMPIN' JIMINY.
THAT STUFF'S ILLEGAL, STRANGER. WHAT MAKES YOU THINK YOU'LL FIND ANY IN OUR LITTLE DIVE?
WORD ON THE STREET IS, THIS IS A WRETCHED DIVE OF SCRUM AND JIMINY.

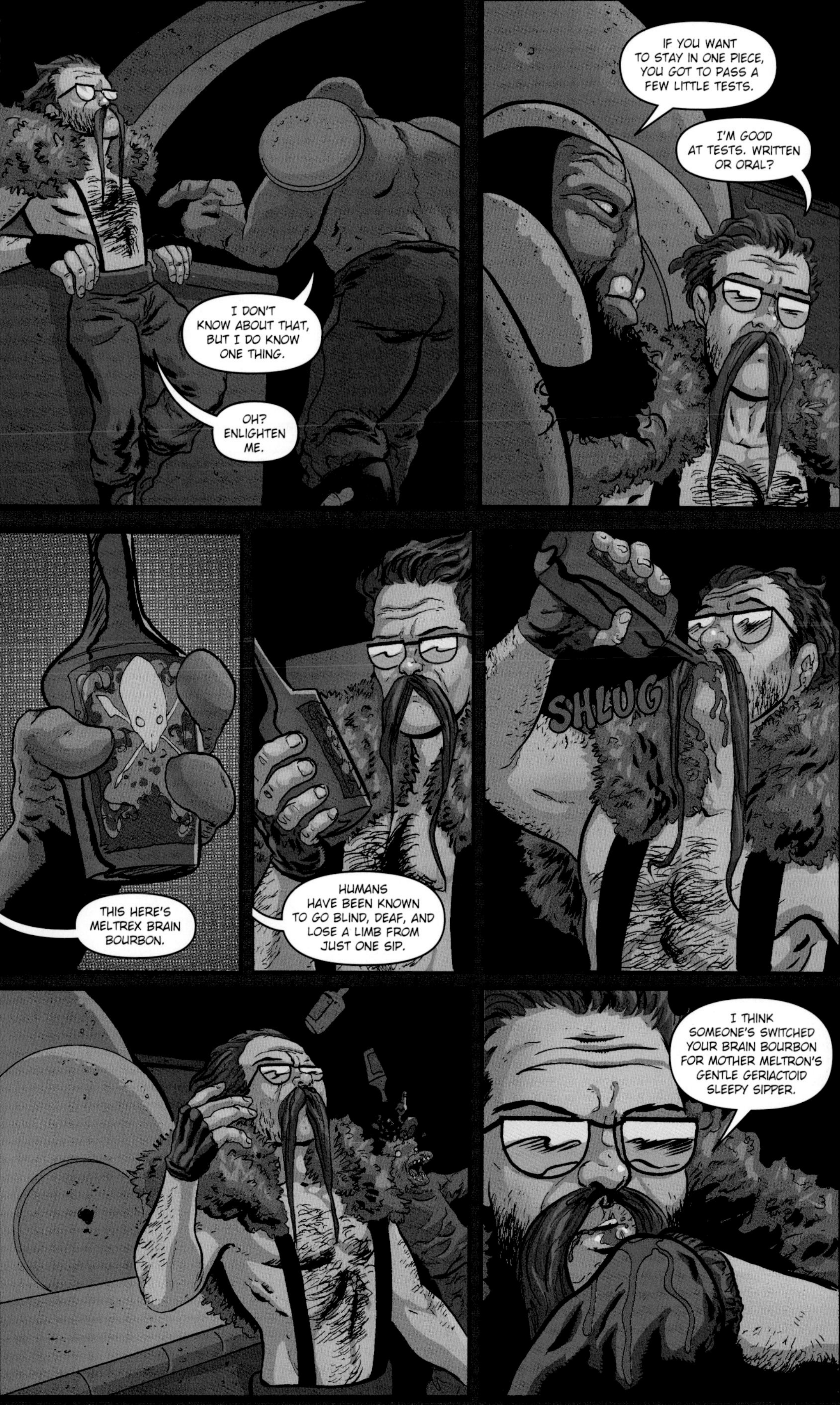
I DON'T KNOW ABOUT THAT, BUT I DO KNOW ONE THING.
OH? ENLIGHTEN ME.
IF YOU WANT TO STAY IN ONE PIECE, YOU GOT TO PASS A FEW LITTLE TESTS.
I'M GOOD AT TESTS. WRITTEN OR ORAL?
THIS HERE'S MELTREX BRAIN BOURBON.
HUMANS HAVE BEEN KNOWN TO GO BLIND, DEAF, AND LOSE A LIMB FROM JUST ONE SIP.
SHLUG
I THINK SOMEONE'S SWITCHED YOUR BRAIN BOURBON FOR MOTHER MELTRON'S GENTLE GERIACTOID SLEEPY SIPPER.

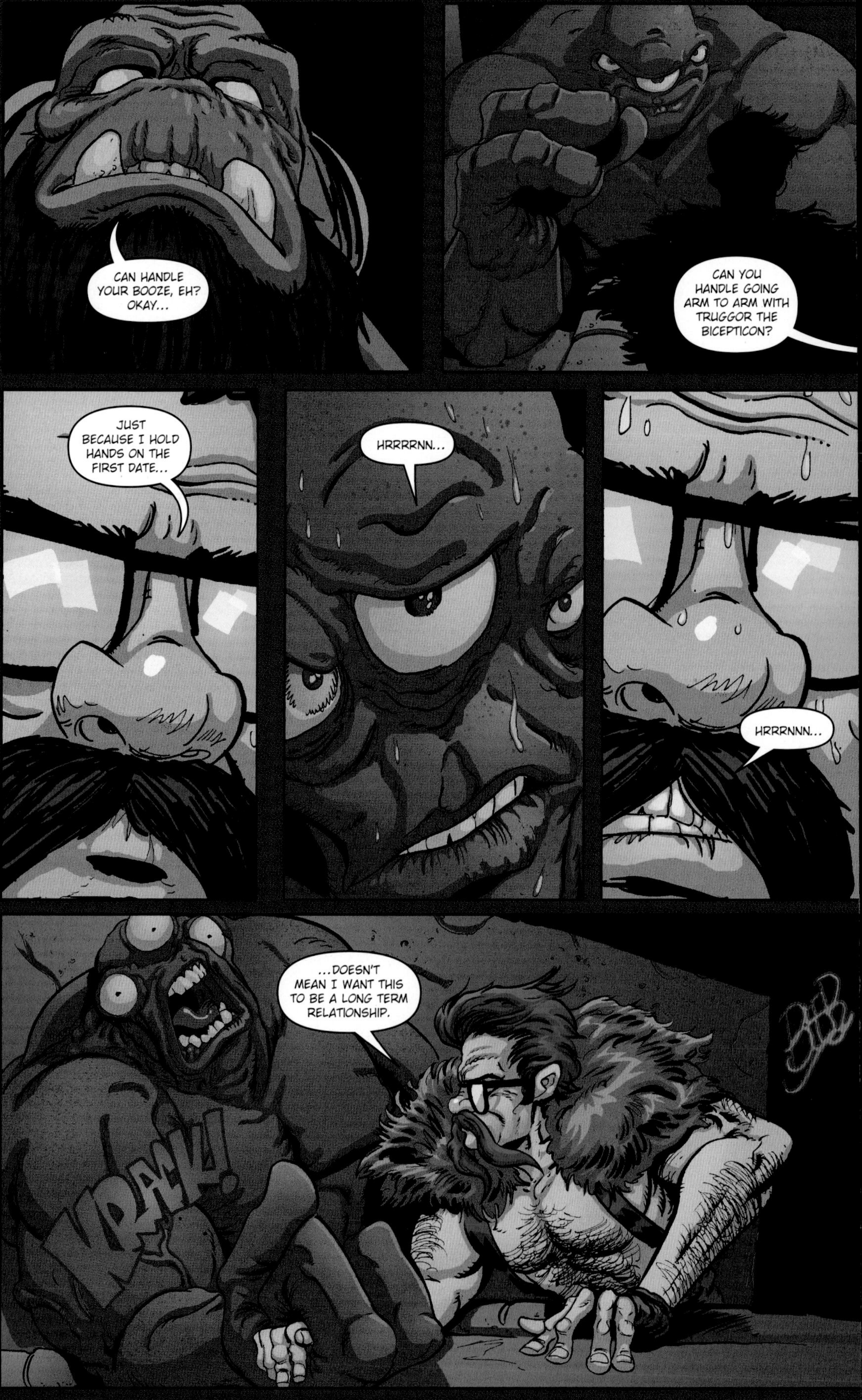
CAN HANDLE YOUR BOOZE, EH? OKAY...
CAN YOU HANDLE GOING ARM TO ARM WITH TRUGGOR THE BICEPTICON?
JUST BECAUSE I HOLD HANDS ON THE FIRST DATE...
HRRRRNN...
HRRRNNN...
...DOESN'T MEAN I WANT THIS TO BE A LONG TERM RELATIONSHIP.

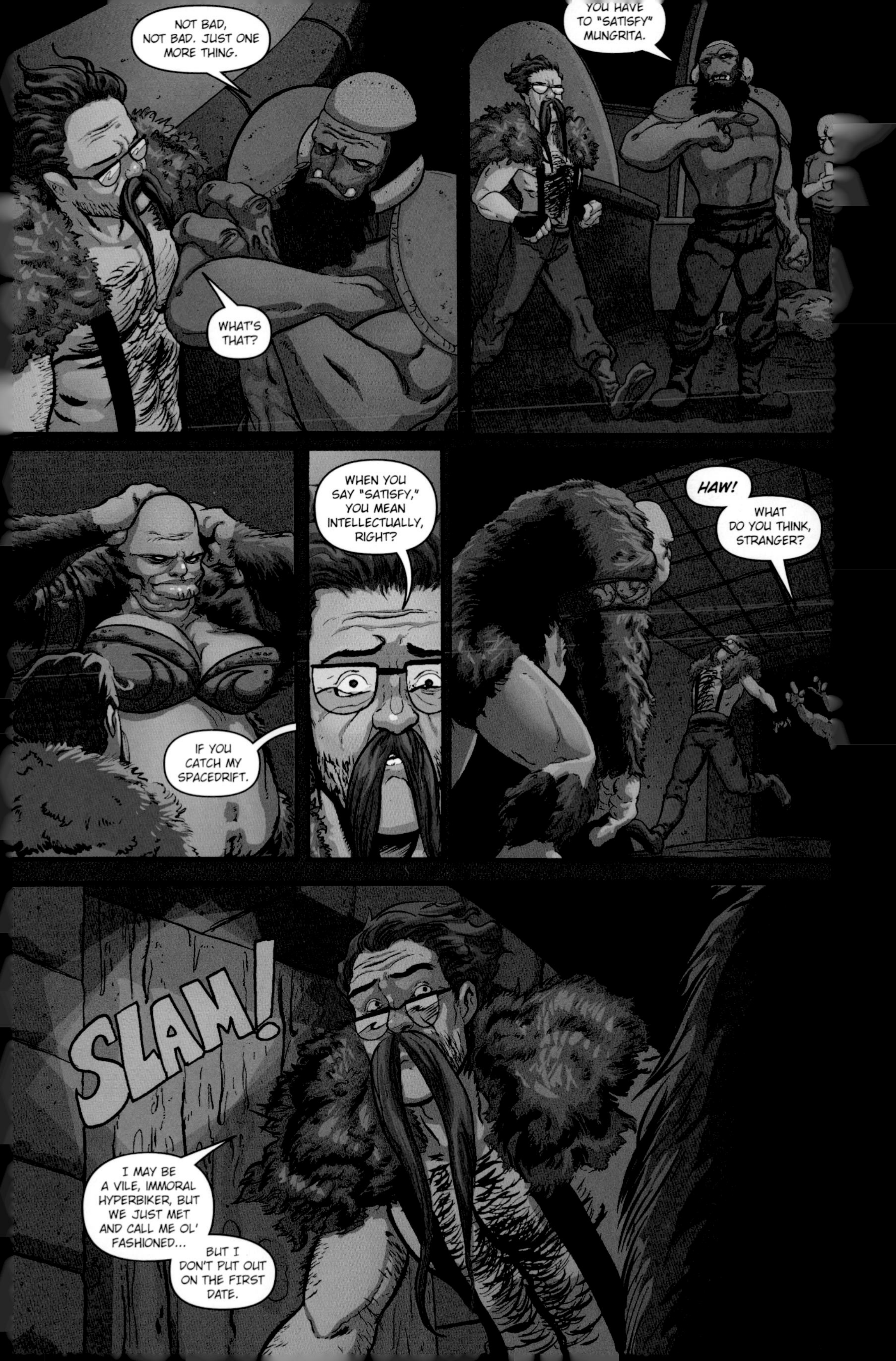
NOT BAD, NOT BAD. JUST ONE MORE THING.
WHAT'S THAT?
YOU HAVE TO "SATISFY" MUNGRITA.
IF YOU CATCH MY SPACEDRIFT.
WHEN YOU SAY "SATISFY," YOU MEAN INTELLECTUALLY, RIGHT?
HAW!
WHAT DO YOU THINK, STRANGER?
SLAM!
I MAY BE A VILE, IMMORAL HYPERBIKER, BUT WE JUST MET AND CALL ME OL' FASHIONED...
BUT I DON'T PUT OUT ON THE FIRST DATE.

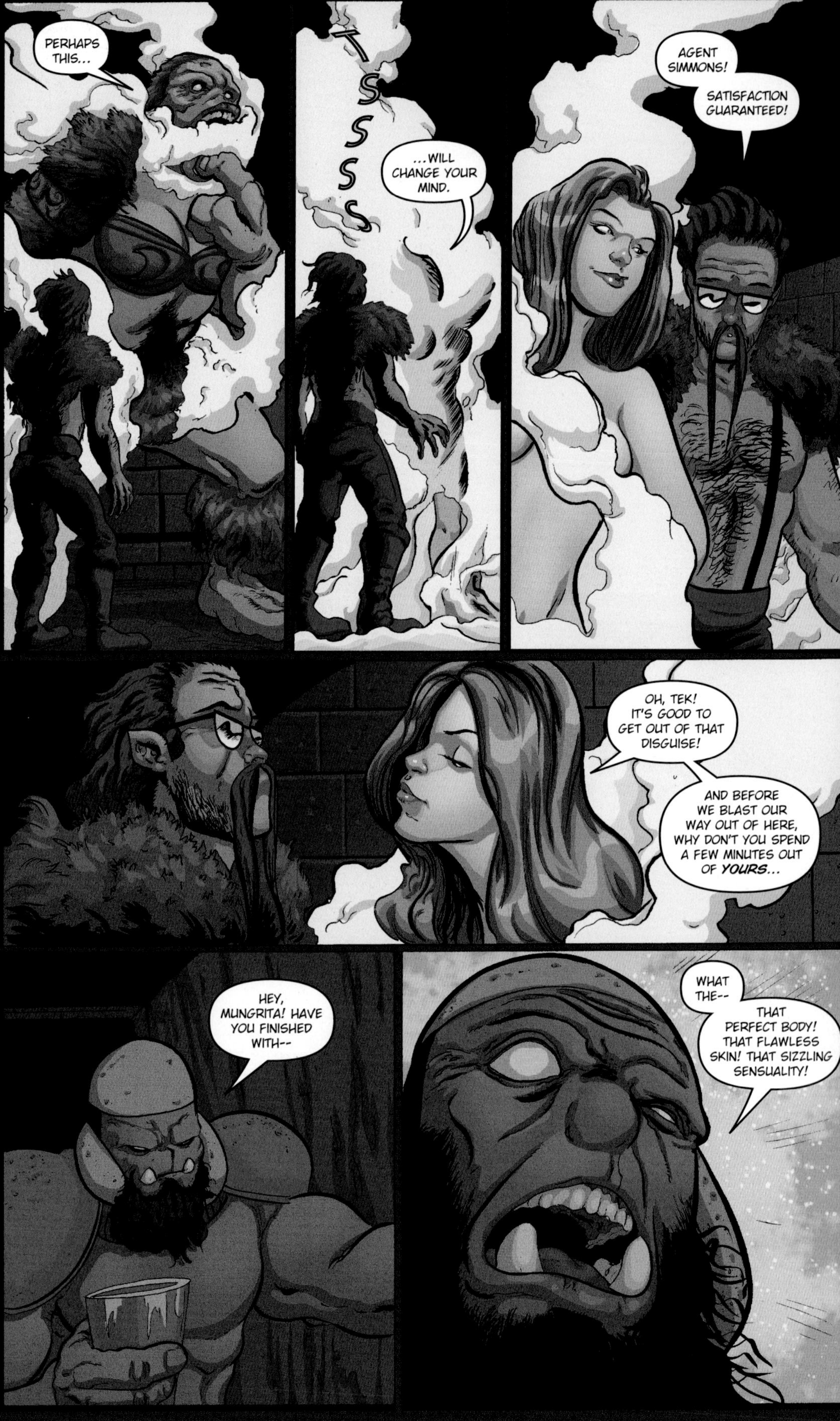
PERHAPS THIS...
TSSSS
...WILL CHANGE YOUR MIND.
AGENT SIMMONS!
SATISFACTION GUARANTEED!
OH, TEK! IT'S GOOD TO GET OUT OF THAT DISGUISE!
AND BEFORE WE BLAST OUR WAY OUT OF HERE, WHY DON'T YOU SPEND A FEW MINUTES OUT OF *YOURS*...
HEY, MUNGRITA! HAVE YOU FINISHED WITH--
WHAT THE--
THAT PERFECT BODY! THAT FLAWLESS SKIN! THAT SIZZLING SENSUALITY!

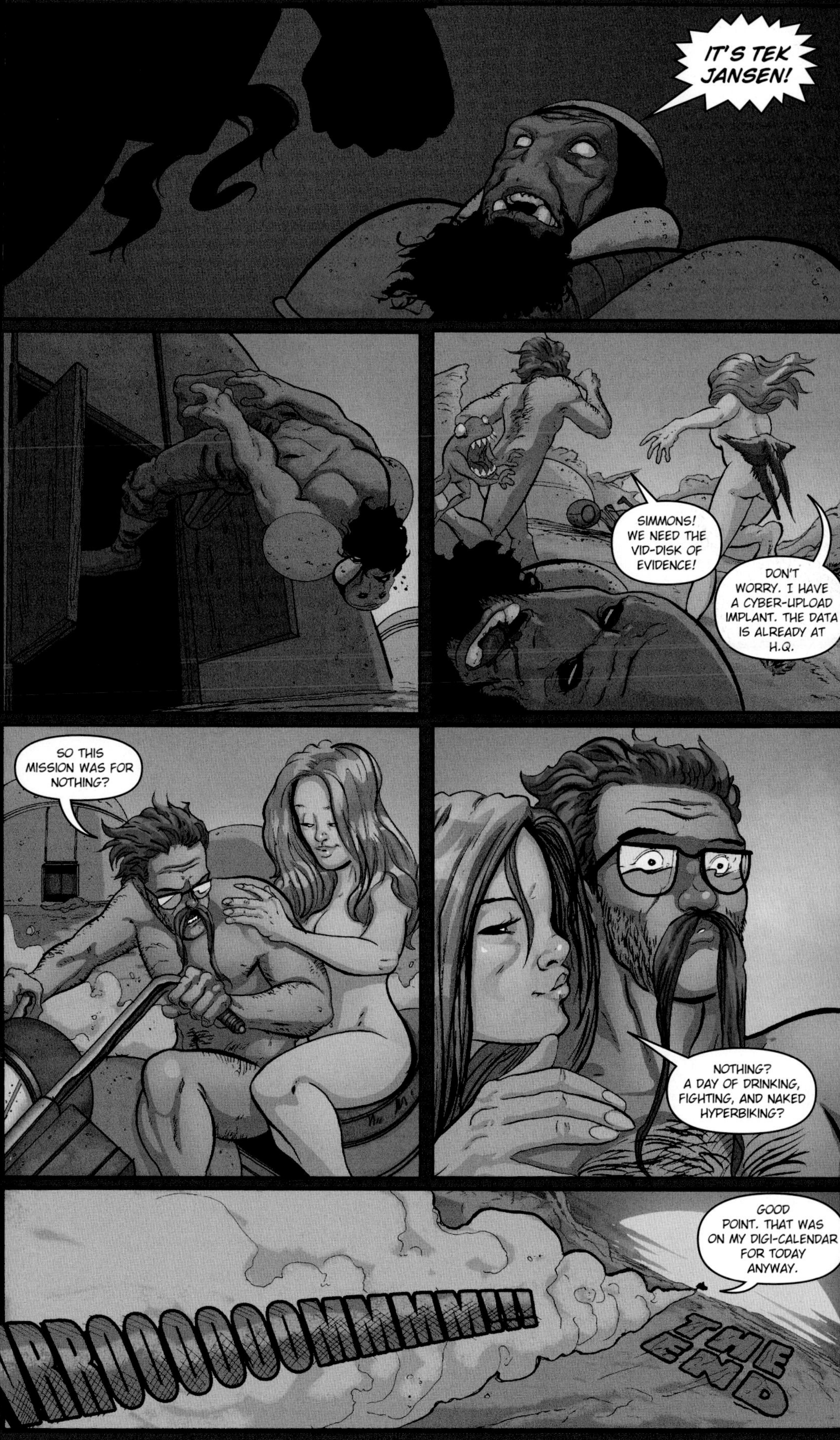
IT'S TEK JANSEN!
SIMMONS! WE NEED THE VID-DISK OF EVIDENCE!
DON'T WORRY. I HAVE A CYBER-UPLOAD IMPLANT. THE DATA IS ALREADY AT H.Q.
SO THIS MISSION WAS FOR NOTHING?
NOTHING? A DAY OF DRINKING, FIGHTING, AND NAKED HYPERBIKING?
GOOD POINT. THAT WAS ON MY DIGI-CALENDAR FOR TODAY ANYWAY.
VRROOOOOOMMMMM!!!
THE END

SQUAD

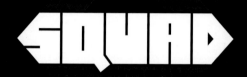

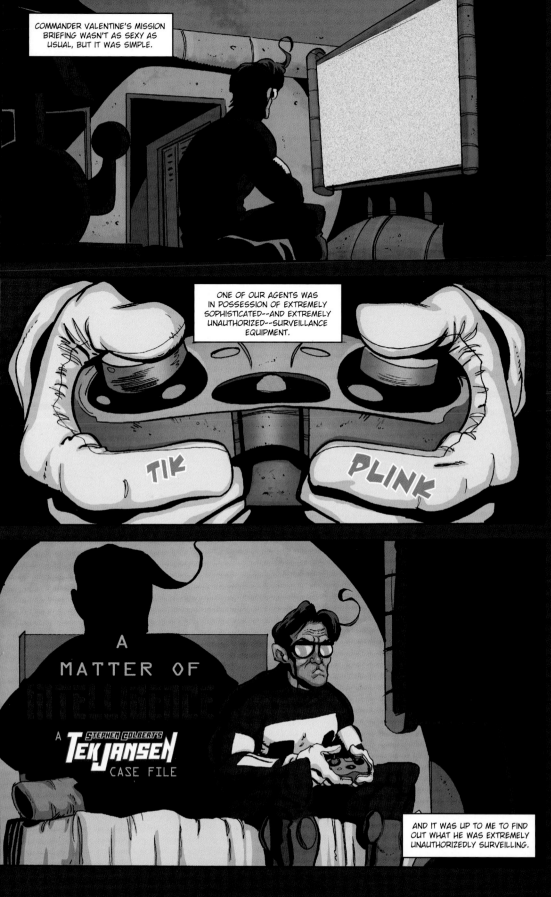

COMMANDER VALENTINE'S MISSION BRIEFING WASN'T AS SEXY AS USUAL, BUT IT WAS SIMPLE.

ONE OF OUR AGENTS WAS IN POSSESSION OF EXTREMELY SOPHISTICATED--AND EXTREMELY UNAUTHORIZED--SURVEILLANCE EQUIPMENT.

TIK

PLINK

A MATTER OF

STEPHEN COLBERT'S
TEK JANSEN
CASE FILE

AND IT WAS UP TO ME TO FIND OUT WHAT HE WAS EXTREMELY UNAUTHORIZEDLY SURVEILLING.

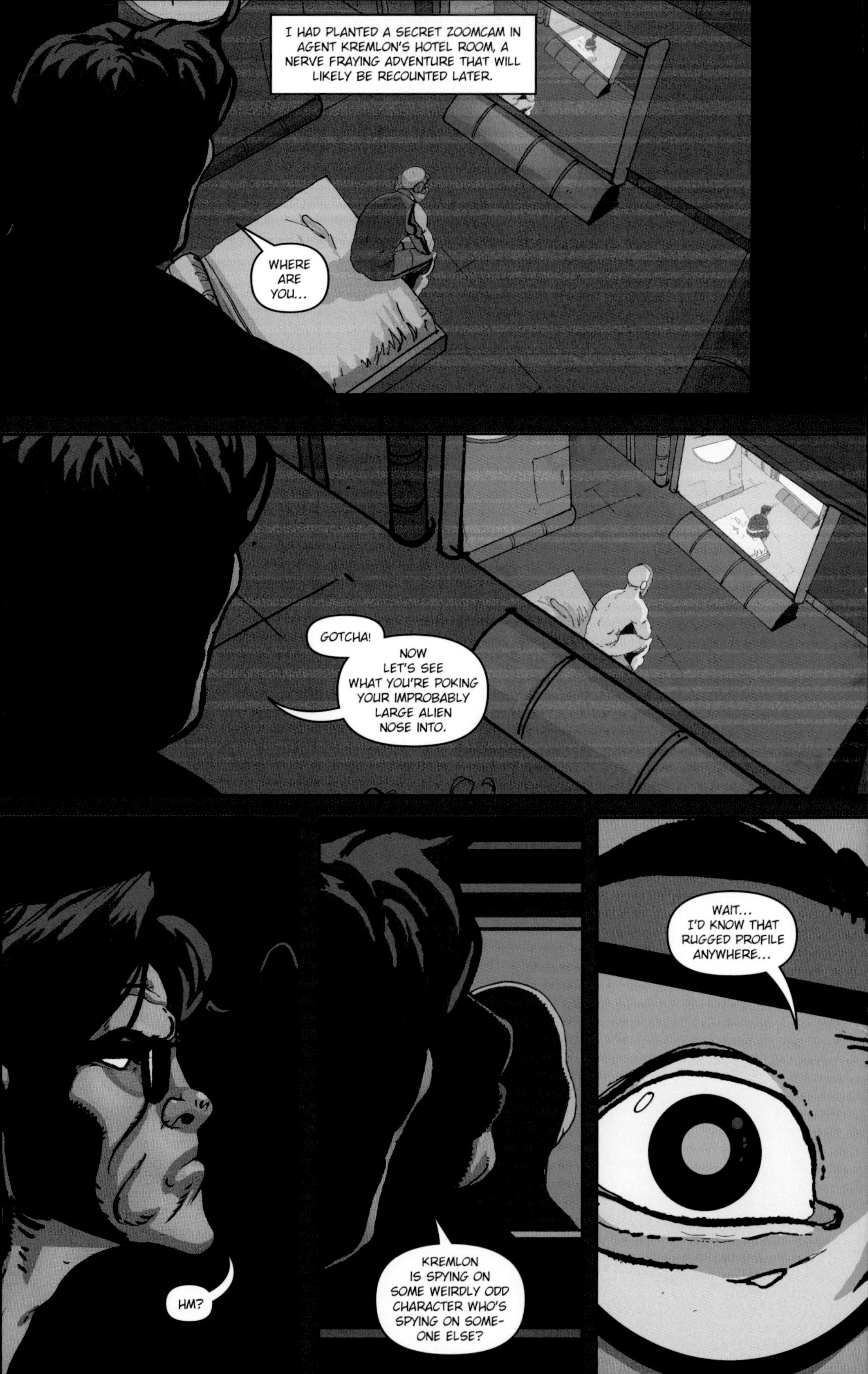
I HAD PLANTED A SECRET ZOOMCAM IN AGENT KREMLON'S HOTEL ROOM, A NERVE FRAYING ADVENTURE THAT WILL LIKELY BE RECOUNTED LATER.
WHERE ARE YOU...
GOTCHA!
NOW LET'S SEE WHAT YOU'RE POKING YOUR IMPROBABLY LARGE ALIEN NOSE INTO.
HM?
KREMLON IS SPYING ON SOME WEIRDLY ODD CHARACTER WHO'S SPYING ON SOME-ONE ELSE?
WAIT... I'D KNOW THAT RUGGED PROFILE ANYWHERE...

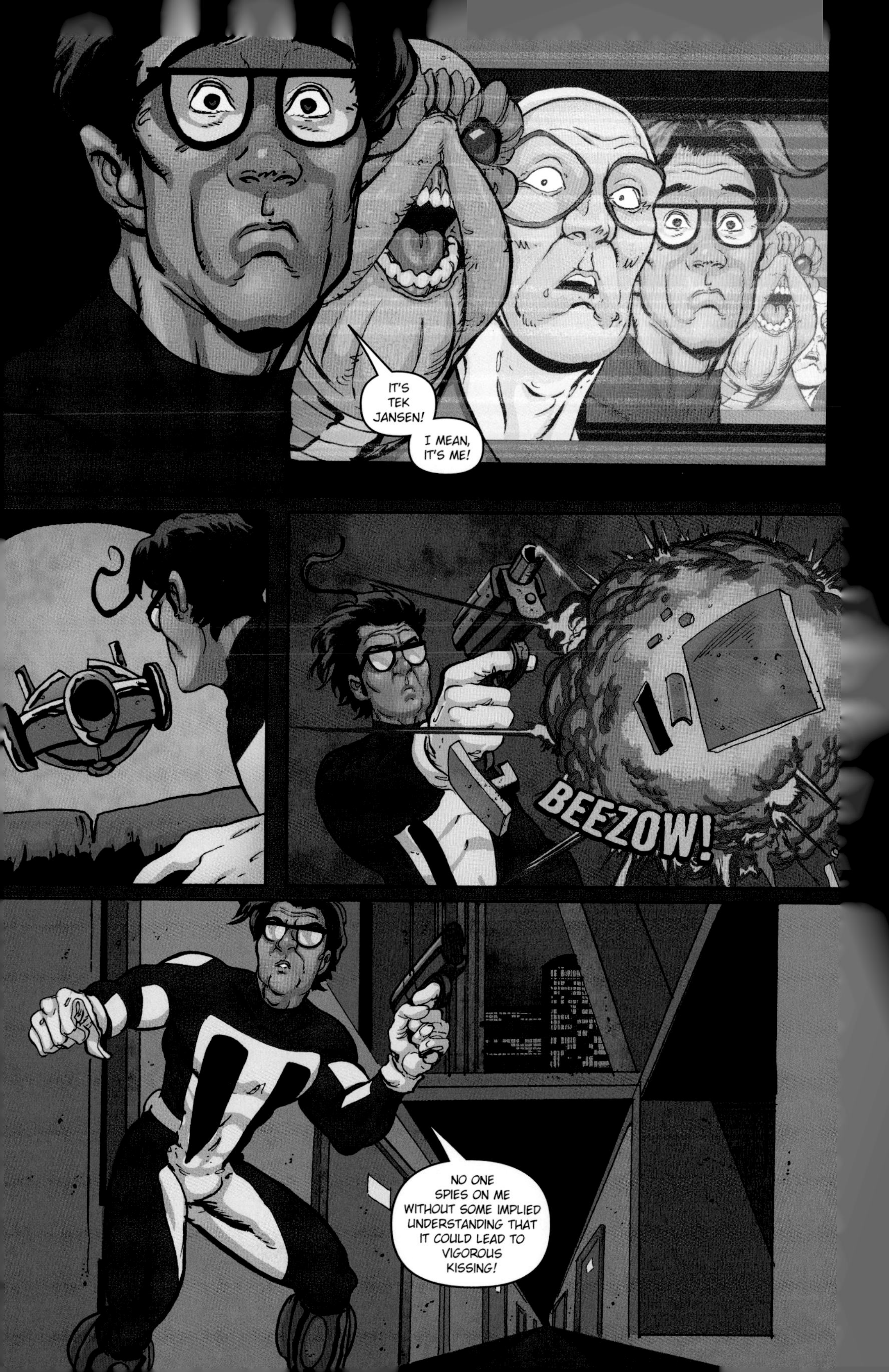
IT'S TEK JANSEN!
I MEAN, IT'S ME!
BEEZOW!
NO ONE SPIES ON ME WITHOUT SOME IMPLIED UNDERSTANDING THAT IT COULD LEAD TO VIGOROUS KISSING!

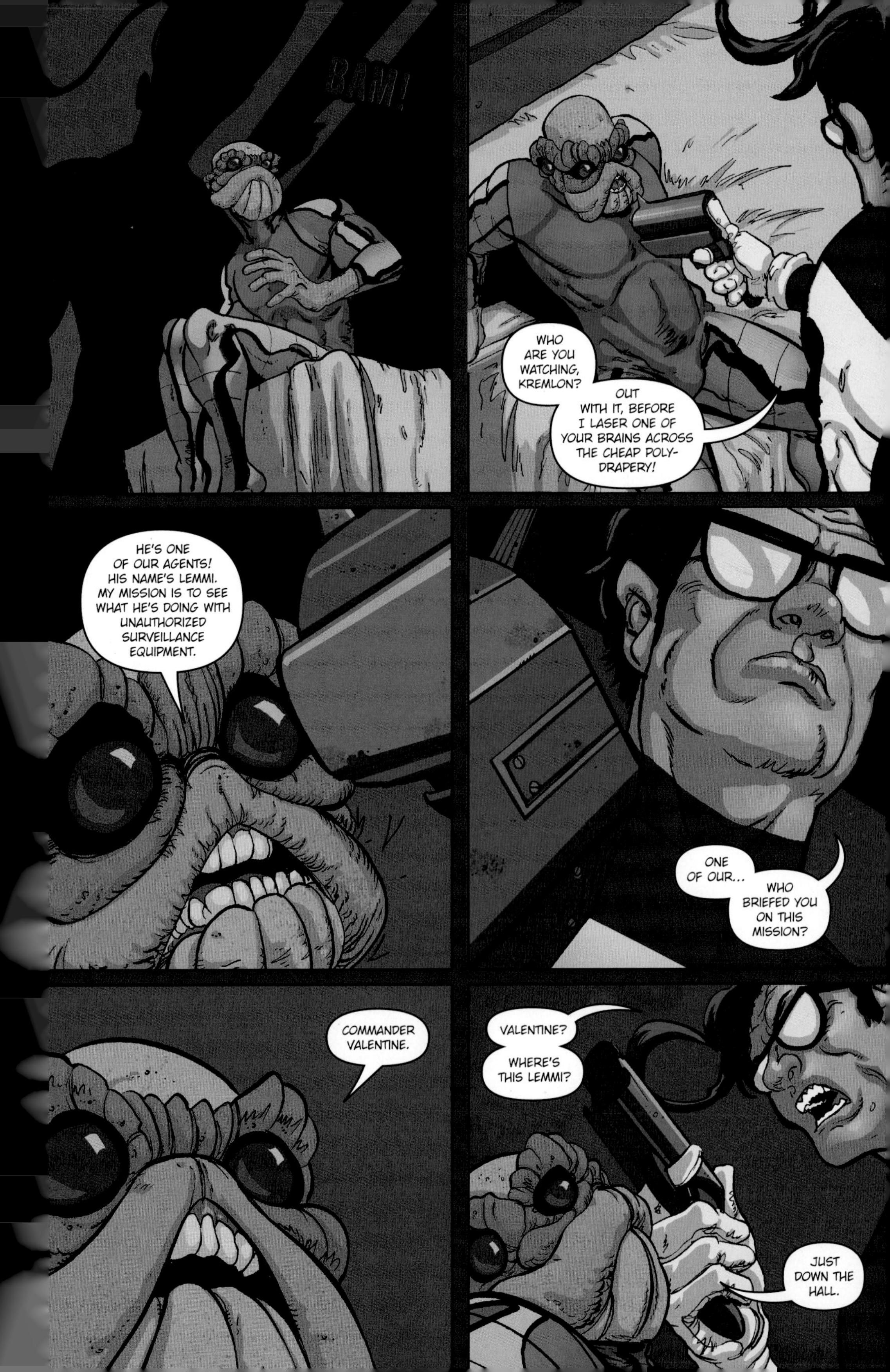
BAM!
WHO ARE YOU WATCHING, KREMLON?
OUT WITH IT, BEFORE I LASER ONE OF YOUR BRAINS ACROSS THE CHEAP POLY-DRAPERY!
HE'S ONE OF OUR AGENTS! HIS NAME'S LEMMI. MY MISSION IS TO SEE WHAT HE'S DOING WITH UNAUTHORIZED SURVEILLANCE EQUIPMENT.
ONE OF OUR...
WHO BRIEFED YOU ON THIS MISSION?
COMMANDER VALENTINE.
VALENTINE?
WHERE'S THIS LEMMI?
JUST DOWN THE HALL.

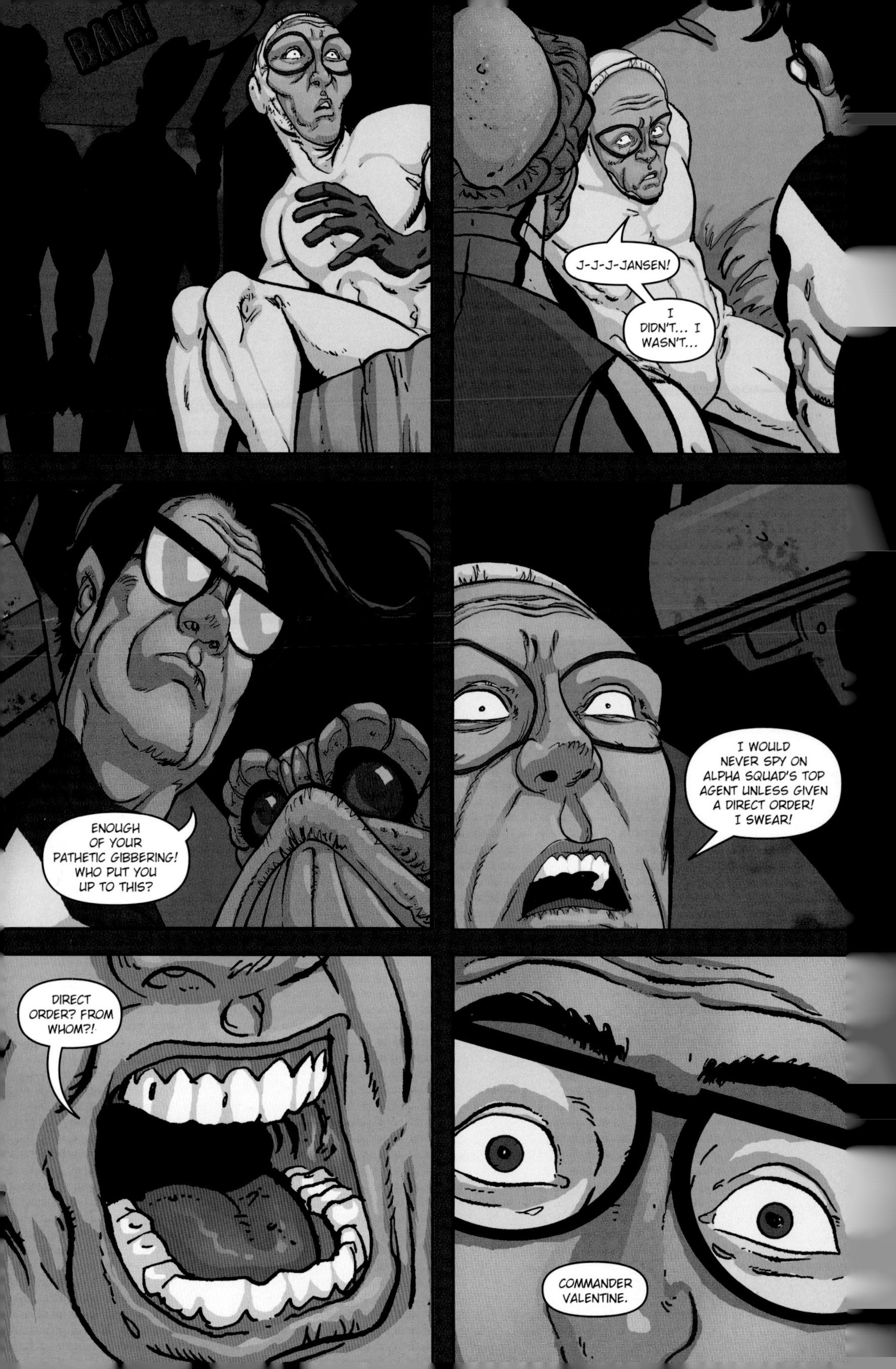
BAM!
J-J-J-JANSEN!
I DIDN'T... I WASN'T...
ENOUGH OF YOUR PATHETIC GIBBERING! WHO PUT YOU UP TO THIS?
I WOULD NEVER SPY ON ALPHA SQUAD'S TOP AGENT UNLESS GIVEN A DIRECT ORDER! I SWEAR!
DIRECT ORDER? FROM WHOM?!
COMMANDER VALENTINE.

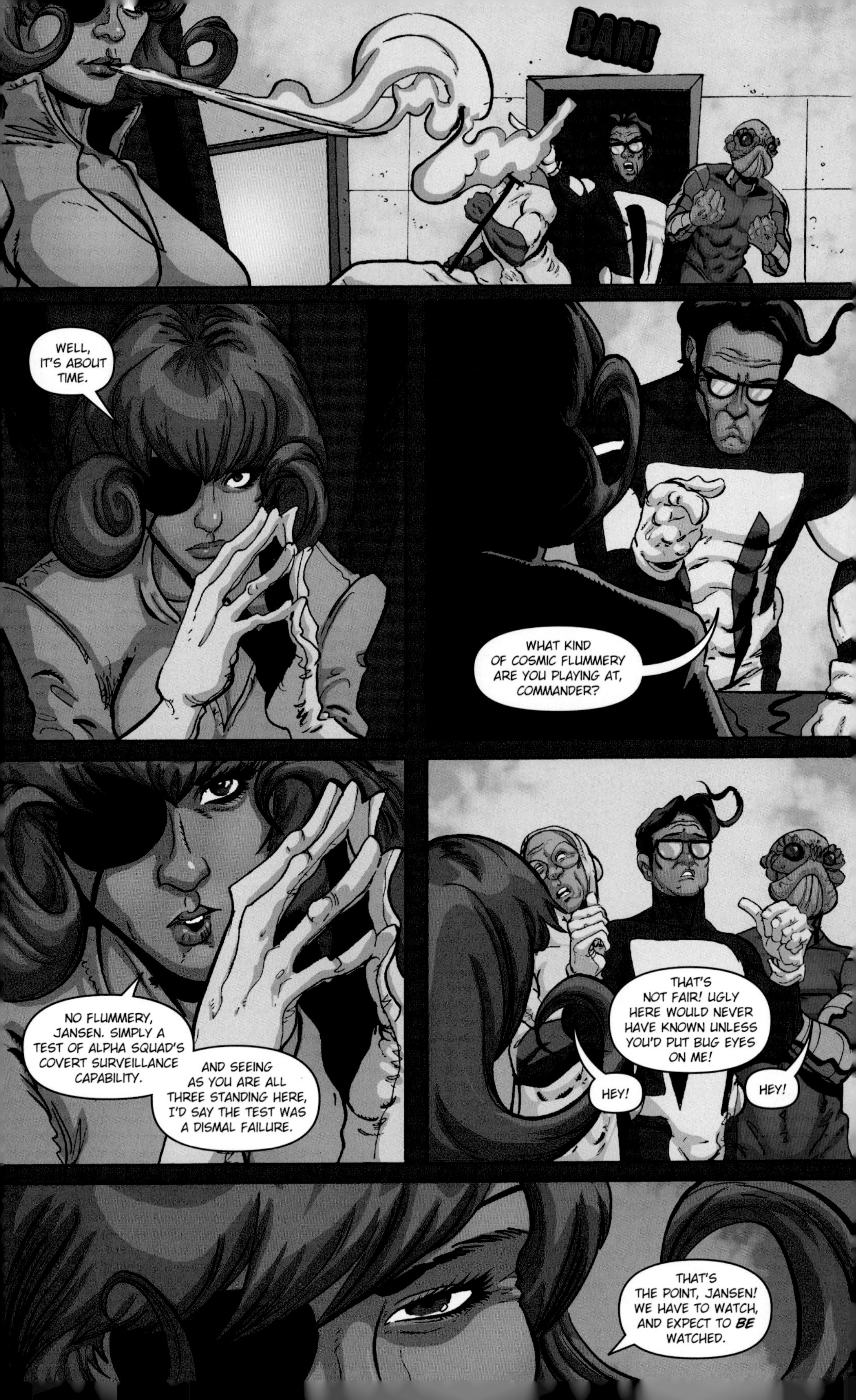
BAM!
WELL, IT'S ABOUT TIME.
WHAT KIND OF COSMIC FLUMMERY ARE YOU PLAYING AT, COMMANDER?
NO FLUMMERY, JANSEN. SIMPLY A TEST OF ALPHA SQUAD'S COVERT SURVEILLANCE CAPABILITY.
AND SEEING AS YOU ARE ALL THREE STANDING HERE, I'D SAY THE TEST WAS A DISMAL FAILURE.
THAT'S NOT FAIR! UGLY HERE WOULD NEVER HAVE KNOWN UNLESS YOU'D PUT BUG EYES ON ME!
HEY!
HEY!
THAT'S THE POINT, JANSEN! WE HAVE TO WATCH, AND EXPECT TO *BE* WATCHED.

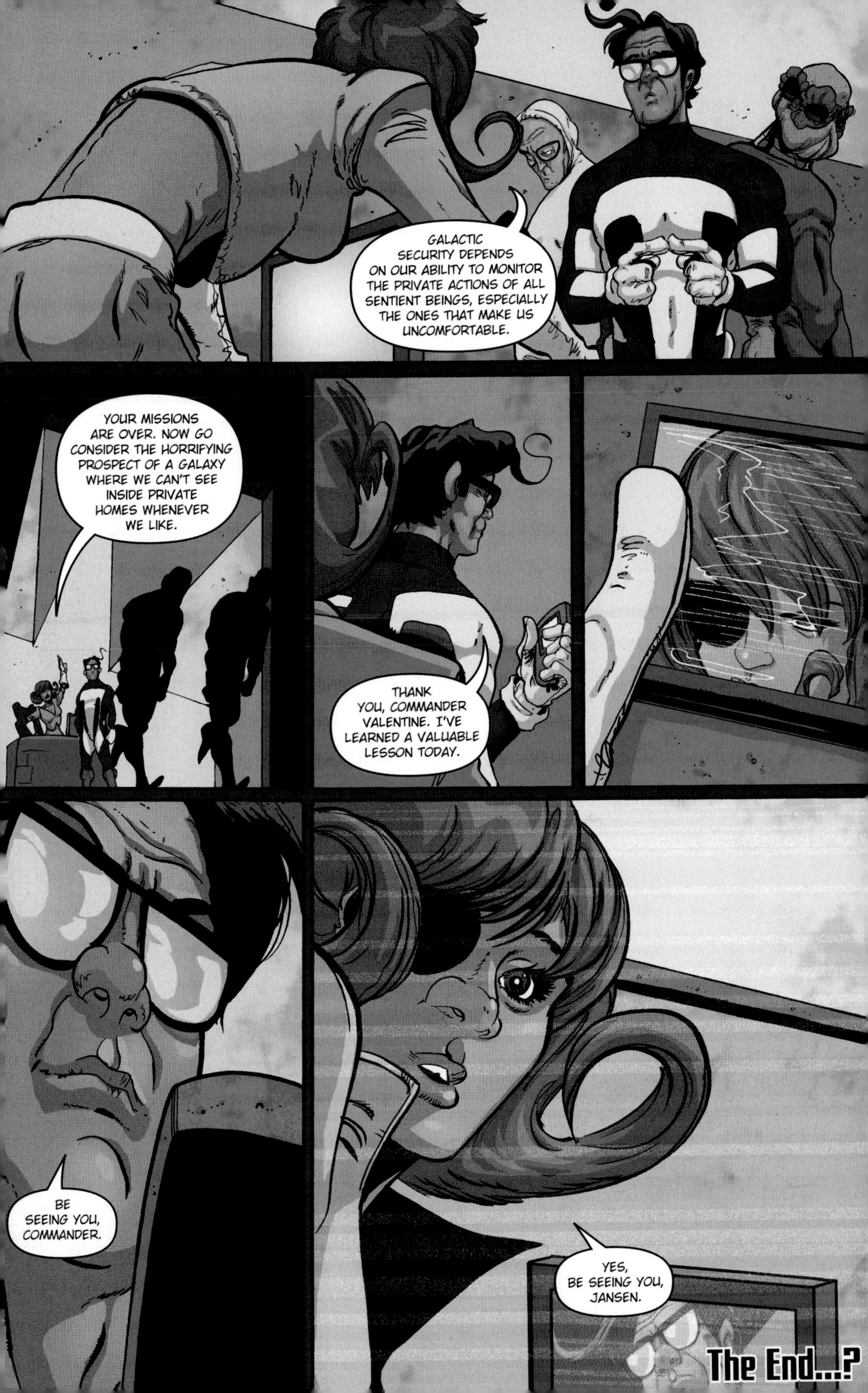
GALACTIC SECURITY DEPENDS ON OUR ABILITY TO MONITOR THE PRIVATE ACTIONS OF ALL SENTIENT BEINGS, ESPECIALLY THE ONES THAT MAKE US UNCOMFORTABLE.
YOUR MISSIONS ARE OVER. NOW GO CONSIDER THE HORRIFYING PROSPECT OF A GALAXY WHERE WE CAN'T SEE INSIDE PRIVATE HOMES WHENEVER WE LIKE.
THANK YOU, COMMANDER VALENTINE. I'VE LEARNED A VALUABLE LESSON TODAY.
BE SEEING YOU, COMMANDER.
YES, BE SEEING YOU, JANSEN.
The End...?

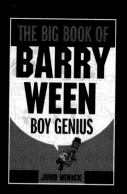

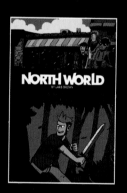